New York
Business Organization Law

The West Legal Studies Series

Your options keep growing with West Legal Studies

Each year our list continues to offer you more options for every area of the law to meet your course or on-the-job reference requirements. We now have over 140 titles from which to choose in the following areas:

Administrative Law	Family Law
Alternative Dispute Resolution	Federal Taxation
Bankruptcy	Intellectual Property
Business Organizations/Corporations	Introduction to Law
Civil Litigation and Procedure	Introduction to Paralegalism
CLA Exam Preparation	Law Office Management
Client Accounting	Law Office Procedures
Computer in the Law Office	Legal Research, Writing, and Analysis
Constitutional Law	Legal Terminology
Contract Law	Paralegal Employment
Criminal Law and Procedure	Real Estate Law
Document Preparation	Reference Materials
Environmental Law	Torts and Personal Injury Law
Ethics	Will, Trusts, and Estate Administration

You will find unparalleled, practical support

Each book is augmented by instructor and student supplements to ensure the best learning experience possible. We also offer custom publishing and other benefits such as West's Student Achievement Award. In addition, our sales representatives are ready to provide you with dependable service.

We want to hear from you

Our best contributions for improving the quality of our books and instructional materials is feedback from the people who use them. If you have a question, concern, or observation about any of our materials, or you have a product proposal or manuscript, we want to hear from you. Please contact your local representative or write us at the following address:

West Legal Studies, 3 Columbia Circle, P.O. Box 15015, Albany, NY 12212-5015

For additional information point your browser at
www.westlegalstudies.com

WEST
✳
THOMSON LEARNING

New York
Business Organization Law

Jeffrey A. Helewitz

WEST

THOMSON LEARNING ™

Australia   Canada   Mexico   Singapore   Spain   United Kingdom   United States

WEST LEGAL STUDIES

New York Business Organization Law
by Jeffrey A. Helewitz

Business Unit Director:
Susan L. Simpfenderfer

Executive Editor:
Marlene McHugh Pratt

Senior Acquisitions Editor:
Joan M. Gill

Developmental Editor:
Rhonda Dearborn

Editorial Assistant:
Lisa Flatley

Executive Production Manager:
Wendy A. Troeger

Production Manager:
Carolyn Miller

Executive Marketing Manager:
Donna J. Lewis

Channel Manager:
Nigar Hale

Cover Design:
Carolyn Miller

For permission to use material from this text or product, contact us by
Tel   (800) 730-2214
Fax   (800) 730-2215
www.thomsonrights.com

Library of Congress Cataloging-in-Publication Data
Helewitz, Jeffrey A. New York business organization law / by Jeffrey A. Helewitz.
    p. cm.
    Includes index.
    ISBN 0-7668-2320-2
    1. Corporation law—New York (State)   2. Business enterprises—Law and legislation—New York (State)   I. Title.
KFN5345 .H45 2001
346.747'065—dc21   2001033857

NOTICE TO THE READER

Publisher does not warrant or guarantee any of the products described herein or perform any independent analysis in connection with any of the production information contained herein. Publisher does not assume, and expressly disclaims, any obligation to obtain and include information other than that provided to it by the manufacturer.

The reader is notified that this text is an educational tool, not a practice book. Since the law is in constant change, no rule or statement of law in this book should be relied upon for any service to any client. The reader should always refer to standard legal sources of the current rule or law. If legal advice or other expert assistance is required, the services of the appropriate professional should be sought.

The Publisher makes no representation or warranties of any kind, including but not limited to, the warranties of fitness for particular purpose or merchantability, nor are any such representations implied with respect to the material set forth herein, and the publisher takes no responsibility with respect to such material. The publisher shall not be liable for any special, consequential, or exemplary damages resulting, in whole or part, from the readers' use of, or reliance upon, this material.

Contents

Preface

All persons involved in law or business are acutely aware of the necessity of having an understanding of the nature of the legal format used to operate the business. Without such knowledge, the businessperson could become engulfed in legal obligations that could have been avoided. *New York Business Organization Law* bridges the gap between law and business to provide the legal professional with the knowledge and skills necessary to make an effective choice in the legal format used to establish a business enterprise in New York.

The purpose of *New York Business Organization Law* is to assist the lawyer, legalassistant, and owner of a small business in determining the most effective operational format for creating a business. Without a basic under-standing of these organizations, the legal professional will be at a disadvantage, not only in representing clients, but also in manag-ing the law office itself.

New York Business Organization Law was developed to integrate theory and practice to provide the legal professional with an understanding of the law to create and operate a business venture in the state of New York. There is no other text available that meets this specific need. Current texts are either designed for general dissemination or merely provide chapters and subnotes in texts dealing with New York law. *New York Business Organization Law* is designed exclusively for the New York law student, paralegal student, and practicing legal professional, to provide a complete yet simple-to-comprehend guide to the world of business organizations. The text is a complement to legal texts on business, bankruptcy, estate planning, and litigation, yet can stand on its own as a primary text for a course de-signed to provide legal students with an understanding of basic New York business organizations.

ORGANIZATION OF NEW YORK BUSINESS ORGANIZATION LAW

The text is divided into twelve chapters and is structured in a manner compatible with any school-established method of course instruction. Most importantly, the text is written in a manner that is comprehensible to law, paralegal, and undergraduate students; its goal is to demystify business organizations.

The twelve chapters are constructed in a similar format. Each chapter begins with an introduction outlining the basic principles that will be covered in the body of the chapter. The chapters are arranged to take the student from the most basic concepts through complex analyses; each chapter provides numerous examples of the principles discussed taken from ordinary, everyday situations, as well as those typically encountered in a legal practice. In this fashion, the examples help the student to comprehend business organizations from a practical point of view. Each chapter includes a chapter summary that pro-vides a concise recapitulation of the subject matter covered.

Unlike most texts that merely provide lists of the terms used in the chapters, *New York Business Organization Law* pro-vides key terms and their definitions in the text margins. These margin notes redefine terms used throughout the text to reinforce the chapter terminology in the mind of the student. Every chapter provides two complete judicial decisions that are germane to the chapter's content to highlight the importance of business organization law to the practice of law, each of which is followed by a set of ques-tions concerning the specific case. Five problem questions designed to test the student's knowledge of the basic concepts discussed conclude each chapter. These exercise questions offer a direct "hands-on" approach to dealing with business organizations in a legal practice.

SUPPLEMENTAL TEACHING AND LEARNING MATERIALS

Instructor's Manual

An Instructors' Manual will be provided for *New York Business Organization Law*. The manual includes the following:

- Sample course syllabi
- Chapter outlines
- Teaching suggestions
- Answers to text exercises and questions
- Sample examinations

Westlaw®

West's on-line computerized legal-research system offers students "hands-on" experience with a system commonly used in law offices. Qualified adopters can receive ten free hours of Westlaw®. Westlaw® can be accessed with Macintosh and IBM PCs and compatibles. A modem is required.

Court TV Videos
West Legal Studies is pleased to offer the following videos from Court TV. Available for minimal fee:

- New York v. Ferguson – Murder on the 5:33: The Trial of Colin Ferguson
- Ohio v. Alfieri – Road Rage
- Flynn v. Goldman Sachs – Fired on Wall Street: A Case of Sex Discrimination?
- Dodd v. Dodd: Religion and Child Custody in Conflict

- Fentress v. Eli Lilly & Co., et al. – Prozac on Trial
- In RE Custody of Baby Girl Clausen – Child of Mine: The Fight of Baby Jessica
- Garcia v. Garcia
- Northside Partners v. Page and New Kids on the Block (Intellectual Property)
- Maglica v. Maglica (Contract Law)
- Hall v. Hall (Family Law)
- Berring Legal Research Videos

About the Author

Jeffrey A. Helewitz received his J.D. and LL.M. in International Business and Trade from Georgetown University Law Center and an M.B.A. in Fi-nance from New York University. He has worked for the National Office of the Internal Revenue Service and has been in private practice for several years. He is the author of nine texts designed for paralegals and lawyers, as well as numerous articles and several other forthcoming texts and a casebook. He has taught at several paralegal institutions in the New York area and is an Adjunct Professor of Law at both C.U.N.Y. School of Law and Touro College Law Center.

Acknowledgments

Thank you to the following reviewers of this text:

Prof. Chelsea Campbell
Lehman College

Prof. Mark Hartwell
Fingerlakes Community College

Prof. Catherine Johns
Genessee Community College

Prof. Scott Myers
Marist College

Jerry Loy
State University of New York
Boone Community College

Judith M. Maloney
Long Island University
C. W. Post Legal Studies Institute

List of Exhibits

Chapter 1

Law of Agency

INTRODUCTION

As a former United States President once said, "The business of America is business," and in no other jurisdiction is this more true than in the state of New York. New York has a reputation in the legal community for being one of the primary jurisdictions to look to for judicial interpretations of business law. For any legal professional working in the state, it becomes imperative that he or she have at least a rudimentary understanding of New York business institutions.

Because almost all businesses operate by means of various individuals who either work for or with the business owner, one of the questions concerned with understanding business law involves the concept of **vicarious liability:** Under what circumstances will a person be held legally liable for injuries resulting to a third person caused not by that individual's actions but by the actions of someone acting for the individual. In almost every business format the business owner may, under certain circumstances, be held liable not only for his or her own actions, but also for the actions of persons who are acting on his or her behalf.

Vicarious liability — one person being held legally responsible for another's actions.

Under traditional legal theory, this concept of vicarious liability is classified under the broad heading of the law of agency; however, such categorization is misleading. The traditional "law of agency" concerns three separate and distinct legal relationships, only one of which is a true agency relationship. To the innocent third party, these distinctions may be difficult to discern. However, it is crucial to be able to differentiate between these three relationships because the liabilities for injuries to third persons are totally different depending on the relationship existing between the business owner and the person acting on or for the owner's behalf.

The three relationships typically included under the concept of the law of agency are the master-servant relationship, independent contractor, and principal-agent relationship. Each of these relationships is created in its own way, and the business owner's potential liability is different or nonexistent, depending on which of the three relationships existed when the injury to the third party occurred. For the business person, the determination of potential liability in operating the business is one of the most important considerations in determining both the nature of the business format selected and the type of legal relationships into which the owner is willing to enter. Because this vicarious liability attaches to all of the different business formats discussed throughout this text, it is necessary to begin an analysis of New York business law with a discussion of the law of agency or, more accurately, the business owner's potential vicarious liability incident to operating a business.

MASTER-SERVANT RELATIONSHIP

Defined

Master-servant relationship — form of employment relationship in which the servant remains under the master's control.

The **master-servant relationship** is one in which a person, known as the servant, is employed to render services of any type, otherwise than in the furtherance of an independent calling, who remains under the control of another, the master, in rendering such services. The master-servant relationship is one of the classical legal business relations and is one of the backbones of tort law.

> *Example: A boss hires a secretary to do the boss's typing, filing, dictation, and greeting customers. The boss is the master, and the secretary is the servant. The secretary is employed to render secretarial services on behalf of the boss who controls the secretary's workday.*

One of the essential elements of the master-servant relationship is the right of the master to control the servant's work. The servant has no independent discretion and must perform the service the master indicates in the manner and order of the master's wishes.

> *Example: One day the secretary from the previous example decides that he or she does not want to do any typing that day and will only file and answer the telephone. The secretary is legally incapable of making such a decision. The control of the secretary's work is within the control and discretion of the boss.*

Note that several years ago, because of the connotative impact of the words "master-servant," some courts and legal scholars were substituting the term "employer-employee" for this type of relationship. This substitution of terms has fallen into disuse because of the proliferation of federal and state statutes that specifically deal with employment law issues. Consequently, the trend has reverted to the term "master-servant."

Liability

Respondeat superior — tort doctrine holding a master liable for his or her servant's torts.

Once it is determined that there is in fact a master-servant relationship, the master will be held liable for the tortious acts committed by his or her servant, provided that the tortious acts occur while furthering the master's business. This concept of vicarious liability is known as **respondeat superior,** "let the master answer." However, in order to hold the master liable, it must be shown that the servant was acting in furtherance of the master's business when the tort occurred.

> *Example: The owner of a flower shop employs a delivery man to deliver floral arrangements ordered by customers. To facilitate the delivery, the owner provides a delivery truck with the shop's name emblazoned on the side. One morning, while delivering*

flowers for his boss, the delivery man realizes that it is almost noon and one of his deliveries is for a luncheon banquet that must be delivered by noon. In speeding across town to make the delivery, the delivery truck hits an elderly woman as she is crossing the street. The owner of the flower shop may be held liable for the woman's injuries because the driver was negligent (speeding) in order to fulfill the owner's business interests.

Frolic of his own — exception to doctrine of respondeat superior.

However, if it can be evidenced that, at the time that the tort occurred, the servant was not furthering the master's business but was on a **"frolic of his own,"** the master will not be held liable for the resulting injuries to third persons.

Example: Assume that, in the previous example, instead of speeding across town to make a delivery for the flower shop, the delivery man, realizing that it is almost noon, decides to race across town to try to catch his girlfriend before she goes to lunch so that they can have lunch together. Now when the van hits the elderly woman, the driver alone will be liable because he is not furthering the master's business but is negligent while on a frolic of his own.

Note that the injured party may either sue the master under the theory of respondeat superior or the servant for his or her own negligent conduct, but the third party may not recover from both.

There are several exceptions to the doctrine of respondeat superior in addition to the servant's frolic of his own which must be addressed:

Fellow servant exception — master is not liable for servant's tortious act committed against another of the master's servants.

1. ***Fellow servant exception.*** This exception to the doctrine of respondeat superior states that a master will not be liable for the negligence of one of his servants that injures another of his servants. The rationale behind this exception is the possibility of collusion among servants to reach the "deep pockets" of the master and the chilling effect that not having such an exception might have on the master's willingness to hire staff.

Example: A worker on an assembly line negligently scatters pipes that she was using as part of her job. The worker standing next to her falls over the pipes and breaks his leg. In this instance, because the injury was caused by the negligence of a fellow servant, the employer will not be liable.

Workers compensation — state statute granting relief from fellow servant exception.

Workers Compensation Board — government agency that administers workers compensation.

Because of the potential injustice that could result because of the fellow servant exception, in which the injured worker's only recourse for potentially serious injuries is to sue a low-income fellow servant, the legislatures have enacted **workers compensation** laws that mandate employers maintain liability insurance and exist to compensate injured workers for job-related accidents that would otherwise not be compensated for because of the fellow servant exception. The statutes provide a comprehensive list of injuries and specify a dollar amount to be paid to the injured worker according to a statutory schedule. N.Y. Work. Comp. Law §§ 11, 29(6). Any worker injured on the job due to a coworker's negligence may seek compensation by filing a claim with the **Workers Compensation Board,** the administrative agency created to adjudicate these claims.

Example: The assembly line worker from the previous example files a claim with the Workers Compensation Board and, after proving the nature and extent of the injury, is awarded a statutorily determined amount as compensation for his injuries.

2. *Intentional torts.* As a general rule, a master is not responsible for injuries to third parties resulting from his or her servant's intentional tortious actions. The doctrine of respondeat superior only applies in instances of negligence. However, there is an exception to this exception: If the intentional tort was committed while furthering the master's business and is reasonably foreseeable as a consequence of the nature of the job the servant is performing, the master may still be held liable.

Example: A nightclub hires a bouncer to maintain control among the patrons. One night, while attempting to remove some rowdy customers, the bouncer hits one the customers, breaking the customer's nose. Even though this in an intentional tort, the nightclub owner may be held liable because such action was reasonably foreseeable based on the type of service the bouncer is employed to perform.

Example: A department store employs a small staff in its customer service department to handle complaints from patrons. During the Christmas week, one of the workers becomes overwhelmed at the crush of complaining customers and, becoming angry at one particularly vociferous customer, reaches over the counter and rips the customer's coat and slaps her face. In this instance, the owner might not be liable because this action was not within the foreseeable scope of the employee's job.

Negligent hiring — master's personal liability when he hires an incompetent servant.

3. *Negligent hiring.* **Negligent hiring** refers to a master employing a person who is not competent to perform the job, and that incompetence causes the injury to the third person. In this instance, the master is not being held vicariously liable but is liable in his or her own right for his or her own negligent conduct.

Example: In the previous example with the department store, if the employee had a history of violent behavior, perhaps even a criminal record for assault, and the employer either failed to research her background or disregarded it and placed her in a situation in which this violent behavior might occur, the owner might be liable for her actions under the concept of negligent hiring.

Bell v. Perrino
67 N.Y.2d 751, 490 N.E.2d 1227 (1986)

Plaintiffs commenced this action to recover damages for injuries sustained by plaintiff Arthur Bell when he was shot and seriously injured by defendant Perrino, an unlicensed taxicab driver, when Bell attempted to escape paying the taxi fare. Plaintiffs sued, among others, Deluxe (the company which dispatched defendant Perrino to pick up Arthur Bell), the City of New Rochelle, and defendant Perrino's employer, Frank Strazza. As to defendant Deluxe, plaintiffs' complaint alleged that it was negligent in failing to supply and/or dispatch and/or hire competent, skillful and licensed taxicab drivers because it knew or should have known that defendant Perrino was given to violence and use of firearms.

The Appellate Division concluded that defendant Deluxe was an independent company providing dispatching services to more than 20 cab companies in New Rochelle; that while Deluxe did recommend that defendant Strazza consider employing Perrino, it was Strazza who actually hired him; that therefore it was clear that plaintiffs had no cause of action against Deluxe under a theory of respondeat superior for negligent hiring; that a dispatcher which owns no cabs and which is an entity independent of those cab companies employing its dispatching services has no obligation to make sure that the drivers it dispatches are qualified and have no vicious propensities, and that as to defendant City of New Rochelle, Special Term properly dismissed the complaint, since absent a special relationship creating a municipal duty to exercise care for the benefit of a particular class of individuals, no liability may be imposed upon a municipality for failure to enforce a statute or regulation, and ordinances such as those at bar, requiring the licensing of the taxicab industry, are enacted for the benefit of the general public, not for the benefit of a limited class of persons.
Affirmed.

---

4. *Personal negligence.* If a master is negligent himself or herself in providing an unsafe environment, the master may be sued in his or her own right by his or her servant or by third persons.

Example: A bookstore owner purchases some inexpensive shelving which he knows is not strong but is very cost-effective. When one of his salespeople places books on the shelf, it collapses, injuring both the employee and a customer. In this instance, the store owner may be personally liable for his or her own negligence in failing to meet an ordinary standard of care in providing unsafe equipment.

INDEPENDENT CONTRACTOR

Defined

Independent contractor — person hired exclusively for the results to be accomplished.

An **independent contractor** is a person who is hired exclusively for the result to be accomplished. The independent contractor is not under the control of the other contracting party, outside of a specific contractual provision, and the independent contractor has total discretion with respect to job performance. Typical examples of independent contractors are doctors, lawyers, accountants, and all other persons who are hired simply to provide a specified result.

Example: A business owner hires a decorator to refurnish the office. Under the terms of the contract, the business owner agrees to pay the decorator a specified amount for services plus an additional specified amount for paint, wallpaper, furniture, and so forth. The decorator is an independent contractor.

Liability

The contracting party is not liable for the actions of the independent contractor that injures third persons, absent a specific contractual obligation to assume such responsibility, unless:

1. the independent contractor is hired to perform an inherently dangerous activity such as using explosives to demolish a building, or

2. the independent contractor agreed to have his or her actions controlled by the other contracting party, or

3. the contracting party provides tools and implements to the independent contractor which is the cause of the injuries to the third person.

As a general rule, the contracting party is not liable, absent an agreement to the contrary, for the tortious acts of the independent contractor or for the contracts the independent contractor enters into in order to perform his or her services. These are the responsibilities of the independent contractor alone.

Example: A businessperson hires a lawyer to incorporate the business. The lawyer fails to pay her secretary who typed the papers used for the incorporation. The secretary cannot sue the businessperson for the money, unless the businessperson specifically agreed to pay for typing. This is the exclusive responsibility of the lawyer.

The same person may act as both a servant and as an independent contractor for the same individual. However, the potential liability of that individual for injuries to third persons is dependent on the activity being performed.

Example: A boss decides the business could use some new letterhead and stationary and knows the secretary has been studying calligraphy. The boss hires the secretary to design the new letterhead for the office for a fee of $1,500, including all costs. Delighted, the secretary goes to the office supply store used by the boss and purchases pens, inks, and paper in order to create the design. Upon leaving, the secretary seizes the bag of supplies in a gesture of glee, and the bag hits another customer causing a black eye. The customer will not prevail in a suit against the boss under the doctrine of respondeat superior. When the injury occurred, the secretary was acting as an independent contractor, not a servant, and so is exclusively liable for any resulting negligence.

Carrion v. Orbit Messenger, Inc.
82 N.Y.2d 742, 621 N.E.2d 692 (1993)

It is well settled that whether an operator of a delivery vehicle is an agent, potentially rendering the principal liable under the doctrine of respondeat superior, or is an independent contractor, is a question for the trier of fact (see, *Johnson v R.T.K. Petroleum Co., 289 NY 101,* rearg denied *289 NY 646; Bratt v Midland Asphalt Corp., 8 NY2d 963, 965*). Here, plaintiffs' pleadings allege that the driver of the truck worked exclusively for defendant, that he was required to use defendant's name and forms when performing work for defendant and to return all defendant's receipts and job tickets. Defendant supplied the truck driver with workers' compensation insurance, paid him, on a weekly basis, 57% of defendant's gross billings, and supplied him with a check cashing card, signed by defendant's representative, on which he was described as an "employee." Because plaintiffs have submitted sufficient proof to raise a question with respect to the nature of the relationship between the tortfeasor and his alleged principal, summary judgment is not warranted.

Rosenberg v. Equitable Life Assurance Society of the United States
79 N.Y.2d 663, 595 N.E.2d 840 (1992)

Plaintiff is the widow of Sidney Rosenberg and the administratrix of his estate. She seeks damages from defendant for her husband's wrongful death from cardiac failure resulting, as the jury found, from a stress electrocardiogram administered during a physical examination ordered by defendant as a precondition to his obtaining life insurance. The examination was performed by Dr. R. Arora, a private physician, who maintained offices in New Jersey and was paid by defendant on a case-by-case basis. He is not a party to this action.

The plaintiff advances two theories for recovery. First, she contends that defendant is vicariously liable for the negligence of Dr. Arora, although he was an independent contractor, because the examination as administered was "inherently dangerous." Second, plaintiff asserts that defendant is liable for its own negligence in ordering the stress exam and in failing to obtain decedent's informed consent to it. The jury agreed with plaintiff on both grounds, awarding her a substantial verdict, and the Appellate Division affirmed. We conclude that defendant is not legally responsible to plaintiff on either ground and, therefore, reverse the judgment and dismiss the complaint.

On this evidence the jury found that decedent underwent a stress EKG during his examination by Dr. Arora and that it was the proximate cause of his death.

The general rule is that an employer who hires an independent contractor is not liable for the independent contractor's negligent acts. There are exceptions, however. For reasons of public policy, the employer's duty is sometimes held to be nondelegable and, though blameless, it is liable for the independent contractor's negligence. The exceptions generally recognized involve situations where the employer (1) is under a statutory duty to perform or control the work, (2) has assumed a specific duty by contract, (3) is under a duty to keep premises safe, or (4) has assigned work to an independent contractor which the employer knows or has reason to know involves special dangers inherent in the work or dangers which should have been anticipated by the employer.

In such instances, the employer cannot insulate itself from liability by claiming that it was not negligent: the employer is vicariously liable for the fault of the independent contractor because a legal duty is imposed on it which cannot be delegated. We are concerned in this case with the fourth exception involving "inherently dangerous" work.

The trial court instructed the jury that Dr. Arora was an independent contractor and that, generally, an employer is not liable for the acts of an independent contractor. It also told the jury of the exception to that general rule fixing liability on the employer "when danger to others is inherent in the acts." The jury was instructed that if it found that defendant should have anticipated the consequences of the negligent acts performed by Dr. Arora, then it could consider defendant responsible for those acts. Although these instructions accurately reflect the rules of vicarious liability when inherently dangerous work is delegated to an independent contractor, we conclude the issue should not have been submitted to the jury in this case but should have been decided as a question of law.

The nature of those acts qualifying as "inherently dangerous" has been stated in a number of ways, not always with perfect consistency. The Restatement explains the rule and the acts within it as follows:

"One who employs an independent contractor to do work involving a special danger to others which the employer knows or has reason to know to be inherent in or normal to the work, or which he contemplates or has reason to contemplate when making the contract, is subject to liability for physical harm caused to such others by the contractor's failure to take reasonable precautions against such danger." (Restatement [Second] of Torts § 427; see also, *McDonald v Shell Oil Co., 20 NY2d 160, 166,* supra; *Rohlfs v Weil, 271 NY 444, 448.)*

Thus, before the exception applies, it must appear not only that the work involves a risk of harm inherent in the nature of the work itself, but also that the employer recognizes, or should recognize, that risk in advance of the contract.

The Appellate Division affirmed the jury's determination here, concluding that the inherently dangerous exception applied "in light of evidence that the doctor was mandated to follow defendant's strict protocol." Although the record supports the finding that defendant requested Dr. Arora to perform the test, defendant could not have "mandated" him to do so because Dr. Arora had not assumed any contractual obligation to do as it bid. In the form letter which was presumably sent to the doctor, it was stated that a stress EKG was required to complete decedent's application for life insurance. However, the letter also stated: "If you cannot complete the test according to our protocol, please return this letter immediately to enable us to make alternate arrangements." More to the point, however, the issue here is not the degree of control exercised over Dr. Arora but whether the act involved was inherently dangerous.

Generally speaking, performing an EKG is not an inherently dangerous activity and plaintiff's evidence that certain dangers accompanied performance of a stress EKG under the circumstances presented was not sufficient to take the case to the jury. Although the stress EKG was ordered for a person with serious heart problems, performance of it, as a matter of law, did not constitute an inherently dangerous activity because defendant's independent contractor was a medical professional under no duty to perform the examination in a manner contrary to his legal and professional responsibilities. That being so, there were no apparent risks involved in defendant requesting him to do so.

Stated another way, the inherently dangerous exception cannot be applied unless a risk inherent in the nature of the procedures is apparent or contemplated by the employer. Dr. Arora, in addition to his professional responsibility embodied in the Hippocratic Oath "to do no harm," had a legal duty common to both New York and New Jersey authority to disclose to his patients inherent risks to them and to perform dangerous procedures only with the patient's consent (see, New York Public Health Law § 2805-d; *Largey v Rothman, 110 NJ 204, 540 A2d 504* [physician has a duty to disclose to patient information as will enable patient to make an evaluation of the nature of the treatment and of any attendant substantial risks]; see also, NJ Stat Annot § 26:2H-12.8 [right of hospital patient to receive from physician information necessary to give informed consent]). Defendant could not reasonably anticipate that Dr. Arora would disregard these responsibilities and administer a stress EKG to decedent if decedent's condition foreclosed doing so safely and it could reasonably expect that the potential risks posed by a stress EKG would be explained to decedent and that he would either give his informed consent or decline to undergo the test. Under the circumstances, the inherent danger exception does not apply and the employer could not be answerable for the negligence of the independent contractor.

It is also worth emphasizing that these exceptions imposing vicarious liability on an employer are grounded on public policy and should have no role when public policy is not served by applying them. In this case, plaintiffs seek to hold defendant liable for requiring Dr. Arora to conduct a stress EKG. However, no medical doctor can be required to render services which, in the doctor's professional judgment, are dangerous or contraindicated and public policy is not served by imposing liability for the doctor's fault in doing so on the insurer. High risk life insurance is an integral part of personal and commercial financial planning. When applicants seek such coverage, insurers must be free, before issuing a policy, to test them in a manner calculated to evaluate the risk presented. In the process, they necessarily rely on members of the medical profession, not only to provide the information required but, also, to perform their duty by refusing to conduct dangerous tests unless the patient is fully apprised of the risks and consents to their administration.

Accordingly, the order of the Appellate Division should be reversed and the complaint dismissed, with costs.

PRINCIPAL-AGENT RELATIONSHIP

Defined

Principal-agent relationship — relationship in which one person has the ability to enter into contracts on another's behalf.

Agent — person who has the legal ability to enter into contracts on another's behalf.

Principal — the person from whom the agent's authority derives.

In the **principal-agent relationship,** an **agent** acts for and on behalf of another person, called the **principal,** in order to enter into contractual relationships with third persons on the principal's behalf. The agent acts as the principal's legal representative with third persons, and the authorized acts of the agent bind the principal contractually to third persons.

There are several essential features of the agency relationship:

1. The agent has the authority to perform legal acts (enter into contracts) on behalf of the principal.

Example: One student asks another student to purchase a textbook for her. When the second student purchases the book from the bookstore, the second student is acting as the agent for the first student—the contract is between the first student and the bookstore.

2. The agent has discretion to perform the legal acts on behalf of the principal in the manner the agent deems most appropriate.

Example: In the previous example, the second student could select any vendor in order to acquire the text; the student did not have to purchase the book at any particular bookstore unless so instructed by the principal.

3. The agent's ability to act is deemed to be both representative and derivative: The agent acts on behalf of the principal (representative) and can only do what the principal can do legally (derivative). The agent's ability to enter into contracts is derived from the principal's ability to do so. For this reason anyone may be an agent, even a minor or an incapacitated person, because the contract is between the principal and the third person, not the agent and the third person.

Example: A mother asks her 10-year-old son to go to the grocery store to buy some bread, having the grocer put the cost on the mother's account with the store. Even though the child is a minor, he may still enter into a valid contract with the store on his mother's behalf.

Example: An incapacitated person, whose financial affairs are under the supervision of a guardian, asks his 35-year-old brother to buy some corporate stock for him. In this instance, even though the brother is legally capable of buying stock, the incapacitated person is not, and so the brother cannot act as the incapacitated person's agent—the "principal" lacks contractual capacity.

It is important to remember that, for the most part (see exceptions following), the agent acts merely as the conduit for the principal when entering into contracts. The agent can be viewed as no more than the principal's pen used to sign the agreement.

Special agent — agent for a particular act or transaction.

General agent — nonspecial agent.

Agents are divided into two broad categories: special and general. A **special agent** is one who is authorized to act for a limited purpose, whereas a **general agent** is defined as all non-special agents—agents for more than just a limited purpose.

Example: The student in the previous example is a special agent. The student is authorized to purchase only one book on one occasion. An example of a general agent would be a management agent who works for a landlord under a two-year contract during which time the agent handles all of the landlord's relations with the tenants.

Creation

There are three methods whereby the principal-agent relationship may be created: by agreement, by ratification, and by estoppel.

Agency by agreement — agency formed by mutual assent.

1. *Agency by agreement.* An agency relationship may be formed simply by the parties, the principal and the agent, agreeing to enter into that relationship. No consideration is necessary; the relationship may be gratuitous. The agreement may be either express or implied, and there are no requisite formalities surrounding the formation of the agreement. The only restrictions are that the agency must be for a lawful purpose and the principal must have contractual capacity. As indicated previously, anyone may be an agent.

Example: A real estate developer hires for a set fee a New York resident to act as his agent for selling residential units in a condominium in Florida. The New York resident has been given the authority to sign sales contracts on behalf of the developer. An agency relationship has been created by agreement.

Erie County Sav. Bank v. Grove
13 N.Y.S.2d 224 (1939)

(a) Motion on notice made under Rule 112 by the plaintiff for judgment on the pleadings; (b) Motion made at time of argument by defendant for judgment on the pleadings.

The disposition of the motions depends on the construction of a power of attorney executed by the defendant, Hattie A. Grove, under which power of attorney her name was attached as an obligor to a certain bond given as collateral with a certain mortgage on real estate, the other obligors being the two other defendants named herein. Insofar as such two other defendants are concerned, judgment has been rendered against them and the action has been severed so far as they are concerned. Such power of attorney which was properly witnessed and acknowledged is in the following language:

'Know All Men By These Presents, that I, Hattie A. Grove, of the Town of Amherst, County of Erie and State of New York, have made, constituted and appointed and by these presents do make, constitute and appoint J. Nelson Grove my true and lawful attorney, for me and in my name, place and stead, giving and granting unto the said J. Nelson Grove full power and authority to do and perform all and every act and thing whatsoever requisite and necessary to be done in and about the premises as fully to all intents and purposes as I might or could do if personally present with full power of substitution and revocation, hereby ratifying and confirming all that said J. Nelson Grove, said attorney or his substitute, shall lawfully do or cause to be done by virtue thereof, and particularly authorizing said attorney to sell, convey, mortgage or lease all real property in which I may have any interest.

'In Witness Whereof, I have hereunto set my hand and seal this 22nd day of May, in the year One Thousand Nine Hundred and twenty-eight.

'Hattie A. Grove L. S.'

Following the execution of such power of attorney, the signatures of the three defendants herein were attached to the bond which is the subject of this suit and its accompanying mortgage, the attachment of the name of the defendant, Hattie A. Grove, being by J. Nelson Grove, as attorney, who, it is claimed, acted under virtue of the power of attorney above recited. In the construction of a power of attorney if there is any ambiguity or doubt, the circumstances which brought about the execution of such power should be considered in determining the scope of the power conferred by the instrument on the attorney. I am of the opinion that there is a question as to whether the language of the power of attorney is such as to convey full authority on the attorney, because, although the first part of the power of attorney apparently is broad and full up to the words 'by virtue thereof,' the words then following 'and particularly authorizing said attorney to sell, convey, mortgage or lease all real property in which I may have any interest' may have been intended as a limitation of the power to one to handle real property of the grantor of the authority and for no other purpose (Restatement Law of Agency, Am.L.I. Section 37(2). If this construction is the correct one, then the attorney did not have a general power and it would be necessary, in order to recover against the defendant, Hattie A. Grove, to establish that she had an interest in the real property covered by the mortgage given as security to the bond on which suit has been brought. The pleadings show no such interest. It may be on trial, such interest can be shown and it may be that on trial if no interest in the real property is shown, that circumstances surrounding the execution of the power of attorney were such as to require the construction of the power of attorney as one of full power. For these reasons, I may not grant either of the motions herein.

Agency by ratification — agency created retroactively when principal affirms unauthorized acts.

2. *Agency by ratification.* This method of creating an agency results when the presumed principal accepts the benefits or otherwise affirms the acts of one who purported to act on his or her behalf. The agency relationship is created retroactively, after the presumed agent has entered into the contract. Be alert to the fact that, since the agent was not authorized to act on behalf of the "principal" when the contract was formed, the "principal" will not be bound to the agreement unless he or she accepts the benefits either expressly or impliedly. Furthermore,

the ratification must be total; the principal cannot selectively ratify portions of the contract.

Example: A paralegal is attending a real estate luncheon. He overhears two real estate tycoons talking, one indicating that she is interested in acquiring a residential unit in a particular area of the city. The paralegal's cousin owns a building in that area that the cousin has been trying to sell unsuccessfully for several years. The paralegal approaches the tycoon, tells her that he is representing the cousin, and tells her about the building, and the tycoon agrees to purchase the property. The agreement is hastily written down on some paper. The paralegal immediately goes to a pay phone and calls his cousin. If the cousin likes the purchase price, the cousin may ratify the agreement. However, if the cousin does not wish to sell the building, the paralegal may be liable to the tycoon because no valid contract has been formed.

Agency by estoppel — agency relationship created by equitable concepts where it would be unjust to permit the principal to deny the agency.

3. ***Agency by estoppel.*** An agency relationship may be created under the auspices of the court's equitable jurisdiction in situations in which the presumed principal has intentionally or negligently caused a third person to believe that another is his agent and the third person relies on such appearance in dealing with the supposed agent. Under these circumstances, the principal will be estopped, or barred, from denying the agency. Note that this method of creation comes about by the acts of the principal, not the agent.

Example: A department store indicates on its directory that it has a watch repair department. A customer who regularly deals with the store goes to the watch repairman to have a watch fixed. The customer receives a department store receipt for the watch. When the customer returns to pick up the watch, the customer pays with the department store's charge card. Two hours later the watch stops running, and the customer returns to the repairman who refuses to do anything. When the customer complains to the store's management, the customer is told that the watch repair department is not part of the store but is an independent contractor who rents store space. In this instance, an agency by estoppel may have been created. The store indicated that the repair department was part of the store—it let the repairman give a store receipt and accept the store charge card for payment. By its own actions, the store has caused the customer to believe that the repairman is acting as the store's agent, and so the store may be held responsible for the damage to the watch.

Types of Authority

Once it has been determined that an agency relationship has been created, the next area of concern is the type of authority the agent possesses. An agent may only act on behalf of the principal if the agent has the authority to so act. There are three types of authority that an agent may have:

Actual authority — agent's ability to act derived from principal's manifestations to the agent.

1. *Actual authority.* **Actual authority** refers to the powers of the agent that the principal has manifested his or her consent that the agent should have. Actual authority results from the principal's manifestations directly to the agent and divides into two areas: **express authority,** which comes about by the specific instructions the principal has given the agent, including any power that would be incidental or

Express authority — ability to act created by direct statements.

Implied authority — ability to act arising from custom, usage, and past.

necessary to carry out that purpose, and **implied authority,** which comes about by custom, usage, or the past conduct of the principal and the agent so that such powers can be implied by their relationship and express conduct.

Example: A clothing manufacturer needs to acquire a specific dye lot of red silk cloth. The manufacturer has employed an agent for the past five years to assist him in these types of acquisitions. The manufacturer contacts the agent and tells her to buy for him 500 yards of the specified fabric, paying no more than $2 per yard. The manufacturer also tells the agent to see that he is billed in the usual manner. The agent has actual authority to purchase fabric for the manufacturer: Her express authority is to buy 500 yards of a specific fabric at no more than $2 per yard; her implied authority is to see that the manufacturer is billed "in the usual manner," which, in this instance based on their past dealings, is to be billed on credit with payments to be made in no less than 90 days after delivery.

As long as the principal has manifested his or her intention by word or deed that the agent has authority to act, the agent has actual authority. This is true even if the principal was mistaken in granting the authority or was misled by the agent into giving the authority. Actual authority is determined by the objective actions of the principal in order to protect third persons who deal with the agent on the principal's behalf. As long as the agent has actual authority, the third party may sue the principal for the full contract price if the agreement is breached.

Example: A real estate developer hires an agent to purchase undeveloped parcels of land. The agent obtains the job by lying on his resume regarding his real estate background which in fact is nonexistent. The agent buys some land for the developer from a third party. The developer feels the price for the land is too high and refuses to go through with the sales contract. The developer claims that he should not be bound because he would never have hired the agent had the agent not lied to him. The seller may sue the developer for breach of contract, and the principal will be bound. The principal's recourse would be against the agent, but the innocent third party is protected.

Apparent authority — ability to act created by principal's manifestations to a third party.

Ostensible authority — apparent authority.

2. *Apparent authority.* **Apparent authority,** also known as **ostensible authority,** results from the principal's manifestations to the third party, not the agent, that the agent is authorized to act on the principal's behalf. The determination of apparent authority rests on the "reasonable" belief of the third party under the circumstances. That is, would the reasonable person believe the agent has the authority to act for the principal?

Example: A farmer enters a grocery store to sell his rutabagas to the owner. The farmer approaches the only person in the store, who is the store's owner. In order to get rid of the farmer, the owner says that the person who makes all produce purchases for the store is a man called Eric, who is not in at the moment. Eric is an employee of the owner who, when the owner is absent, acts as the owner's agent in making sales to customers. Later in the day when the owner is out and Eric is in charge, the farmer returns and, ascertaining that the man is Eric, convinces Eric to buy the rutabagas. In this instance, the owner would be liable to the farmer for the purchase price of the vegetables because the owner told the farmer that Eric had the authority to make such purchases.

Because apparent authority is created by the principal's manifestations to the third person, such authority can only be rescinded by the principal manifesting to the third person that the agent no longer has the authority to act. Any statement to the agent alone is ineffective with respect to the third person who is relying on the representation of authority the principal has made to him or her.

Example: The grocery store owner from the previous example, furious at what Eric did, tells Eric never to buy rutabagas again. Several weeks later the farmer returns and convinces Eric to buy arugula for the store. The owner is still liable to the farmer—the farmer was never told by the owner that Eric could no longer make such purchases, and Eric did not buy rutabagas, which is what he was told not to do by the grocer.

If the agent has apparent authority, just as with actual authority, the principal is liable to the third person who dealt with the agent for the full contract price.

Authority by estoppel — agent's ability to act created under equitable concepts when it would be unjust to permit the principal to escape liability.

3. *Authority by estoppel.* **Authority by estoppel** results when the principal intentionally or negligently causes or allows a third person to believe that his agent is authorized to do that which in fact he is not authorized to do *and* the third person detrimentally relies thereon to such an extent that it would be unjust to allow the principal to deny the authority. Authority by estoppel differs from apparent authority in that it comes about without direct manifestations to the third person and the third person must detrimentally rely on the perceived action, meaning that the third person must suffer some economic loss. If the agent is only imbued with authority by estoppel, the third party is limited in his or her recovery to actual loss rather than the contract price.

Example: The grocery store owner from the previous examples has now forgiven Eric. Several months later, Eric asks for a raise, but the owner does not wish to part with money. Instead, the owner makes Eric the "Store Manager," giving him a jacket with a name tag indicating his new title. A different farmer enters the store while the owner is absent, sees Eric in the jacket, and approaches him to sell some produce, believing that the store manager would have the ability to make such purchases for the store. Eric buys some fruit. In this instance, the owner is liable for the economic loss to the farmer if he breaches the agreement because the owner provided Eric with the indicia of authority—the jacket and the name tag—which was relied on by the farmer. However, if the contract called for buying the fruit at $2 per barrel but the farmer's actual cost was $1 per barrel, the farmer may only receive $1 per barrel from the owner—the actual loss, not the contract price.

Standard Funding Corp. v. Lewitt
89 N.Y.2d 546, 678 N.E.2d 874 (1997)

Plaintiff Standard Funding Corporation, an insurance premium financing company, entered into a series of financing agreements with Lewitt Agency, Inc. to finance the premiums on insurance polices of defendant Public Service Mutual Insurance Company. Standard Funding had provided Lewitt with its financing agreement forms which Lewitt and the prospective insureds were to complete and sign. Before entering into the first financing agreement with Lewitt, Standard Funding contacted Public Service Mutual whose personnel confirmed that Lewitt was an agent in good standing with the company, licensed to sell all lines of business.

At issue on this appeal are four such agreements that Standard Funding and Lewitt entered into in October and December 1989 to finance premiums ranging from $15,500 to $153,500 for policies purportedly issued by Public Service Mutual. Each form, which was signed by Lewitt and the insured, indicated that Public Service Mutual had issued policies to the insureds and that the insureds had paid approximately 25% of the premiums to the insurance company.

After Standard Funding failed to receive payments from the alleged insureds, it contacted Public Service Mutual who investigated the matter and discovered that these four financing agreements covered fictitious policies and false insureds. No policies were ever issued in connection with these agreements and Public Service Mutual received no premiums for them. Public Service Mutual thereafter terminated Lewitt's agency contract.

Standard Funding commenced this damages action against Lewitt and Public Service Mutual. The claim against Public Service Mutual was premised on the theory that the insurer was liable for the fraudulent acts of Lewitt acting as its agent. After Lewitt filed for bankruptcy, the claim against Public Service Mutual proceeded to trial. Following a nonjury trial, Supreme Court entered judgment in favor of Standard Funding in the amount of $227,325 plus interest. The Appellate Division affirmed, holding that although the financing agreements between Lewitt and Standard Funding were outside the scope of Lewitt's actual authority, Standard Funding had reasonably relied upon Lewitt's authority to issue Public Service Mutual policies and collect premiums in tendering its checks to Lewitt, and thus, Public Service Mutual was liable under the doctrine of apparent authority. Because we conclude that Lewitt had neither actual nor apparent authority to enter into the financing agreements on behalf of Public Service Mutual, we now reverse.

There is no basis to conclude that the agency contract between Lewitt and Public Service Mutual endowed Lewitt with actual authority to procure on behalf of Public Service Mutual the financing of premiums for proposed insureds. The agency agreement granted Lewitt authority to "solicit and accept proposals for insurance covering such risks as the Company may authorize to be insured in the [agent's] territory . . . subject [to] all the terms, covenants and conditions of this agreement." Under the terms of its agency agreement, Lewitt was also endowed with "full power and authority to receive, collect and receipt for premiums on insurance tendered by the Agent to and accepted by the Company." Thus, Lewitt was expressly authorized only to issue insurance policies and to receive and collect premiums; nothing in the agency agreement authorized Lewitt to negotiate or enter into premium financing agreements on behalf of Public Service Mutual.

We reject plaintiff's contention that premium financing is an activity incidental to or reasonably necessary for the performance of those express powers. In the case of *First Trust & Deposit Co. v Middlesex Mut. Fire Ins. Co. (284 NY 747,* affg *259 App Div 80),* a copartnership acted as agent for the defendant insurance company for whom it was authorized to issue insurance policies and collect premiums. As required by law, the insurance company had certified to the State Insurance Department "the good reputation and integrity of the copartnership" as its agent *(259 App Div, at 82).* Just as Lewitt here, the agency in First Trust tendered a fictitious insurance policy and instrument of indebtedness to an institution engaged in premium financing and vouched for their genuineness. When both the policy and the debt instrument turned out to be fraudulent, plaintiff, as assignee of the financing company, sought recovery from the insurance company on an agency theory.

The Appellate Division rejected plaintiff's argument that the insurance agent had been acting as agent for the defendant insurance company in procuring premium financing for proposed insureds. Instead, the Court held that the debt instrument and warranty "were given in a transaction on behalf of the copartnership as an entity, or on behalf of ostensibly insured, or on behalf of the investment corporation, and not in behalf of the copartnership as agent for the defendant" (*id., at 88* [emphasis supplied]). This Court agreed, affirming "on the ground that the fraud of the defendant's agent was not perpetrated in the course of the agent's employment" *(284 NY, at 748).* Likewise here, we hold that Lewitt's activities in entering into the premium financing agreements with Standard Funding fall outside the scope of activities authorized by its agency agreement.

Nor do we find any record support for a determination that Lewitt had apparent authority to enter into or procure financing agreements on behalf of Public Service Mutual. "Essential to the creation of apparent authority are words or conduct of the principal, communicated to a third party, that give rise to the appearance and belief that the agent possesses authority to enter into a transaction."

Public Service Mutual made no representations regarding Lewitt's authority to procure on its behalf premium financing for its proposed insureds. Rather, Public Service Mutual's representations were limited to Lewitt's power to write insurance policies and accept premiums for them. Moreover, all representations in the premium financing agreements were purely those of the agent. The financing agreements set forth the obligations of the insured and contained a warranty clause entitled "Brokers and/or Agents Representations and Undertaking" whereby the signatory agent or broker agreed to "warrant[ ] the validity of this agreement and the truth of the facts contained therein," including the genuineness of the insured's signature and the fact that an individual policy had been issued. The only signatures required on the form were those of the "Broker or Agent" and the "Insured." Correspondingly, the checks issued by Standard Funding pursuant to the financing agreements were payable solely to Lewitt. Under these circumstances, the very terms of the agreements belie Standard Funding's allegation that from its perspective, Lewitt appeared to be acting as agent for Public Service Mutual.

The only explicit representation Standard Funding can point to in order to establish apparent authority is Public Service Mutual's certification that Lewitt was an agent in good standing authorized to write all lines of business for it. In *First Trust (supra),* however, where the insurance company had certified to the State Insurance Department "the good reputation and integrity of the copartnership" as the insurance company's agent, the Appellate Division held this very type of representation insufficient to support application of the doctrine of apparent authority *(259 App Div, at 82, 87–88).* We agree with the reasoning of that Court and hold that, in merely confirming Lewitt's good repute and status as an agent to write insurance policies, Public Service Mutual did not clothe Lewitt's representations in the premium financing agreements with apparent authority (see, *Ford v Unity Hosp., 32 NY2d, at 473,* supra).

Finally, plaintiff's reliance on the fact that Public Service Mutual received notices of financing as a basis for imposing liability on Public Service Mutual is also unavailing. The notices of financing stated that payment from Standard Financing was "subject to your acceptance of the terms and conditions of the premium finance agreement." It is undisputed that Public Service Mutual never signified any acceptance of the terms and conditions of the financing agreements, as the notices required.

Thus, no express ratification by Public Service Mutual ever took place (see, Restatement [Second] of Agency § 82 and comment a [principal may become liable for its agent's unauthorized acts by adopting the agent's actions and electing to become a party to the transaction]). Moreover, the rule that ratification may be implied where the principal retains the benefit of an unauthorized transaction with knowledge of the material facts, has no application here, since it is undisputed that Public Service Mutual received no premiums or any other benefit in connection with the fraudulent financing agreements.

Accordingly, the order of the Appellate Division should be reversed, with costs, and the complaint against Public Service Mutual dismissed.

Scope of Authority

Once the nature of the agent's authority has been established, the courts will only obligate the principal to acts of the agent performed on the principal's behalf which fall within the scope of the authority so granted, and the courts strictly construe the scope of the agent's authority. Furthermore, the law imposes an affirmative duty on third persons who deal with agents to determine in advance the scope of the agent's authority to act. Under New York law, an agent may only collect the selling price for the principal's goods sold by the agent if the agent possesses the goods. Furthermore, the agent may only accept cash for the payment; the agent may not take a check or extend credit unless that has been specifically agreed to or is part of the custom or past practices of the parties.

Heffernan v. Marine Midland Bank, N.A.
1999 N.Y. App. Div. LEXIS 12990

The complaint alleges that from 1985 through 1996 a former employee (Helliwell) of defendant bank perpetrated a "Ponzi" scheme, in which he solicited plaintiffs (many of whom appear to have been friends and family members) to invest in a purported "Trust B" account. Helliwell falsely represented to plaintiffs that the funds would be used to purchase notes issued and guaranteed by the bank. The funds plaintiffs entrusted to Helliwell were allegedly deposited into Helliwell's personal accounts at the bank and converted to his personal use.

We affirm the dismissal of plaintiffs' causes of action against the bank for fraud and breach of contract on the ground that, assuming the truth of the facts alleged in the complaint, the guaranteed rate of return on risk-free bank notes that Helliwell promised was so extraordinary as to require plaintiffs to make reasonable inquiry into the scope of Helliwell's actual authority (see, *Collision Plan Unlimited v Bankers Trust Co., 63 N.Y.2d 827, 831, 482 N.Y.S.2d 252, 472 N.E.2d 28*). Plaintiffs do not claim to have made such inquiry. Accordingly, their reliance on any appearance that Helliwell had authority to act for the bank with respect to the represented investment opportunity was unreasonable as a matter of law (cf., *Hallock v State of New York, 64 N.Y.2d 224, 231, 485 N.Y.S.2d 510, 474 N.E.2d 1178*).

We also conclude that the doctrine of authority by estoppel (see, Restatement [Second] of Agency § 8B) is inapplicable, since reasonable reliance, which as indicated is lacking, is essential to establishing such authority (see, *Matter of Karavos Compania Naviera v Atlantica Export Corp., 588 F.2d 1, 11*). Nor can liability be imposed on the bank based on the doctrine of respondeat superior, since Helliwell's scheme cannot be considered to have been within the scope of his employment (see, *Overton v Ebert, 180 A.D.2d 955, 957, 580 N.Y.S.2d 508,* lv denied *80 N.Y.2d 751; City of New York v Corwen, 164 A.D.2d 212, 218, 565 N.Y.S.2d 457).* Regarding plaintiffs' negligence-based causes of action, we find they were properly dismissed as plaintiffs fail to allege any facts showing a special duty running from the bank to them (see, *Gottlieb v Sullivan & Cromwell, 203 A.D.2d 241, 242, 609 N.Y.S.2d 344).*

However, we reinstate plaintiffs' sixth cause of action, for conversion, insofar as it is based on acts allegedly perpetrated in or after April 1991, on the ground that the complaint alleges facts, which, if proven, could support imposition of liability on the bank as a joint tortfeasor. If a bank, having actual notice or knowledge that a fiduciary is misappropriating trust funds on deposit with it, cooperates in the diversion, it may be held liable as a participant in the wrongdoing.

An agent is considered to be a fiduciary of the principal, meaning that the agent is held to a higher standard of care than ordinary care. As a result of being a fiduciary, an agent is required to fulfill his or her duties personally, and as a general rule agents are precluded from delegating their authority. However, there are three exceptions to this general rule of non-delegability for agents:

1. An agent may delegate any act that is considered to be mechanical or ministerial.

   Example: An agent may negotiate and enter into contracts on behalf of the principal, but the agent does not have to type the contract, a mechanical task, nor personally deliver the contract to the third party, a ministerial task.

2. An agent may delegate any act that the agent may not lawfully perform himself or herself.

   Example: As part of his duties as a management agent for a corporate landlord, the agent is required to sue tenants for breaches of their leases. A court rule requires that corporations be represented by a licensed attorney. If the agent is not a lawyer, he may hire one to fulfill this function.

3. An agent may delegate any duty where such delegation is customary or necessary. What is customary or necessary is determined by the court on a case by case basis.

In addition to the preceding, an agent is possessed of emergency powers to cover unforeseen emergency situations in furthering the authorized duties.

Because an agent is a fiduciary, he or she owes the principal the following specified duties:

1. *Duty to perform.* Once a person has agreed to be an agent, the person must perform the task so assumed.

2. *Duty to notify.* An agent must keep the principal informed of all actions the agent takes on the principal's behalf.

3. *Duty of loyalty.* The agent must be loyal to the interests of the principal and may not "self-deal," that is, make a profit (other than the agreed on compensation) for acting on the principal's behalf.

The principal may sue the agent for a breach of any of these duties, as well as for a breach of any general fiduciary obligation.

The principal also owes three duties to the agent, and the agent may seek judicial relief against the principal if the principal fails to meet these obligations:

1. *Duty to compensate and reimburse the agent.* This duty exists if such compensation and reimbursement has been agreed to by the parties.

2. *Duty to cooperate.* The principal must provide the agent with all information and documents in his or her control that the agent needs to fulfill his or her functions.

3. *The ordinary duty of care.* A principal may be liable to the agent for any negligence on the part of the principal that injures the agent, such as providing an unsafe work space for the agent to use.

Liabilities

As a general rule, the agent is not liable to the third person with whom he or she contracts on the principal's behalf because the contract is between the principal and the third person. However, there are two instances in which the agent may be liable to the third person:

1. *Ratification.* When the agent is acting without authority, if the principal does not ratify the contract, the agent may be liable to the third person for any loss or injury the third person incurs by reason of the failure of the contract. Furthermore, in order for the principal's ratification to be effective, the principal must have complete knowledge of all of the details of the arrangement and must agree to all of them—there can be no partial ratification of a contract entered into by the presumed agent. Also, the ratification relates back to the date of the contract. Therefore, if another person acquires rights in the interim, the principal may be precluded from ratifying the agreement because it would unfairly interfere with the fourth person's rights. If in the interim, the arrangement has become unlawful because of a supervening change in the law, the principal will also be precluded from ratifying the agreement.

Undisclosed principal — third person believes agent is acting on his or her own behalf.

Partially disclosed principal — agency relationship is disclosed, but not the identity of the principal.

2. *Undisclosed principal.* If the agent misleads the third party into believing that he or she is acting on his or her own behalf and not as an agent, the third party may avoid the contract with the principal or hold the agent to the agreement. This is known as an **undisclosed principal**. As a subset of this situation, there is the possibility of the **partially disclosed principal** in which the agent informs the third person that he or she is acting as an agent but does not disclose the identity of the principal. If the third person agrees to enter into a contract under these circumstances, the third person and the principal will be bound.

Termination

At some point the agency relationship will terminate, and the law recognizes four methods of such termination:

1. *By the expiration of the term of the agency.* By its own terms, the agency relationship may end.

   Example: A landlord hires a management agent for a two-year contract. At the end of the two years the agency relationship is terminated.

2. *By the loss or destruction of the subject matter.* The agency may terminate if the subject matter is lost or destroyed.

   Example: A horse owner hires an agent to contract for the horse's stud services. The horse dies. The agency is terminated because the subject matter no longer exists.

3. *By the death or insanity of the principal or the agent.* The death of the parties would obviously terminate the agency. However, under New York Gen. Oblig. Law § 3-501, the death of a member of the armed forces does not terminate the agency until the parties have actual knowledge of the death. Once the principal becomes adjudicated incapacitated, he or she no longer possesses contractual capacity so that the agent cannot contract on the principal's behalf. If the agent becomes incapacitated, the agency also terminates, even though a principal may select an incapacitated person as an agent. The difference lies in the fact that the agent had capacity when the agency relationship was created and subsequently became incapacitated, thereby permitting the principal to reconsider the relationship. If the parties are unaware of the incapacity, the contract entered into with third persons are considered valid.

4. *By the act of the agent or the principal.* A principal may terminate the agency by **revocation,** and the agent may terminate the agency by **renunciation.** However, if the agency relationship included a **power coupled with an interest**—supported by consideration as in a contract—the parties may have relinquished their ability to renounce or revoke, and such action may be considered a breach of the agency contract. Of course, the parties may always voluntarily agree to terminate the relationship.

Revocation — principal's act to terminate agency.

Renunciation — agent's act to terminate agency.

Power coupled with an interest — supported by legal consideration.

CHAPTER REVIEW

A study of the law of business must begin with a study of the law of agency. Most businesses operate by utilizing the services of persons other than the owner, and as a consequence, the business owner may be liable to third persons for injuries resulting from acts performed by persons acting on the owner's behalf.

There are three types of relationships usually classified under the heading of the law of agency: the master-servant relationship in which the master is held vicariously liable for the negligent acts of his or her servant that injure third persons while the servant is furthering the master's business; the independent contractor who generally does not engender liability for the other contracting party unless the contractor is involved in highly dangerous activities or is being supervised by the other party; and the principal-agent relationship in which a principal will be held liable for the contracts the agent enters into on the principal's behalf, provided that the agent is acting within the scope of his or her authority.

An agency relationship may be created by agreement of the parties, by the principal's retroactive ratification of the agent's unauthorized acts, or by estoppel in which the principal is barred from denying the agency because of the inequity such denial would occasion for an innocent third party.

An agent's authority to act may be either actual, resulting from the principal's manifestations directly to the agent; apparent, resulting from the principal's manifestations to the third person; or by estoppel, resulting from the principal's actions that cause a third person to believe that the agent is authorized to act on the principal's behalf. Regardless of the nature of the agent's authority, the courts construe the scope of that authority very strictly.

An agent is a fiduciary to the principal and owes the principal the fiduciary duties of performance, loyalty, care, and notification. Conversely, the principal owes the agent the duties of cooperation, compensation and reimbursement, and the ordinary standard of care.

An agency relationship may terminate in one of four ways: by agreement of the parties, by the death or destruction of the subject matter, by the death or insanity of the parties, or by the term of the relationship itself.

KEY TERMS

Actual authority
Agency by agreement
Agency by estoppel
Agency by ratification
Agent
Apparent authority
Authority by estoppel
Express authority
Fellow servant exception
Frolic of his own
General agent
Implied authority
Independent contractor
Master-servant relationship

Negligent hiring
Ostensible authority
Partially disclosed principal
Power coupled with an interest
Principal
Principal-agent relationship
Renunciation
Respondeat superior
Revocation
Special agent
Undisclosed principal
Vicarious liability
Workers compensation
Workers Compensation Board

EXERCISES

1. Why is a principal unable to ratify only a portion of the unauthorized contract the agent enters into on his or her behalf?
2. Go to the library and find sample agency agreements.

3. Explain in detail the difference between the three types of authority an agent may have.

4. Give three examples of situations in which a master would be liable for his or her servant's acts.

5. Why does the law impose a duty on third persons who deal with agents to determine the scope of the agent's authority? Explain.

FACTUAL PROBLEM

The president of a corporation leaves the corporate checkbook and corporate seal out on her desk overnight. When the janitor comes in to clean, he sees the items and writes out several checks using the seal. The next day he cashes the checks. What is the liability of the corporate president?

Sole Proprietorship

INTRODUCTION

The remainder of this text examines the various legal formats that may be used to create and operate a business in the state of New York. The various business formats are presented in chronological order, from the earliest of the business formats to the most recent; as each is introduced and discussed, the reader should be aware of the benefits and detriments associated with operating a business under that format. Each new form was developed in order to rectify what was perceived as detriments of the existing formats while retaining or expanding the perceived benefits.

The earliest form of business was the **sole proprietorship,** the situation in which one person owns and operates a business for himself or herself. However, even though the business is owned by just one individual, this does not mean that just one person operates it. The owner may employ servants and agents and also utilize the services of an **independent contractor** in order to further his or her business interests.

In discussing all of the various business formats available in New York, it is imperative that a distinction be made between the legalities surrounding the creation of the entity and the those surrounding the operation of the entity. The legal rights and obligations that apply to the operation of a business only come into play once the business has been legally created. In legal terms, the creation of the entity is the **condition precedent** to the application of the operational rules.

Sole proprietorship — person who owns and operates a business on his or her own.

Independent Contractor — person hired exclusively for the results to be accomplished.

Condition precedent — act or event that gives rise to an absolute duty to perform.

CREATION

The sole proprietorship is probably the easiest of the business formats to create because legally there are absolutely no requirements needed to create a sole proprietorship. As soon as an individual decides to go into business for himself or herself, the sole proprietorship is created.

Example: A paralegal student decides to increase her income while at school. Being an accomplished pianist, the student decides to give private piano lessons. As soon as the decision is made, the sole proprietorship is created.

The distinguishing characteristic of a sole proprietorship is that it is owned and operated by just one person. Consequently, sole proprietorships have no existence separate and distinct from the owner. The owner and the business are deemed to be one. Because of this individual identity, the sole proprietorship presents two major advantages as a business format:

1. *Ease of formation.* Because no legal requirements exist to create the entity, as exemplified previously, the decision to create the business is the act of formation.
2. *Flexibility in management.* Because the business is owned and operated by just one person, that person can make automatic management policy decisions without seeking approval from anyone else and can implement these decisions immediately.

Example: A woman has decided to try to sell her home-baked cookies to small restaurants and private individuals. Her first attempt is chocolate chip cookies. The cookie sales are brisk, but she is getting tired of just making chocolate chip cookies. One day while stirring a batter, she decides that she will start baking oatmeal raisin cookies. She has made a major policy decision; she has changed the product line. This decision can be immediately implemented.

Before going further, an explanation is necessary regarding the term *management*, as used in the context of legally creating and operating a business entity. "Management" refers to policy decision-making, not supervising personnel. Therefore, all reference to management concerns administrative decision-making.

In addition to the two advantages of operating a sole proprietorship, there may also be some tax benefits for the owner. Because the business and the owner are inseparable, all income from the business is deemed ordinary taxable income to the owner. However, the owner is entitled to take deductions from the gross income for all expenses associated with operating the business. Sole proprietors file a tax form called a **Schedule C** which is attached to their regular income tax return. This schedule is designed especially for sole proprietorships and permits the sole proprietor to deduct such items as rent, utilities, insurance, one-quarter of his or her health insurance premiums, travel and entertainment expenses, repairs, purchases of equipment, and so forth that are associated with operating the business. If the sole proprietor operates the business out of his or her home, he or she can consequently deduct various ordinary expenses that would otherwise not be deductible from his or her income, such as rent or mortgage payments.

Schedule C — the form used by sole proprietorships to report income.

Example: A lawyer operates his practice out of his house. He can deduct a portion of his rent for the space used for the practice, plus a portion of his utilities, telephone, and so forth that are attributable to the operation of the business used to generate income. If he worked for someone else, he would still have these expenses, but he would not be deducting them from his income for tax purposes.

The sole proprietor may also use the losses resulting from the business to offset other ordinary income. The sole proprietor is required to file **estimated taxes** on a quarterly basis because no taxes are withheld on the income of the owner of the business. However, if the sole proprietor employs servants, the sole proprietor is required to deduct and withhold income taxes for the wages he or she pays to the employee.

Estimated taxes — quarterly income tax obligation.

Operating a sole proprietorship also engenders several detriments for the owner, as well as the benefits discussed previously.

1. *Unlimited personal liability.* This is the greatest detriment associated with owning and operating a sole proprietorship. Because the business exists solely as an extension of the owner's existence, the owner's assets may be reached by any person injured by the operation of the business in contract, property, or tort. There is no way to shield the owner's assets, but the sole proprietor may purchase insurance to cover this potential liability. The insurance premiums are a deductible expense on Schedule C.

Anti-Hydro Company, Inc. v. Castiglia
92 A.D.2d 741, 461 N.Y.S.2d 87 9 (1983)

Memorandum: Defendant established T. C. Supply & Rentals, a sole proprietorship, by filing a business certificate in the Chautauqua County Clerk's office on December 4, 1975. Thereafter he commenced purchasing certain materials from plaintiff. On March 29, 1976, at the request of plaintiff, defendant forwarded to plaintiff a letter signed by him, and duly notarized, stating the following: "In consideration of the agreement by the Anti-Hydro Company to ship merchandise on open account, at their request to: T. C. Supply and Rentals, 156 Newton Street, Fredonia, NY, 14063, the Undersigned Parties do hereby agree that they will personally guarantee the payment of all Anti-Hydro invoices by due date, and if the above named purchaser, T. C. Supply and Rentals fails to make payment of such invoices, the Parties Undersigned will individually or collectively make payment of same. This guarantee will be continued until the Undersigned Parties shall notify the Anti-Hydro Company in writing of its termination, when and after full payment of account has been made."

In December, 1976 defendant's wife formed a corporation named Fredonia T. C. Supply and Rentals, Inc. Defendant was not an incorporator, director or stockholder of the corporation, but he acknowledged serving as "part-time manager." Thereafter plaintiff sold materials on credit to the corporation. All purchases made by the sole proprietorship prior to January 1, 1977 were paid for in full and all purchases thereafter were made by the newly formed corporation.

In this brief trial, plaintiff's bookkeeper at least twice acknowledged that plaintiff was aware from and after January, 1977 that its credit transactions were with the corporation. The purchases for which judgment was first recovered against the corporation were made between June 30, 1978 and August 29, 1978. That judgment was not paid and plaintiff then brought this action premised upon defendant's purported "guarantee." The trial court held that it would be inequitable to relieve the defendant of his obligation under the "guarantee" because: (1) the change from sole proprietorship to a corporation was de minimis; (2) there was no significant change in the operations and management of the company; and (3) defendant failed to fulfill his obligation to give plaintiff written notice of termination of the guarantee. We reverse.

Under suretyship principles, a guarantor relationship arises when one party becomes bound to satisfy an obligation owed by another. "The principal debtor, of course, is not a party to the guaranty, and the guarantor is not a party to the principal obligation, with the result that a suretyship or other contract is not a guaranty unless there is a primary or principal obligation to which the surety's agreement is collateral." (57 NY Jur, Suretyship and Guaranty, § 15, pp 206-207.) Since a sole proprietor is personally liable for his business debts, the letter purporting to guarantee payment of debts of the sole proprietorship was nothing more than a promise by defendant that he would pay debts which he personally incurred. It is not a promise to pay the debts of another. Even if we were to view the writing as a valid guarantee, it would not bind defendant to pay debts of the corporation. It is well settled as a general rule that a guarantee does not extend to a subsequent entity if there has been a true change in the composition or structure of the enterprise (57 NY Jur, Suretyship and Guaranty, § 314). Here, a new corporate entity was created in which defendant was not a shareholder, officer or director. There was a distinct change in identity; a new name was adopted and new and different checks, invoices and stationery were used. The change to corporate character was so obvious that plaintiff concedes it was aware that it was doing business with a corporation. Plaintiff claims, and the court found, that defendant should be estopped from using the cloak of the corporate entity to relieve himself of liability on his written promise. There is no evidence here, however, of a representation made by defendant upon which plaintiff relied to its detriment; thus there is no basis for an estoppel (see *Nassau Trust Co. v Montrose Concrete Prods. Corp., 56 NY2d 175).* Defendant's written promise related only to the debts of the sole proprietorship and it would be wholly unreasonable to conclude that plaintiff relied upon that promise as guaranteeing payment of the corporate debts when plaintiff was knowingly transacting business with the corporation.

Wolberg Electrical Supply Company, Inc. v. Frisch
145 A.D.2d 800, 535 N.Y.S.2d 784 (1988)

On June 24, 1977 defendant, a licensed electrician who had for a number of years been doing business as sole proprietor of D. L. Frisch Company, established a continuous line of credit for electrical supplies with plaintiff. The credit application was signed by defendant as owner and contained an unlimited guarantee of all liability. Some seven years later, on or about October 26, 1984, D. L. Frisch Company was incorporated as D. L. Frisch Company, Inc., with Barbara Frisch, defendant's wife, as president, and this corporation continued to do business with plaintiff without informing plaintiff that the sole proprietorship had been incorporated.

Defendant was sued individually, by summons and complaint served on January 19, 1987, for the balance due in the amount of $52,173.48 for goods sold to D. L. Frisch Company, Inc. between July 1986 and November 1986. On April 9, 1987 a default judgment was entered against defendant for his failure to appear, answer or move with respect to the process that was served upon him. On April 14, 1987 defendant was served with notice of entry of the default judgment taken against him, which clearly indicated that "[judgment] has been entered against you in this case as shown above." An information subpoena was thereafter mailed to defendant on May 12, 1987 by certified mail, return receipt requested, and was signed for by Barbara Frisch on May 13, 1987. Entry of judgment against defendant for the total sum of $61,929.03 is clearly stated therein. On June 12, 1987 a second copy of the information subpoena was forwarded to defendant, with a cover letter advising him of the consequences of his failure to respond.

Assuming that defendant has alleged a sufficient excuse for the default (see, *Clark v Sherwood, 117 AD2d 973),* we find that he has failed to establish the existence of a

meritorious defense. The record conclusively establishes that the parties' business relationship began as one between plaintiff and defendant, who was acting as sole proprietor
of D. L. Frisch Company. According to plaintiff's allegations, the relationship continued as
such through and including the period at issue, July 1986 through November 1986.
Defendant concedes that he executed an unlimited guarantee with plaintiff for the debts
of D. L. Frisch Company, but alleges that prior to the period at issue his wife had formed
a corporation and that the corporation thereafter obtained credit from various suppliers,
including plaintiff. Defendant submitted no documentary evidence to support either of
these allegations, but more importantly, there is nothing in the record to indicate that
defendant ceased doing business as D. L. Frisch Company or that the goods purchased
from plaintiff during the period at issue were purchased by defendant in his capacity as
an agent or officer of the corporation, rather than in his capacity as the proprietor of D. L.
Frisch Company (see, 15 NY Jur 2d, Business Relationships, § 1028, at 288). On the
contrary, the statements of account for the period at issue contain no indication that
defendant purchased the goods as anything other than the sole proprietor of the business with which plaintiff had dealt for years. Accordingly, defendant has failed to establish the existence of a meritorious defense and Supreme Court's order should, therefore,
be affirmed.

---

2. *Difficult to fund.* Once again, because of the unity of identity between the owner
and the business, the business never acquires its own credit. In order to fund the
business, the owner must either contribute his or her own money or borrow
money based on his or her own credit worthiness. If someone else contributes
funds and takes a share of the business in consequence thereof, the business may
be considered a partnership rather than a sole proprietorship (see Chapter 3).

3. *Estate planning concerns.* Because the owner and the business are considered one
person, if the business provides the support for a family and the owner dies, there
may be no one capable of operating the business for the surviving family members.
Therefore, a sole proprietor must be sure to make some testamentary provisions for
the care of his or her family because the business terminates with his or her death.
If a surviving spouse or child continues the business, it is deemed to be a new sole
proprietorship. There is no continuity of existence for the business.

Once the sole proprietorship is formed, the owner must be alert to the laws governing
its operations.

OPERATION

Although there are no formalities involved in creating a sole proprietorship, there may be
laws and regulations incident to operating the business:

DBA form — document
used to register an assumed
business name.

1. *Registration of the name.* If the sole proprietor wants to operate the business under
an assumed name, he or she is required to file an Assumed Name Form, generally
referred to as a **DBA form** (Doing Business As), with the county clerk's office in
the county in which the business will operate (see Exhibit 2–1). Gen. Bus. Law

§ 130. The sole proprietor is prohibited from doing business under any name that includes the word "company" or "and Associate" because such words might mislead the public into believing that the business is other than a sole proprietorship. Also, the name must be unique within the county. The county clerk will check the name and charge a fee for the filing.

Example: A woman wishes to start a business by selling hand-knit sweaters. She decides to call the business "Knockout Knits" and files a DBA form with the county clerk's office. She is now legally allowed to use "Knockout Knits" as her business name.

Mark — word, symbol, or group of words that designates a specific product or service.

Service mark — government grant of exclusive use of a name designating a service.

Trademark — government grant of exclusive use of a name designating a good.

2. *Marking a name.* If the sole proprietor wishes to protect the name he or she is using for the business, thereby precluding other persons from using that name, the name must be marked. A **mark** is a word, symbol, or group of words that designate a particular product or service, distinguishing it from similar products and services. A mark is called a **service mark** if it represents a service, or a **trademark** if it represents a good. The word or symbol may be marked after it has been used in interstate commerce by filing it with the federal government in Washington, D.C. In order to be afforded protection, the mark must be unique in the industry.

Example: The woman from the previous example wishes to use the name "Knockout Knits" as her label and wants to protect her use of the name. She sells a sweater with the name on the label to a friend in New Jersey and then registers the trademark in Washington, D.C. Because no one else in the knitwear industry uses that name, the mark is hers.

Marks are valid for a 10-year period and may be continually renewed by the holder.

3. *Regulatory filings.* Depending on the nature of the business, the sole proprietor may be required to file several documents with the government:

(a) Under New York's General Business Law and/or the Education Law, many types of businesses must be licensed or registered in order to operate in the state. The scope of the occupations covered by these laws is very broad and must be individually checked.

Example: The woman from the previous example decides that she would like to sell her sweaters outdoors during nice weather. In order to sell her products in the street, she must first obtain a peddler's license.

(b) Many occupations must be licensed by the state of New York before the occupation can be practiced. These occupations are specified in the General Business Law and the Education Law. Before the sole proprietor can practice one of these occupations, the state license must be obtained.

Example: In order to implement his income, a paralegal wishes to act as a massage therapist in his spare time. In order to work as a massage therapist legally, he must first obtain licensing from the state of New York.

(c) In addition to the foregoing, New York requires certain businesses to obtain special licensing for various purposes, such as selling liquor in a restaurant or employing a minor. Before operating, the sole proprietor must check the New York statutes to determine whether he or she needs a special license.

Example: During the busy tax season, an accountant who operates as a sole proprietor hires his 15-year-old daughter and her school friend to help out after school and on the weekends. Because he is employing minors, he must obtain a special license from the state.

(d) *Business taxes.* If the sole proprietor sells goods to the public, he or she is responsible for collecting New York state sales taxes pursuant to section 1132 of the New York State Tax Law. The sole proprietor must file an Application for Registration as a Sales Tax Vendor (see Exhibit 2–2) with the Department of Taxation and Finance, and the taxes so collected must be reported and paid over to the state on a quarterly basis.

If the sole proprietor is engaged in manufacturing a product or engaged in other specified activities, the owner may be exempt from paying sales taxes on the goods he or she purchases in order to make his or her product. The list of products and services that are exempt from paying sales taxes appear in section 1115 of the Tax Law. If the sole proprietorship comes within the statute, the owner should file a Resale Certificate (see Exhibit 2–3) with the Department of Taxation and Finance to avoid having to pay sales tax.

Example: The owner of "Knockout Knits" must purchase her yarn and notions from other businesses. Because she is not the ultimate consumer but uses the goods to manufacture her product, she may be able to avoid paying sales tax on her purchases if she files the Resale Certificate with the Tax Department.

Zoning — government regulation of land use.

Variance — permitted divergence from zoning regulations.

Zoning board — government agency administering zoning laws.

Cartage — business's obligation to dispose of waste.

Tax Identification Number — issued by the IRS for income tax purposes.

Business tax — franchise tax.

5. *Zoning.* Local governments zone geographic areas for particular uses. Before opening a business, the sole proprietor must make sure the area in which the business is to operate is zoned for such a business enterprise. If it is not, he or she must either seek a **variance,** legal permission from the **zoning board** to operate despite the zoning restriction, or seek another location.

6. *Cartage.* **Cartage** refers to waste disposal. Businesses must pay for such services; they are not permitted to use the regular garbage collection service provided to noncommercial residents.

7. *Employer taxes.* If the sole proprietor employs persons, he or she must obtain a **Tax Identification Number** from the Internal Revenue Service and must withhold income taxes from the wages he or she pays to the employees. This withheld tax must be placed into a special trust account for the benefit of the government. Furthermore, the employer is required to contribute to Social Security and Unemployment Insurance on behalf of the workers and is mandated to Maintain Workers Compensation Insurance as well.

8. *Business tax.* Certain municipalities impose an operation **business tax** on any business that rents commercial space. This can be a serious financial consideration for the sole proprietor in obtaining a suitable location.

Shaw, DBA Shaw Fuel Oil & Kerosene v. State of New York Tax Appeals Tribunal
203 A.D.2d 720, 610 N.Y.S.2d 971 (1994)

Proceeding pursuant to CPLR article 78 (initiated in this court pursuant to Tax Law § 2016) to review a determination of respondent Tax Appeals Tribunal which canceled petitioner's registration as a distributor of diesel motor fuel under Tax Law article 12-a.

Petitioner operated two businesses as sole proprietorships; one was a tavern known as the Stage Coach Inn and the other was as a vendor of oil and kerosene as well as some contracting work under the name of Shaw Fuel Oil & Kerosene (hereinafter Shaw Oil). The Stage Coach Inn was duly registered as a sales tax vendor under Tax Law article 28 and petitioner filed sales tax returns reporting and remitting taxes. Shaw Oil was not registered as a sales tax vendor but was audited by respondent Department of Taxation and Finance in March 1988 regarding its sales tax liability from December 1983 through February 1988. In 1988 Shaw Oil registered as a distributor of diesel motor fuel with the Department of Taxation and Finance (see, Tax Law § 283 [2]).

The Department's audit of Shaw Oil resulted in the issuance of notices of determination assessing Shaw Oil an additional $31,263.24 in sales and use taxes due. The audit also revealed evidence of altered invoices and the failure to collect, report and remit sales tax. These matters were referred to the Office of Tax Enforcement for criminal investigation. On September 18, 1990 petitioner entered a negotiated plea of guilty to filing a false instrument in the second degree, a class A misdemeanor. Petitioner was sentenced to serve 30 days in jail, pay a fine of $2,500 and make restitution of $19,666.40.

In October 1990, a field audit of Shaw Oil's diesel motor fuel tax and petroleum business tax liability was conducted for the period from September 1988 through August 1990. The audit revealed that petitioner filed no diesel motor fuel tax returns for September, October and November 1988 and that taxable sales of fuel were not reported. The auditor concluded that Shaw Oil made unreported taxable sales regarding some 78,700 gallons of fuel oil, taxable at a rate of 10 cents per gallon, and assessed a tax due of $7,870 plus penalties and interest. The audit also revealed that Shaw Oil had given its suppliers residential use certificates stating that 93% of the product purchased from them was for residential use. This allowed the suppliers to deduct almost all of the proceeds of their sales to Shaw Oil from their gross receipts subject to tax liability. Shaw Oil's actual sales indicated that only 66% of its product was sold for residential use. Thus, Shaw Oil was assessed a penalty at the statutory rate of 5% of the difference, amounting to an added tax liability of $6,180.

The Department issued Shaw Oil a notice of proposed cancellation of its registration as a diesel motor fuel distributor on February 12, 1991 based on five different failures to comply with the provisions of the Tax Law:

1. Failure to report and remit sales taxes collected on the sales of diesel motor fuel.
2. Filing false sales tax returns relating to sales of diesel motor fuel.
3. Failure to collect sales tax on taxable sales of diesel motor fuel.
4. Delivery and disclosure of falsified sales invoices to representatives of the Department.
5. Failure to file returns or pay tax for the months of September, October and November 1988 relative to excise tax on diesel motor fuel.

Following a conciliation conference the notice was sustained on April 10, 1992. A hearing was thereafter scheduled before an Administrative Law Judge (hereinafter

ALJ). Five days prior to the hearing, however, petitioner's counsel was notified that a sixth ground for cancellation would be presented at the hearing in addition to the five already stated—that of petitioner's submission of false residential use certificates to its suppliers.

After the hearing the ALJ issued a determination finding that cancellation of petitioner's registration as a diesel motor fuel distributor was supported by sufficient grounds and sustained the notice of proposed cancellation. The ALJ found it "clear from the facts" that petitioner committed fraud and deceit in his operations as a distributor of diesel motor fuel (see, Tax Law § 282-a [2] [i]). The ALJ also upheld the added sixth ground for cancellation based on adequate notice and adequate time to prepare a defense.

Petitioner filed a notice of exception with respondent Tax Appeals Tribunal which issued a decision upholding the ALJ's determination. The Tribunal concluded that it was unnecessary to decide whether petitioner's argument that the criminal conviction, standing alone, was an insufficient basis for cancellation because "the record reveals so much other evidence of deceit by petitioner" that, in any event, cancellation was warranted. The Tribunal also found that the punishment was not out of proportion to petitioner's many persistent acts of misconduct and termed petitioner's claim that the auditor had advised him to alter invoices incredible, noting that, had petitioner believed that the auditor would corroborate his statements, he could have subpoenaed her to appear at the hearing.

We initially reject petitioner's argument that his acts did not rise to the level of fraud and/or deceit to justify revocation of his registration as a motor fuel distributor. Examination of the record reveals overwhelming evidence supporting the cancellation of petitioner's registration as a diesel motor fuel distributor pursuant to Tax Law § 283 (4) (i). The proof demonstrates that petitioner, inter alia, criminally filed false sales tax returns, failed to file tax returns, falsified documents, failed to collect sales tax and failed to remit taxes actually collected. These acts constitute "fraud or deceit in [petitioner's] operations as a distributor" (Tax Law § 283 [4] [i]). Any of the six grounds proven is sufficient to support cancellation. Petitioner's explanations and excuses for his actions lack credibility and the Tribunal did not abuse its discretion in rejecting them.

We also find without merit petitioner's contention that the additional or sixth ground for cancellation was improperly raised at the hearing because petitioner did not have sufficient time to prepare an adequate defense to the allegation (see, *Matter of Diamond Term. Corp. v New York State Dept. of Taxation & Fin.*, 158 AD2d 38, 40–41, 557 N.Y.S.2d 962, lv denied 76 NY2d 711). Moreover, petitioner could have requested an adjournment, if needed. Rather, petitioner made no such request. Petitioner also argues that the Department's failure to call the auditor at the hearing requires a finding of fact that petitioner's testimony with regard to the alteration of receipts is true. The failure to call the auditor in the circumstances, however, does not warrant the inference that her testimony would not contradict that of petitioner. The record indicates that her sales tax audit was not in issue and was offered only as a foundation or background. Thus, she was not anticipated to be a witness at the hearing by the Department and, if petitioner required her testimony, he could have subpoenaed her. It was not known that petitioner would claim at the hearing that the auditor gave him the advice to alter the invoices, which was inconsistent with the fact that she called petitioner's activities to the attention of the Office of Tax Enforcement with a view to criminal prosecution. In any event, there was sufficient proof of other grounds for cancellation to sustain the determination of the Tribunal.

CHAPTER REVIEW

The sole proprietorship is one of the most common forms of business that exists in the state. Many people are unaware of the extent of the number of sole proprietorships because there are no requisite formalities to create the entity, and only the government may be aware of the actual number because of the use by the owner of Schedule C on his or her income tax return.

Although there are certain benefits incident to creating a sole proprietorship, such as the ease of formation and the flexibility in its management, the greatest detriment incident to this business format is the unlimited personal liability of the owner for the obligations of the business. Many entrepreneurs seek other business formats simply to avoid this potential liability.

Despite the fact that the sole proprietorship is probably the easiest business entity to create, in terms of operation, it is as complex, legally, as all of the other formats discussed throughout this text.

KEY TERMS

Business Tax	Service mark
Cartage	Sole proprietorship
Condition precedent	Tax Identification Number
DBA form	Trademark
Estimated taxes	Variance
Mark	Zoning
Schedule C	Zoning board

EXERCISES

1. Go to the library and read the General Business Law and the Education Law to determine whether the following businesses and occupations must be licensed: massage therapist, hairdresser, legal consultant, legal assistant, and dental assistant.

2. With all of the potential liabilities, discuss why a person would wish to operate a business as a sole proprietorship. Which types of businesses would be best to operate as a sole proprietorship? Why?

3. Check your locality for its zoning restrictions to determine the types of businesses that may operate in your neighborhood. Indicate how you could have the zoning ordinances changed.

4. Discuss why a person might wish to create a trademark.

5. A client wants to start a business from her house to sell herbs by direct mail. Discuss why operating the business as sole proprietorship may or may not be beneficial.

FACTUAL PROBLEM

A debtor in bankruptcy has been operating a business which he asserted was a sole proprietorship, and he has used the services of an independent contractor to help him. Now, in bankruptcy, he is claiming that he is a partner with the contractor and therefore the contractor should also be held liable for half of the debts. Discuss the merits of his argument.

X 201— Certificate of Conducting Business under an Assumed Name
For Individual. 11-98

BlumbergExcelsior, Inc.
PUBLISHER NYC 10013

𝔅usiness Certificate

I HEREBY CERTIFY *that I am conducting or transacting business under the name or designation*

of

at

City or Town of   **County of**   **State of New York.**

My full name is*

and I reside at

I FURTHER CERTIFY *that I am the successor in interest to*

the person or persons heretofore using such name or names to carry on or conduct or transact **business.**

IN WITNESS WHEREOF, *I have signed this certificate on*

....

* Print or type name.
* If under 21 years of age, state "I am................years of age".

ACKNOWLEDGMENT IN NEW YORK STATE (RPL 309-a)   **ACKNOWLEDGMENT OUTSIDE NEW YORK STATE (RPL 309-b)**

State of New York
County of   } ss.:

State of
County of   } ss.:

On   before me, the undersigned,
personally appeared

On   before me, the undersigned,
personally appeared

personally known to me or proved to me on the basis of satisfactory evidence to be the individual(s) whose name(s) is (are) subscribed to the within instrument and acknowledged to me that
he/she/they executed the same in his/her/their capacity(ies), and
that by his/her/their signature(s) on the instrument, the individ-
ual(s), or the person upon behalf of which the individual(s) acted,
executed the instrument.

personally known to me or proved to me on the basis of satisfactory evidence to be the individual(s) whose name(s) is (are)
subscribed to the within instrument and acknowledged to me
that he/she/they executed the same in his/her/their capacity(ies),
and that by his/her/their signature(s) on the instrument, the indi-
vidual(s), or the person upon behalf of which the individual(s)
acted, executed the instrument, and that such individual made
such appearance before the undersigned in

_____
(signature and office of individual taking acknowledgment)

*(insert city or political subdivision and state or county or other place acknowl-
edgment taken)*

_____
(signature and office of individual taking acknowledgment)

Exhibit 2–1

Business Certificate *(Forms may be purchased from BlumbergExcelsior, Inc. or any of its dealers. Reproduction prohibited.)*

DTF-17 (8/00)

New York State Department of Taxation and Finance

Application for Registration as a Sales Tax Vendor

Department use only

Please print or type

1 Type of certificate you are applying for
(You must check one box; see instructions): ☐ Regular ☐ Temporary ☐ Show ☐ Entertainment

2 Legal name of vendor

3 Trade name or DBA (if different from item 2)

4 Federal employer identification number

5 Address of business location (show/entertainment or temporary vendors use home address)
Number and street   City   County   State   ZIP code   Country, if not U.S.

6 Business telephone number (include area code)   **7** Date you will begin business in New York State *(see instructions)*   **8** Temporary vendors: Enter the date you will end business in New York
( )

9 Mailing address, if different from business address on line 5
c/o name   Number and street   City   State   ZIP code

10 Type of organization: ☐ Individual (sole proprietor) ☐ Partnership ☐ Trust ☐ Governmental ☐ Exempt organization ☐ Corporation ☐ Limited Liability Partnership ☐ Limited Liability Company ☐ Other *(specify)*

11 Reason for applying: ☐ Started new business ☐ Purchased existing business ☐ Adding a new location ☐ Change in organization ☐ Other *(specify)*

12 Regular vendors — Will you operate more than one place of business?
☐ Yes *(check appropriate box below)* ☐ No
A ☐ Separate sales tax return will be filed for each business location.
B ☐ One sales tax return will be filed for all business locations *(complete Form DTF-17-ATT and attach it to this application).*

13 List all owners/officers. Attach a separate sheet if necessary. All applicants must complete this section.

Name	Title	Social security number
Home address	City	State	ZIP code	Telephone number ( )
Name	Title	Social security number
Home address	City	State	ZIP code	Telephone number ( )
Name	Title	Social security number
Home address	City	State	ZIP code	Telephone number ( )

14 If your business currently files New York State returns for the following taxes, check the box for the appropriate tax type and enter the identification number used on the return:
☐ Corporation tax   ID # _____
☐ Withholding tax   ID # _____
☐ Other *(explain)* _____ ID # _____

15 If you have ever registered as a sales tax vendor with New York State, enter the information shown on the last sales tax return you filed:
Name _____ Identification number _____

16 Do you expect to **collect** any sales or use tax or **pay** any sales or use tax directly to the Department of Taxation and Finance? ☐ Yes ☐ No

17 Describe your major business activity and enter your six-digit NAICS code:

Describe your business activity in detail *(attach a separate sheet if necessary)*	North American Industry Classification System (NAICS)

18 Are you a sidewalk vendor? ☐ Yes ☐ No
If *Yes*, do you sell food? ☐ Yes ☐ No
19 Do you participate solely in flea markets, antique shows, or other "shows"? ☐ Yes ☐ No
20 Do you intend to make retail sales of cigarettes or other tobacco products? ☐ Yes ☐ No
21 If you withhold or will withhold New York State tax from employees, do you need withholding tax forms or information? ☐ Yes ☐ No

Exhibit 2–2

Application for Registration as a Sales Tax Vendor *(Courtesy of the New York State Department of Taxation and Finance.)*

DTF-17 (8/00) (back)

22 If you acquired this business from a registered vendor, did you file Form AU-196.10, *Notification of Sale, Transfer or Assignment in Bulk*, with the Tax Department? ..... ☐ Yes ☐ No
Former owner's name _____ Address _____ ID # _____

23 Have you been notified that you owe any New York State tax? .... ☐ Yes ☐ No

Type of tax	Amount due	Assessment number (if any)	Assessment date	Assessment currently being protested? ..... ☐ Yes	☐ No

24 Do any responsible officers, directors, partners, or employees owe New York State or local sales and use taxes on your
behalf, on behalf of another person, or as a vendor of property or services? .... ☐ Yes ☐ No

Individual's name		Street address	City	State	ZIP code

Social security number	Amount due	Assessment number (if any)	Assessment date	Assessment currently being protested? ..... ☐ Yes	☐ No

25 Have you been convicted of a crime under the Tax Law during the past year? .... ☐ Yes ☐ No

Date of conviction	Court of conviction	Disposition (fine, imprisonment, probation, etc.)

26 During the past year, has any responsible officer, director, partner, or employee of the applicant been convicted of a crime
under the Tax Law? .... ☐ Yes ☐ No

Individual's name		Street address	City	State	ZIP code

Social security number	Date of conviction	Court of conviction	Disposition (fine, imprisonment, probation, etc.)

27 If previously registered as a New York State sales tax vendor, was your *Certificate of Authority* revoked or suspended
during that past year? ☐ Yes ☐ No If *Yes*, please indicate why_____ .
_____

Questions 28, 29, and 30 apply to corporations only.

28 If any shareholder owns more than half of the shares of voting stock of the applicant, has this shareholder ever owned
more than half of the shares of voting stock of another corporation? ☐ Yes   ☐ No **If *Yes*, complete questions 29 and 30.**

29 Did this shareholder own these shares of another corporation when the corporation had a tax liability that remains unpaid? .... ☐ Yes ☐ No

Shareholder's name		Corporation name	Federal identification number	
Street address		City	State	ZIP code

Type of tax	Amount due	Assessment number (if any)	Assessment date	Assessment currently being protested? ..... ☐ Yes	☐ No

30 Did this shareholder own these shares of another corporation at a time during the past year when the corporation was
convicted of a crime under the Tax Law? .... ☐ Yes ☐ No

Corporation name		Federal identification number	
Street address		City	State	ZIP code

Date of conviction	Court of conviction	Disposition (fine, imprisonment, probation, etc.)

I certify that the information in this application is true and correct. Willfully filing a false application is a misdemeanor punishable under the Tax Law.

Signature	Title	Telephone number	Date

☐ Check this box if you want your sales tax returns mailed to a tax preparer rather than the address on the front of this application. Enter
preparer information in the box below:

Name of preparer	Street Address	City	State	ZIP code

This application will be returned if it is not signed or if any other information is missing.
Mail your application to: NYS Tax Department, Sales Tax Registration Unit, W A Harriman Campus, Albany NY 12227, at least 20 days (but not more than 90 days) before you begin doing business in New York State.

Exhibit 2–2
Continued *(Courtesy of the New York State Department of Taxation and Finance.)*

New York State Department of Taxation and Finance

Resale Certificate

ST-120 (6/99)

☐ **Single-use certificate**   ☐ **Blanket certificate**   **Date issued** _____

Temporary vendors must issue a single-use certificate.

Seller information - *please type or print*

Seller's name

Address

City   State   ZIP code

Purchaser information - *please type or print*

I am engaged in the business of _____ and principally sell _____

(Contractors may not use this certificate to purchase materials and supplies.)

Part 1 - To be completed by registered New York State sales tax vendors

I certify that I am:

☐   a New York State vendor (including a hotel operator or a dues or admissions recipient), show vendor or entertainment vendor. My valid Certificate of Authority Number is _____

☐   a New York State temporary vendor. My valid Certificate of Authority Number is _____ and expires on _____

I am purchasing:

A ☐   Tangible personal property (other than motor fuel or diesel motor fuel)
- for resale in its present form or for resale as a physical component part of tangible personal property;
- for use in performing taxable services where the property will become a physical component part of the property upon which the services will be performed, or the property will actually be transferred to the purchaser of the taxable service in conjunction with the performance of the service, or

B ☐   A service for resale, including the servicing of tangible personal property held for sale.

Part 2 - To be completed by non-New York State purchasers

I certify that I am not registered nor am I required to be registered as a New York State sales tax vendor. I am registered to collect sales tax or value added tax (VAT) in the following state/jurisdiction _____ and have been issued the following registration number _____ . (If sales tax or VAT registration is not required and a registration number is not issued by your home jurisdiction, indicate the location of your business and write ***not applicable*** on the line requesting the registration number.)

I am purchasing:

C ☐   Tangible personal property (other than motor fuel or diesel motor fuel) for resale, and it is being delivered directly by the seller to my customer or to an unaffiliated fulfillment services provider in New York State.

D ☐   Tangible personal property for resale that will be resold from a business located outside New York State.

Part 3 - Certification

I, the purchaser, understand that:
- I may not use this certificate to purchase items or services that are not for resale.
- If I purchase tangible personal property or services for resale, but I use or consume the tangible personal property or services myself in New York State, I must report and pay the unpaid tax directly to New York State.
- I will incur tax liabilities, in addition to penalty and interest, for any misuse of this certificate.

Please type or print

Purchaser's name as it appears on the sales tax registration	Name of owner, partner, or officer of corporation, authorizing the purchase
Street address	Purchaser's signature
City State ZIP code	Title

Substantial penalties will result from misuse of this certificate.

Exhibit 2–3

Resale Certificate *(Courtesy of the New York State Department of Taxation and Finance.)*

ST-120 (6/99) (back)

Instructions For Use of Resale Certificates

Form ST-120, *Resale Certificate*, is a sales tax exemption certificate. **This certificate is only for use by a purchaser who:**

A - is registered as a New York State sales tax vendor and has a valid Certificate of Authority issued by the Tax Department and is making purchases of tangible personal property (other than motor fuel or diesel motor fuel) or services that will be resold or transferred to the purchaser's customers, **or**

B - is not required to be registered with the New York State Tax Department;

- is registered with another state, the District of Columbia, a province of Canada, or other country, or is located in a state, province, or country which does not require sellers to register for sales tax or VAT purposes; and

- is purchasing items for resale that will be either:

  1) delivered by the seller to the purchaser's customer or to an unaffiliated fulfillment service provider located in New York State, or

  2) delivered to the purchaser in New York State, but resold from a business located outside the state.

Note: For purposes of 1) above, delivery by the seller includes delivery in the seller's own vehicle or by common carrier, regardless of who arranges for the transportation.

If, among other things, a purchaser has any place of business or salespeople in New York State, or owns or leases tangible personal property in the State, the purchaser is required to be registered in New York State. If you need help determining if you are required to register because you engage in some other activity in the State, contact the Department (see the **Need Help** section). However, a purchaser who is not otherwise required to be registered in New York may purchase fulfillment services from an unaffiliated New York fulfillment service provider and have its tangible personal property located on the premises of the provider without being required to be registered in New York State.

If you meet the registration requirements and engage in business activities in New York State without possessing a valid Certificate of Authority, you will be subject to penalty of up to $500 for the first day on which you make a sale or purchase, and up to $200 for each additional day, up to a maximum of $10,000.

Limitations on use

Contractors cannot use this certificate. They must either:

● issue Form ST-120.1, *Contractors Exempt Purchase Certificate*, if the tangible personal property being purchased qualifies for exemption as specified by the certificate, or

● issue Form AU-297, *Direct Payment Permit*, or

● pay sales tax at the time of purchase.

Contractors are entitled to a refund or credit of sales tax paid on materials used in repairing, servicing or maintaining real property, if the materials are transferred to the purchaser of the taxable service in conjunction with the performance of the service. For additional information, see Publication 862, *Sales and Use Tax Classifications of Capital Improvements and Repairs to Real Property.*

To the Purchaser

Enter all the information requested on the front of this form.

You may check the *Blanket certificate* box to cover all purchases of the same general type of property or service purchased for resale. If you do not check the *Blanket certificate* box, the certificate will be deemed a *Single-use certificate*. Temporary vendors may not issue a blanket certificate. A temporary vendor is a vendor (other than a show or entertainment vendor), who, in no more than two consecutive quarters in any 12-month period, makes sales of tangible personal property or services that are subject to tax.

This certificate does not exempt prepaid sales tax on cigarettes. This certificate may not be used to purchase motor fuel or diesel motor fuel.

If you intentionally issue a fraudulent exemption certificate, you will become liable for penalties and interest, in addition to the sales tax initially due. Some penalties that may apply:

● 100% of the tax due

● $50 for each fraudulent exemption certificate issued

● a misdemeanor penalty consisting of fines not to exceed $10,000 for an individual or $20,000 for a corporation

● loss of your Certificate of Authority

To the Seller

If you are a New York State registered vendor and accept an exemption document, you will be protected from liability for the tax, if the certificate is valid.

The certificate will be considered valid if it was:

● accepted in good faith,

● in the vendor's possession within 90 days of the transaction, and

● properly completed (all required entries were made).

A certificate is accepted in good faith when a seller has no knowledge that the exemption certificate is false or is fraudulently given, and reasonable ordinary due care is exercised in the acceptance of the certificate.

You must get a properly completed exemption certificate from your customer no later than 90 days after the delivery of the property or the performance of the service. When you receive a certificate after the 90 days, both you and the purchaser are subject to the burden of proving that the sale was exempt, and additional documentation may be required. An exemption certificate received on time that is not properly completed will be considered satisfactory if the deficiency is corrected within a reasonable period. You must also maintain a method of associating an invoice (or other source document) for an exempt sale made to a customer with the exemption certificate you have on file from that customer.

Invalid exemption certificates - Sales transactions which are not supported by valid exemption certificates are deemed to be taxable retail sales. The burden of proof that the tax was not required to be collected is upon the seller.

Retention of exemption certificates - You must keep this certificate for at least three years after the due date of the return to which it relates, or the date the return was filed, if later.

 Need Help?

Tax information: 1 800 972-1233
Forms and publications: 1 800 462-8100
From outside the U.S. and outside Canada: (518) 485-6800
Fax-on-demand forms: 1 800 748-3676
Internet access: http://www.tax.state.ny.us
Hearing and speech impaired: 1 800 634-2110

Exhibit 2–3
Continued *(Courtesy of the New York State Department of Taxation and Finance.)*

Chapter 3

General and Limited Partnerships

INTRODUCTION

General partnership — business operated and owned by two or more persons with unlimited personal liability.

Uniform Partnership Act (UPA) — statute governing general partnerships.

As indicated in Chapter 2, one of the greatest drawbacks of operating a business as a sole proprietorship is the unlimited personal liability of the business owner for the obligations of the business. In order to attempt to relieve this liability, the next format that came into existence was the general partnership. A **general partnership** is defined as an association of two or more persons engaged in business for profit as co-owners. This definition comes from the **Uniform Partnership Act (UPA),** the statute governing general partnerships in the state of New York since 1919.

The UPA operates as a safety net for the partners. Under the UPA, all partners are deemed to be equal owners, and consequently, all rights and obligations are evenly distributed. However, the partners themselves are always free to enter into an agreement that varies this concept, and if found valid, the partners' agreement will supersede the provisions of the UPA. Absent an agreement to the contrary on any point, the UPA will prevail.

Contribution — appointment of liability between partners.

Limited partnership — partnership with one or more general partners and one or more limited partners.

General partner — person who manages a limited partnership or who is a partner in a general partnership.

Pursuant to New York and general law, all general partners have unlimited personal liability for the obligations of the business. However, unlike the sole proprietorship, the general partners may seek **contribution** from the other partner(s) which helps to minimize that unlimited liability, a great advantage over the sole proprietorship. Funding for the general partnership is similar to the method of funding the sole proprietorship: The general partners either contribute the funds, or they borrow the funds based on their own credit worthiness. A general partnership, like a sole proprietorship, is not considered for most purposes to be a separate entity from its owners.

In order to increase funding options, as an outgrowth of the general partnership, another form of business was created known as a limited partnership. A **limited partnership** is defined as an association of two or more persons engaged in business for profit as co-owners, with one or more general partners and one or more limited partners. The **general partner** retains unlimited personal liability for the obligations of the business, whereas the

Limited partner —
investor in a limited partnership.

**Uniform Limited
Partnership Act (ULPA)**
—former New York limited
partnership law.

**Revised Uniform Limited
Partnership Act (RULPA)**
— current New York lim-
ited partnership law.

Statute of Frauds — law
requiring certain contracts
to be in writing to be
enforceable.

limited partners are legally considered investors who do not have a say in management but who only share in the business profits or losses. In New York, limited partnerships are governed by two statutes: the **Uniform Limited Partnership Act (ULPA)** for limited partnerships formed prior to July 1, 1991, and the **Revised Uniform Limited Partnership Act (RULPA)** for limited partnerships formed on or after July 1, 1991.

This chapter discusses the creation, operation, and potential benefits and detriments of operating a business as one of these two legal entities.

GENERAL PARTNERSHIP

Creation

Under the UPA, there are no formalities necessary to create a general partnership. As soon as two or more persons agree to form a business relationship, the partnership comes into existence.

Example: Mickey and Judy want to raise some money. They decide to use an old barn on Mickey's property to produce a show. Mickey and Judy are now partners.

Under the UPA, any two persons may agree to become partners; they do not need to be natural persons. Corporations, trusts, associations, other partnerships, and so forth can all join to form a basic partnership. The primary requirement is simply that these persons have legal capacity to form a partnership and they actively intend to do so. However, even though the UPA does not require any creating documents to form a general partnership, pursuant to the **Statute of Frauds,** in order for the agreement to be enforceable, it must be in writing if the subject matter of the agreement relates to an interest in real property or cannot be performed within one year (among other subjects not relevant to forming business partnerships).

Example: Two friends decide to form a partnership to develop commercial real estate. Because this agreement covers interests in realty, to be enforceable, it must be in writing. Furthermore, if the friends intend the partnership to continue for several years, this also requires the agreement to be in writing to be enforceable.

Kellogg v. Kellogg
185 A.D.2d 426, 585 N.Y.S.2d 824 (1992)

A more detailed recitation of the facts in this matter can be found in this court's prior decision in this case *(169 AD2d 912).* Briefly stated, the parties are brothers who executed a document entitled "Partnership Agreement" on August 13, 1984, after a series of events which resulted in plaintiff providing a loan and other help to defendant to operate an expanded service station in the City of Ithaca, Tompkins County. Thereafter, the parties worked together at the service station until disputes arose between them. Plaintiff left the business and was issued monthly checks of $3,000 from defendant until February 1989. Eventually, plaintiff commenced this action alleging that a partnership had been formed and seeking, inter alia, dissolution of the partnership and an accounting. In defendant's answer, he asserted that the document signed by the parties was actually a security agreement for a $15,000 loan from plaintiff. Defendant also asserted numerous affirmative defenses and counterclaims. The parties' cross motions for summary judgment were denied by Supreme Court and that decision was affirmed by this court on appeal *(169 AD2d 912,* supra). Subsequently, a nonjury trial was held after which Supreme Court found, among other things, that no partnership between the parties had been created. Judgment was entered dismissing the complaint and the counterclaims and these cross appeals ensued.

Initially, plaintiff essentially contends that Supreme Court's finding that no partnership existed between the parties was against the weight of the credible evidence. Therefore, he urges this court to examine the record, reverse the judgment and grant relief in his favor. We disagree. While it is true that in reviewing a verdict from a nonjury trial this court has authority as broad as Supreme Court to grant judgment in one party's favor, we are nonetheless generally deferential to Supreme Court's credibility determinations, especially in a close case or on sharply contested issues (see, *Northern Westchester Professional Park Assocs. v Town of Bedford, 60 NY2d 492, 499; Monette v Monette, 177 AD2d 802, 802-803).* Significantly, in this case the question of whether a partnership existed was harshly disputed and potentially credible evidence was submitted on both sides. Among the factors to be considered in determining whether a partnership was created are "'the intent of the parties (express or implied), whether there was joint control and management of the business, whether there was a sharing of the profits as well as a sharing of the losses, and whether there was a combination of property, skill or knowledge'" *(Boyarsky v Froccaro, 131 AD2d 710, 712,* quoting *Ramirez v Goldberg, 82 AD2d 850, 852).*

Here, while plaintiff certainly presented evidence which supported his contention that a partnership was created, there was ample proof at trial to support Supreme Court's decision. Although plaintiff testified that a partnership was unequivocally created, he admitted on cross-examination that a tax identification number was never applied for, the insurance and alcohol license were never changed into the partnership name, and plaintiff's name was never added to the lease for the premises. The parties' accountant testified that the parties' income tax returns and any financial statements drawn up for the business were prepared as though the business was a sole proprietorship. The attorney who prepared the "Partnership Agreement" admitted that he had drafted earlier agreements between the parties which, although titled otherwise, were intended to be security agreements that would protect plaintiff's loan only if defendant died or became disabled. Defendant testified that he understood that the subject agreement was only meant to be a security agreement to protect plaintiff's interests in case he died. An examination of the agreement itself indicates that, although it contains clauses resembling those typically found in partnership agreements, it also uncharacteristically leaves all control of the business to plaintiff and states that its primary purpose is to protect the parties in case of death or disability of the other. Further, the arrangement whereby plaintiff received monthly checks of $3,000 instead of splitting the business's profits was inconsistent with a partnership. Because this and other evidence supports the decision, we decline to disturb the judgment of Supreme Court which had the advantage of hearing the witnesses and assessing their credibility for itself (see, *Monette v Monette, supra).*

The remaining arguments of the parties have been reviewed and are either lacking in merit or were rendered academic by this court's resolution of the foregoing issue. Despite defendant's contentions otherwise, his counterclaims were properly dismissed because the record is devoid of any proof of any wrongdoing on the part of plaintiff who was paid pursuant to the parties' agreements. Notably, defendant admitted at trial that the compensation he paid to plaintiff was a gift to show defendant's appreciation for plaintiff's help with the business.

Once the partnership is formed, the parties are deemed to be partners with the incident partnership rights. The **partnership rights or interests** are:

1. the right to the physical assets of the business
2. the right to manage and control the partnership business
3. the right to the income, profits, and losses of the business

1. *Partnership property.* Unless otherwise designated, all property acquired by the partnership is deemed to be held in a **tenancy in partnership,** a form of multiple ownership of property that was developed exclusively for business partnerships. The following restrictions are placed on all property held in this manner:

   (a) No one partner may possess the partnership property for other than partnership purposes without the other partners' consent.

   (b) No one partner may sell the partnership property (excluding the business inventory) without the other partners' consent.

   (c) The personal creditors to the individual partners may not apply claims to the partnership property.

   (d) The heirs of a deceased partner have no right to the partnership property; title to the property passes to the surviving partners who are required to compensate the heirs of the deceased partners for the value of the property so acquired.

Tenancy in partnership is an outgrowth of both joint tenancies and tenancies in common. Under a **joint tenancy,** which must be created with the **four unities** of time, title, interest, and possession, all **joint tenants** have equal rights of possession to the property and a right of survivorship to the property without the necessity of paying off the heirs of the deceased joint tenant. Under a **tenancy in common,** the title may be created over time, and the tenants' interests do not have to be equal (except for an equal right of possession). There is no right of survivorship among **tenants in common,** and each tenant in common is free to alienate his or her interest.

If the partnership intends to hold property other than in a tenancy in partnership, such title should be explicitly indicated. This is especially true if one of the partners is merely loaning property to the partnership, intending to retain title personally. In such a situation, the partner should draft a rental agreement specifying that the title is to remain with the lending partner but liability for rent (which may be minimal) and maintenance, insurance repairs, and so forth for the property is the responsibility of the partnership during the period of the loan. If no such indication is made, the law may assume the property was a gift or contribution to the business and title may change to a tenancy in partnership.

The right to the physical assets of the partnership is a personal right and may not be assigned by the partners.

2. *Management.* Under the UPA, all partners are considered equal partners with equal say in management. However, as a practical consideration, in very few partnerships are the partners equal in management and control. The basic partnership usually

---

Partnership rights or interests — rights to manage, to assets, and to income, profits, and losses.

Tenancy in partnership — title for partnership property.

Joint tenancy — multiple ownership of property with rights of survivorship.

Four unities — time, title, interest, and possession.

Joint tenant — title holder of a joint tenancy.

Tenancy in common — form of multiple ownership of property with divisible portions.

Tenant in common — title holder to a tenancy in common.

comes into existence when one person has the expertise and the other person has the money. The party with the expertise usually manages the day-to-day operations of the business, whereas the party with the money usually controls the finances. If this is the intent of the parties, they should so indicate in a written agreement.

Example: The sole proprietor who is baking cookies as a small business out of her house has become a great success. In order to expand, she needs capital, and her husband agrees to contribute $50,000 to become a partner. The couple executes an agreement whereby the wife will control the operations and the husband will control the finances. Under the UPA, this agreement will prevail over the statute's provisions.

Under partnership law, all general partners are considered to be agents for the partnership, meaning that the contracts one partner enters into on behalf of the partnership with third persons binds all of the partners under general agency law principles. However, under the UPA there are five agreements that must have the consent of all of the partners in order for them to be bound. These agreements are:

(a) assignment of partnership property in trust for creditors—basically putting partnership property up as collateral to secure a loan for the business.
(b) sale of the goodwill of the business—agreeing to have the partnership as the guarantor, surety, and so forth for a third person.
(c) submitting a partnership claim to arbitration—because the decision of the arbitrator is binding and final, thereby precluding a day in court; in order to forgo the right to adjudicate the matter, the partners must specifically agree.
(d) confession of judgment—agreeing to the liability alleged in a lawsuit without trying the issue; this may arise in certain contractual clauses known as a **cognovit** provisions.
(e) any act that would make it impossible to carry on the business—this is a catchall provision that is determined on a case by case basis because the legislature could not anticipate every situation in which this might occur.

cognovit — contract provision confessing judgment.

The right to manage and control the business is a personal right and cannot be assigned by the partners.

3. *Income, profits, and losses.* Under partnership law, partners are precluded from receiving compensation for services they perform on behalf of the partnership. Partners are expected to be compensated by a division of the profits. However, the parties may agree to a modification of these rules, and many times partners receive income as a "draw against profits" throughout the year. The right to the income and profits is not considered a personal right, and therefore, the partners may assign such rights. The assignees of the partners' income and/or profits do not thereby become partners. However, under New York law the receipt of such profit may be considered as an indication of being a partner, and so to limit the assignee's liability, an assignment should be drafted indicating all rights and obligations.

Operation

Once the partnership is formed, each partner is subject to unlimited personal liability for the obligations of the business. This is **joint liability**, if the cause of action arises out of a contractual claim, or **joint and several liability**, if the basis of the claim lies in tort. Joint liability means that all of the partners must be made parties to the action in a court that has jurisdiction over all the partners (usually the state in which the business is located). Under the CPLR section 1025, a partnership may sue and be sued in a partnership name and may hold property in that name as well. Joint and several liability means that the injured party may sue any partner in any court that has jurisdiction over any partner for the full amount of the injury. The partner so sued may seek contribution from the other partners but is still fully liable to the injured party for the full amount.

Joint liability — partners' liability for contract actions.

Joint and several liability — partners' liability for tort actions.

> *Example: Persons from New York, New Jersey, and Connecticut form a partnership that operates a store in New York. If the partnership fails to pay a supplier, the supplier must sue them in New York, the only state that would have jurisdiction over all three partners because the cause of action is in contract and the partners' liability is joint. Conversely, if a customer slips on the floor of the store owned by the partnership, the customer may sue a partner either in New York, New Jersey, or Connecticut, bringing into court the partner with the deepest pockets because the action, based in tort, holds the partners jointly and severally liable.*

In New York, before a general partnership can operate, it is required to file a Business Certificate in the county clerk's office of every county in which the partnership will operate. The **Business Certificate for Partners** (see Exhibit 3–1) is the document the partnership will also use if it intends to operate under an assumed name.

Business Certificate for Partners — document that must be filed before a partnership can operate.

All of the operational requirements discussed in Chapter 2 with respect to licensing and sales tax apply to the general partnership, as well as to the sole proprietorship. General partnerships, like sole proprietorships, are not considered to be taxable entities. The general partnership files an informational return, Form IT-204 (see Exhibit 3–2), with the New York State Department of Taxation and Finance which indicates its income, expenses, and ultimate profit or losses. This form also indicates the names and Social Security numbers of the partners who receive a copy of this form to file with their own personal income tax returns. The profits and losses of the partnership are passed through to the partners. If there is a profit, each partner reports and pays taxes on the profits for the profit attributable to his or her ownership interest. If there is a loss, the partner is entitled to use that loss to offset his or her other income. The partners must report and pay taxes on the profit, even if the profit is not actually distributed to them but is put back into the business for expansion and development.

Kraus v. Kraus
250 N.Y. 63, 164 N.E. 743 (1928)

By an interlocutory judgment, the existence of a partnership has been established between the plaintiff, his father and a brother. The father, directed to account, has been found by the final judgment to have overpaid the complaining son. The balance in the father's favor is $5,033.17. He filed a stipulation waiving an affirmative judgment with the result that none was rendered. The Appellate Division held that two items, one for income taxes, $6,505.84, and the other for rental value of partnership land, $1,466.66, had been charged against the son in error. Subtraction of these items would yield a balance the other way.

(1) Under both State and Federal law the income tax return by a member of a partnership should include his share of the partnership income, whether distributed or not (Tax Law [Cons. Laws, ch. 60], § 364; U. S. Code, title 26, § 1068-30). The return by the partnership as such is one for information only (Tax Law, § 368; U. S. Code, title 26, § 1068-36). The members of this partnership did not conform to that requirement. The business was in the father's name. To the world he was its owner, and so for many purposes he was treated by the sons. In making his returns for taxes, he included the whole income of the business, and paid the tax accordingly. By so doing, he paid nearly $13,000 in excess of the tax that would have been due if computed on his share alone. Under the ruling of the referee, one-half of this excess was charged against each of the two sons.

We think the charge was proper. The plaintiff knew how the returns were made, and in substance, if not in form, approved them. He was told by his brother, who made out the statements, that his father, reporting individually, would include the income of the firm, and that the brothers might thus exclude it from their personal returns. The plaintiff acted on that advice, and made return accordingly. He omitted from his own return all mention of his interest in the income of the partnership, and reduced by so much the total of his yearly earnings. We think the substance of the transaction was a request by plaintiff to his father to assume the tax on the excess and lay it out for his account.

The argument is made that the effect of this allowance is to deprive the plaintiff of the benefit of exemptions and deductions that might conceivably have been his if the excess has been included in his own reports of income. He does not attempt to show to what extent, if at all, the result would thus be changed. He insists that the burden is on the defendant to prove the precise extent to which the payment by the partnership resulted to his benefit. We think his acquiescence bars him from limiting so narrowly the measure of the charge against him. If he believed that through the aid of exemptions or deductions he could reduce the tax upon his interest in the business, or wipe it out altogether, by making his own return, he should have sounded a timely warning against the method of return and payment in use with his assent. With full knowledge of the method, he told his father to go on. He will not now be heard to urge that the expense thereby incurred is not a charge upon his share.

(2) Land, bought with partnership money, was held during the life of the partnership for partnership use. After dissolution, the plaintiff and his brother, and later the plaintiff solely, used it for their own profit to the exclusion of the father. A charge against the plaintiff for an equitable share of the value thus appropriated, was allowed by the referee, and rejected on appeal.

We think the charge should be upheld. The plaintiff was not tenant in common with the defendants in the occupation of this land. If that had been the relation, the rule might apply that between one tenant in common and another an accounting is not due for the fruits of occupation in the absence of ouster or a claim of hostile right *(LeBarron v. Babcock, 122 N. Y. 153)*. The plaintiff was not tenant in common, but "tenant in partnership" (Partnership Law [Cons. Laws, ch. 39], § 51). The incidents of this tenancy are stated in the statutes. "The incidents of this tenancy are such that * * * a partner, subject to the provisions of this chapter and to any agreement between the partners, has an equal right with his partners to possess specific partnership property for partnership purposes; but he has no right to possess such property for any other purpose without the consent of his partners." The plaintiff did possess the partnership property for purposes not partnership without the consent of his partner, the appellant. He is accountable like any stranger for the value of the usufruct thus wrongfully engrossed *(Legore v. Peacock, 109 Ill. 94)*. A different question would be here if the plaintiff had held possession after the partnership had been wound up, and the equities between the partners adjusted and satisfied. Then, but not till then, the tenancy might cease to be a tenancy in partnership, and take to itself the quality of a tenancy in common *(Darrow v. Calkins, 154 N. Y. 503, 514)*. The equities between the partners had not been satisfied or adjusted when the plaintiff used the land for the transaction of his private business. They have not been satisfied even now, for a balance owing to the appellant is even now unpaid. We think the plaintiff was a trustee for the partnership while in occupation of the property, and that he is chargeable accordingly.

The order of the Appellate Division should be reversed, and the judgment of the referee affirmed, with costs in this court and in the Appellate Division.

Section 62 of the UPA sets out three broad categories of grounds for terminating a general partnership:

1. A general partnership may terminate without violating the partnership agreement if::
    (a) the time period specified in the agreement has expired.
    (b) it is the express wish of *any* of the partners.
    (c) a partner is expelled from the business.

As a general proposition, any time a partner withdraws from the business the partnership is deemed terminated. If the remaining partners continue the business, it is deemed to be a new partnership. If the remaining partners wish to continue the business, they must give personal notice to all of their business creditors and publish a notice in the newspaper for the general public to terminate liability for the withdrawing partner. The withdrawing partner remains liable for any cause of action that arose while he or she was a partner up to the date of the withdrawal. Conversely, if a person joins an existing partnership, he or she is only liable for causes of action that arise after the date of joining unless the new partner signs an agreement specifically assuming all existing obligations.

2. A partnership terminates if it or any of the partners engages in activities that violate the partnership agreement.
3. A general partnership terminates on the death or bankruptcy of a partner or by court order if the court decides:
    (a) a partner has engaged in misconduct.
    (b) a partner has become incapacitated.
    (c) there has been a breach of partnership.
    (d) the business has become too unprofitable to continue.
    (e) any other equitable grounds.

Note that the personal bankruptcy of a partner will terminate the partnership so that the creditors can attach the assets of the partnership attributable to the bankrupt partner.

Remember that under a tenancy in partnership the property so held is not subject to claims of the partners' personal creditors; so to avoid a fraud on such creditors, the law terminates the partnership, thereby making the assets available for attachment.

Once the partnership has been terminated, the partners may not accept new business and must wind up its affairs.

Benefits and Detriments

A general partnership affords the partners the following benefits over a sole proprietorship:

- By having partners with different areas of expertise, the partnership can create a better business.
- The business can be funded by contributions from more than one person and can acquire loans based on the creditworthiness of more than just one individual.
- Although personal liability remains unlimited, the partners may seek contribution for such liability from the other partners, thereby limiting the actual amount each partner would have to pay.
- The partners can take advantage of using partnership losses to offset other personal income.

A general partnership may be more detrimental than a sole proprietorship in the following ways:

- Because each partner is an agent for the partnership, each partner's vicarious liability is increased because of the acts of the other partners.
- A partner has less than complete control over the management of the business because management must be shared with the other partners.
- The partners must report and pay income taxes on partnership income even though the partners may not actually receive the income.

LIMITED PARTNERSHIP

Creation

Unlike sole proprietorships and general partnerships, in order to form a limited partnership, New York imposes several stringent requirements. Two laws govern the formation of a limited partnership depending on the date of its creation. The revised statute was enacted in order to simplify some of the requirements of the earlier laws and to afford more simplicity in the way a limited partnership may operate.

Under both statutes, in order to form a limited partnership, the partners must file a **Certificate of Limited Partnership** (see Exhibit 3–3). Under the ULPA, the certificate could have been filed either at the county clerk's office where the business was located or with the Secretary of State. Under the RULPA, the certificate must be filed with the Secretary of State. Under both laws, the limited partnership must have a name that is unique for limited partnerships in the state of New York, and it must contain the words "Limited Partnership" or "LP" to alert the public that they are dealing with a limited partnership. The Certificate

Certificate of Limited Partnership — document that must be filed to create a limited partnership.

of Limited Partnership also serves as the DBA for limited partnerships. Certain words are prohibited from being used in the limited partnership name; a complete list of such prohibited terms appears in section 121-102(3) of the Limited Partnership Law.

The limited partnership is required to appoint the New York Secretary of State as agent for service of process and must appoint a natural person living or working in New York or a New York corporation as its registered agent. Any change in the limited partnership requires the filing of an Amended Business Certificate (see Exhibit 3–4) with the Secretary of State.

Both laws mandate a publication requirement for limited partnerships (there is an exception for theatrical enterprises under section 23.03(4) of the New York Arts and Cultural Affairs Law). The publication must indicate the name and address of the limited partnership, as well as the names and addresses of the general and limited partners. The notice must be published once a week in two newspapers for a six-week period. The county clerk's office provides a list of approved newspapers that can be used for the publication requirement, and proof of such publication must be filed with the state.

Limited partnership agreement — contract used to form a partnership.

Under both the ULPA and the RULPA, a limited partnership is required to have a **limited partnership agreement** signed by all general and limited partners (Partnership § 121-110).

Limited partnership share — evidence of ownership interest.

The general partner manages and controls the business and has unlimited personal liability for the obligations of the limited partnership. The limited partner is considered to be an investor only and is precluded from participating in the management of the business. By giving up management rights, the limited partner's liability is limited to the amount he or she contributed to obtain his or her **limited partnership share.** His or her personal assets are exempt from business creditors unless he or she does something, such as participate in management or hold himself or herself out as being a general partner, to lose that status as a limited partner. Pursuant to the RULPA, limited partners may engage in the following activities on behalf of the limited partnership without losing their status as limited partners:

(a) act as a contractor for the business
(b) provide professional consulting services
(c) act as a surety for the business
(d) participate in voting

Gonzalez v. Chalpin
77 N.Y.2d 74, 565 N.E.2d 1253 (1990)

Plaintiff Gonzalez sued defendant Excel Associates (Excel) and its limited and general partners for breach of contract seeking damages for unpaid compensation for renovation work he performed, at the request of defendant-appellant Chalpin, on an apartment building owned by Excel. Excel, a New York limited partnership, has one individual general partner, defendant Lipkin; one corporate general partner, defendant Tribute Music, Inc. (Tribute); and one limited partner, Chalpin. Chalpin is also the president, sole shareholder and director of Tribute.

The general restriction on the liability of limited partners is not controlling here because, if the partner "in addition to the exercise of [the partner's] rights and powers as a limited partner * * * takes part in the control of the business," the limited partner becomes liable as a general partner (Partnership Law § 96). Chalpin cannot challenge the trial court's affirmed factual determination that he took part in the control of Excel's business. Instead, he attempts to skirt the individual and general responsibility imposed by Partnership Law § 96 by claiming that he acted at all times solely in his capacity as an officer of Tribute.

Irrefutably, individual liability should not be imposed on a limited partner merely because that person happens also to be an officer, director and/or shareholder of a corporate general partner (see, *Frigidaire Sales Corp. v Union Props., 88 Wash 2d 400, 562 P2d 244).* But that is not this case. Moreover and conversely, a limited partner who "takes part in the control of" the limited partnership's business should not automatically be insulated from individual liability merely by benefit of status as an officer and sole owner of the corporate general partner. That is this case.

A limited partner who assumes such a dual capacity rightly bears a heavy burden when seeking to elude personal liability. For once a plaintiff meets the threshold burden of proving that a limited partner took an active individual part in effectuating the limited partnership's interests *(Continental Natl. Bank v Strauss, 137 NY 148, 151),* the fulcrum shifts. The limited partner in such a dual capacity must then, at least, prove that any relevant actions taken were performed solely in the capacity as officer of the general partner.

Defendant in this case failed to adjust to the shift and did not overcome the proof of involvement and responsibility for his actions undertaken in his individual capacity. Chalpin's only evidence, offered to support his claim that he acted as an officer of Tribute in the employment dealings with Gonzalez on behalf of Excel, was Excel's certificate of limited partnership. The certificate states that Chalpin is a limited partner and was signed by Chalpin on behalf of Tribute, and the attached certification states that Chalpin is the president of Tribute.

Chalpin essentially would have the Court adopt a rule of law according the piece of paper conclusive weight on the critical issue. This is not a sensible rule and would not make a difference in this case, in any event, where there is no evidence that Chalpin ever asserted his identity and authority as a corporate officer of Tribute when conducting Excel's affairs with Gonzalez—except his own testimony, which was expressly discredited and characterized as unbelievable by the trial court. The clinching documentary evidence shows Chalpin signing Excel's checks in payment to Gonzalez in his own name and without naming Tribute or indicating that he was signing in any representative capacity.

Chalpin also invites the Court to incorporate into Partnership Law § 96 a requirement that a plaintiff seeking to hold a limited partner individually liable must prove reliance on the limited partner's personal conduct. This argument is not supportable or sound (see, *Delaney v Fidelity Lease, 526 SW2d 543* [Sup Ct Tex]). Such a significant qualification on the statutorily regulated liability pattern of Partnership Law § 96, if nevertheless deemed worthy of consideration, must come from the Legislature so that reasonable certainty and reliability in these business relationships and transactions could be reflected in the statutory formulation.

In sum, the trial court and Appellate Division properly rejected Chalpin's limited liability defense and imposed individual liability on him. We have examined the remaining arguments and conclude they are without merit or consequence on the outcome of this case.

Accordingly, the order of the Appellate Division should be affirmed, with costs.

Blue sky laws — state security laws.

It is important to note that because limited partners are deemed to be investors, limited partnerships may be subject to regulations pursuant to the state securities law (**blue sky laws**). In New York, if the entity has forty or more investors, it comes within the purview of the securities laws.

The general partners manage and control the business. However, the law requires them to obtain the consent of the limited partners in the following circumstances in order for the limited partnership to be bound:

1. Any act in contravention of the limited partnership agreement—this would be a breach of contract unless the contracting parties agree.
2. Confession of judgment—because of precluding a day in court, just as with general partnerships.
3. Possession of partnership property for other than partnership purposes—because the property is held in tenancy in partnership.
4. Any act that would interfere with the general operation of the business.
5. Admission of a new general partner—because the general partner manages the business, a new general partner will have a direct impact on the limited partner's interest in the investment.

As a general proposition, limited partners may sell their shares and may be added to the limited partnership as long as it is provided for in the limited partnership agreement because as investors only they do not have a direct effect on the investment. In New York, the same person may be both a general and a limited partner in the same limited partnership.

Operation

All of the laws, rules, and regulations that apply to general partnerships apply to limited partnerships as well.

Pursuant to section 121-801 of the Partnership Law, a limited partnership terminates:

1. at the time specified in the Certificate of Limited Partnership.
2. on the happening of any event specified in the Limited Partnership Agreement that acts as a termination.
3. with the written consent of all of the general partners and two-thirds of the limited partners.
4. on the withdrawal of the general partner or when there are no surviving general partners.

On termination, the limited partnership is dissolved and must wind up its affairs. In distributing its assets, after all creditors have been paid, the limited partners have a priority over the general partners in receiving the business assets.

Savasta v. 470 Newport Associates
82 N.Y.2d 763, 623 N.E.2d 1171 (1993)

Plaintiffs' predecessors in interest sold a property containing two apartment buildings to defendant general partnership and took back a mortgage. Subsequently, the general partnership had difficulty in making its mortgage payments to plaintiffs. For consenting to the refinancing of the mortgage, plaintiffs were made limited partners with a 20% interest in the partnership's profits. Under the partnership agreement, plaintiff limited partners' interest was to terminate on January 31, 1985. At the center of this dispute is paragraph 4 of the partnership agreement, which provided that "should the partnership prior to January 31, 1985, dispose of [the property] by sale or otherwise . . . then this partnership shall terminate upon any partner hereto giving written notice to that effect to the other partners." The agreement was silent with respect to the period within which the written notice was to be served.

In November 1982, the general partnership created a corporation and transferred its sole asset, the apartment complex, to the corporation and converted the property to cooperative apartments. At the closing, defendant general partners paid in full the original mortgage held by plaintiffs. Then or shortly thereafter, the corporation sold approximately 20% of the cooperative shares to individual apartment owners.

Plaintiff limited partners, however, did not give notice to terminate the partnership at that time. Indeed, on March 3, 1983, they accepted $45,073.32 as the full amount the general partners owed them as of that date, representing their 20% share of the partnership profits, including their share of the proceeds from the sale of the cooperative apartments. For the next 18 months, the limited partners accepted, without objection, monthly payments of their 20% share of the partnership profits. Finally, on September 6, 1984 (about 22 months after the alleged "disposition"), they sent the general partners a purported notice of termination of the limited partnership. Even then, they continued to accept monthly payments from the general partners until January 31, 1985 when the limited partnership terminated pursuant to its terms.

When a contract does not specify time of performance, the law implies a reasonable time *(Webster's Red Seal Publs. v Gilberton World-Wide Publs., 67 A.D.2d 339, 343, 415 N.Y.S.2d 229, affd 53 N.Y.2d 643, 438 N.Y.S.2d 998, 421 N.E.2d 118)*. What constitutes a reasonable time for performance depends upon the facts and circumstances of the particular case *(Ben Zev v Merman, 73 N.Y.2d 781, 783, 536 N.Y.S.2d 739, 533 N.E.2d 669)*. In the present case the Appellate Division concluded that in light of all the circumstances, plaintiffs' 22-month delay before seeking termination of the partnership was unreasonable. We agree with that determination, and accordingly, even if plaintiffs are correct that the cooperative conversion triggered the right to terminate under paragraph 4 of the partnership agreement, they would be entitled to no relief because of their unreasonable delay in exercising that right.

Benefits and Detriments

The benefits of operating a limited partnership over a general partnership are:

- A person may acquire ownership of a business without engendering unlimited personal liability.
- Financing can be obtained by selling additional limited partnership shares, an option not available for sole proprietorships or general partnerships.
- The profits and losses pass through to the partners in the same fashion as with general partnerships.

The detriments of operating a limited partnership are:

- formalities in creation
- loss of control for limited partners

- potential regulation under state securities laws
- formalities required to make changes in the limited partnership
- increased operating costs due to increased formalities

The People of the State of New York v. Zinke
147 A.D.2d 106, 541 N.Y.S.2d 986 (1989)

This appeal presents the issue of whether a general partner with virtually unfettered management control and investment discretion may be held criminally accountable for misappropriating a limited partnership's funds.

In April 1981, defendant, an investment adviser for small pension and profit-sharing funds, formed a limited partnership, SIN (Stonehenge Investment Notes) 1, Ltd., in which he was the general partner and about 20 to 25 pension funds or profit-sharing plans were limited partners. The partnership's purpose, as defined in the partnership agreement, was to invest in "negotiable notes, mortgages and other evidences of indebtedness secured by real property." The partnership assets were invested basically in second mortgages on properties located in California. Defendant invested about $40,000 of his own money in the partnership when it started and another $360,000 in 1985, after the incidents which led to his conviction had occurred.

As general partner, defendant controlled the partnership's books, records and cash. Although the limited partners had the right to inspect all partnership records and to receive yearly certified balance sheets and profit and loss statements, they did not have the right to review the investments defendant selected or countersign partnership checks. Nor did they have any voice in the running of the partnership.

In order to establish defendant's guilt of larceny, the People were required to prove that, with the intention of disposing of the same for his own benefit, he wrongfully withheld property from its owner, SIN 1. The People's proof shows that defendant withdrew $1,050,000 from the partnership account in two installments in order to make payments on a building that he was purchasing for himself. His motive in looting the partnership account in such manner was transparent. He had been unable to close on the purchase of the building on two separate occasions, and, by the terms of his agreement with the seller, risked forfeiting $700,000 of his own money if he did not make the payments required to extend the closing dates. Defendant ultimately purchased the building in part with the $1,050,000 in partnership moneys he had withdrawn from the partnership account, sold it seven months later at a gross profit of $2,000,000, used that profit entirely for his own account and never repaid the partnership. Indeed, in his own testimony, defendant conceded these basic facts. Thus, there was no doubt that he had appropriated to himself the partnership's funds.

Fiduciaries such as corporate officers or directors who divert stockholders' funds for their own private purposes are guilty of embezzlement under the larceny statute. In this case, defendant, the general partner of a limited partnership, stood in precisely the same fiduciary relationship to the limited partners and was obligated to manage the partnership's assets for their benefit. Defendant, however, citing the common-law principle that it is not larceny to take property of which the taker is a part owner (see, e.g., 3 Torcia, Wharton's Criminal Law § 393, at 391-392 [14th ed 1980]), claims an exemption from criminal prosecution for misappropriating partnership property. He argues that New York has consistently followed the common-law rule (see, *People v Hart, 114 App Div 9; People v O'Brien, 102 Misc 2d 246; People v Dye, 134 Misc 689)* and points to the

Legislature's rejection, in enacting the current Penal Law in 1965 (L 1965, ch 1030), of the position of the Model Penal Code, which abrogated the common-law rule by defining larceny as stealing the "property of another," and the latter as any property "in which any person other than the actor has an interest * * * regardless of the fact that the actor also has an interest in the property" (Model Penal Code § 223.0 [7]; § 223.2 [1]).

Defendant's claim that New York law prohibits a larceny prosecution of a partner for stealing partnership funds is, in our view, itself incorrect since under New York law a partner is a "co-owner" of partnership property only when he is using it for the partnership's purposes. (Partnership Law § 51 [2] [a].) Moreover, the common-law rule loses its vitality outside the context of a traditional partnership in which each member has equal control over the business, as well as an equal opportunity to protect himself from another partner's theft. Here, the limited partners entrusted their funds to defendant to manage for their benefit, and he committed a theft when he used those funds for himself.

Pursuant to Penal Law § 155.05, a person is guilty of larceny if he takes, obtains or withholds property from an owner thereof. An "owner" of property is statutorily defined as a person who "has a right to possession * * * superior to that of the taker." (Penal Law § 155.00 [5].) By statute, one "joint or common owner of property shall not be deemed to have a right of possession thereto superior to that of any other joint or common owner thereof." (Penal Law § 155.00 [5].) Thus, a joint or common owner of property cannot be prosecuted for larceny if he steals that property from another joint or common owner, because the person from whom the property was taken is deemed by statute to have an equal, not superior, right of possession.

Partners, however, are "co-owners" of partnership property only when they possess the property in furtherance of the purposes of the partnership. Section 50 (a) of the Partnership Law describes the property of a partner to include "his rights in specific partnership property," such as the partnership bank accounts involved in this case. Section 51 (1) provides that "[a] partner is co-owner with his partners of specific partnership property holding as a tenant in partnership." If such "co-ownership" of a tenancy in partnership gave each partner an equal right to possess partnership property under all circumstances, as does co-ownership under other types of tenancies in common, then the proposition that partners can never steal from each other would be correct. No partner would ever have a possessory right superior to another, and none would be "owners" under the larceny statute.

Partnership Law § 51 (2) (a), however, provides that a tenancy in partnership gives partners "an equal right * * * to possess specific partnership property for partnership purposes." Section 51 (2) (a) just as clearly denies to any partner the "right to possess such property for any other purpose without the consent of his partners." Thus, a partner who diverts property from the partnership for his own purposes does so without a possessory right under the tenancy in partnership.

This limitation on the possessory rights appurtenant to a tenancy in partnership is a natural concomitant of the legal principle codified in section 43 of the Partnership Law, namely, that every partner must act as a fiduciary for the other partners when dealing with partnership property. *(Meinhard v Salmon, 249 NY 458, 463-469.)* Such fiduciary relationship among partners is not generally imposed on other joint owners of property. (See, e.g., *Streeter v Shultz, 45 Hun 406, 409* [3d Dept 1887], affd *127 NY 652.)* Thus, it is not surprising that a tenancy in partnership has been described as a unique form of co-ownership. (Moynihan, Real Property, ch 10, § 1, n 1 [1965]; see also, *Matter of Minton Group (46 Bankr 222* [SD NY 1985].)

Defendant's insistence that partners are joint owners under section 155.00 (5) of the Penal Law is based almost entirely on the commentary to that section (Hechtman,

Practice Commentaries, McKinney's Cons Laws of NY, Book 39, at 104 [1975 ed]), which is not itself premised on the Partnership Law's definition of co-ownership, but, rather, on two old appellate cases, both decided before the 1919 enactment of the Partnership Law with its limited definition of a partner's ownership rights. Moreover, since neither of those cases unambiguously holds that partners are the type of joint owners who cannot be held criminally responsible for stealing from one another, they hardly provide a persuasive basis to exempt from criminal liability conduct that would in nonpartnership contexts be regarded as embezzlement.

For example, in *Holmes v Gilman (138 NY 369, 377),* the Court of Appeals stated that a misappropriation of partnership funds could not be regarded in law as an embezzlement. The statement, which was entirely unnecessary to resolve the issues of civil liability before the court, is dicta and provides only the weakest support for defendant's position. The other authority, *People v Hart (114 App Div 9,* supra), does not provide any stronger support. There, the trial court had instructed the jury that it could not find the defendant guilty of larceny if he was a partner of his victim, but then refused to answer the jury's question as to how to determine whether the two were in fact partners. In reversing, this court did not hold that such instruction was required or adopt its content as a principle of law. Instead, it apparently ruled that since the Trial Judge's instruction was the law of the case, it was error to fail to elucidate for the jurors the legal principles relevant to the issue. Even if construed as an endorsement of the principle that one partner cannot steal from another, the holding is too tangential to be viewed as decisive authority.

Thus, in our view, the language of the Partnership Law shows that a partner is not exempted from criminal liability for theft when he diverts partnership property to his own purposes. But we need not decide whether this logical principle applies to a traditional partnership since what is involved here is an entirely different situation, one in which defendant, as the general partner, was primarily a manager of the limited partners' money, and only secondarily an investor in or owner of the business. That role difference, we believe, clearly takes defendant and other general partners out of the "joint ownership" exemption from criminal liability.

Technically, all partners are fiduciaries of one another. In the traditional partnership, however, each partner has an absolute and equal statutory right to manage the business. (Partnership Law § 40 [5]; § 50 [c].) Therefore, each partner has an opportunity to protect himself from another partner's theft, because each has a right to supervise the business to insure that partnership funds are being spent only for partnership purposes.

By contrast, in a limited partnership only the general partner has any right to manage the business. (Partnership Law §§ 96, 98.) Unlike regular partners with equal management rights, limited partners are mere passive investors, entirely dependent on the good faith and integrity of the general partner to whom they have entrusted their investment. They thus stand in the same position in regard to the general partners as stockholders in regard to corporate officers and directors, who are not exempt from a larceny prosecution when they embezzle corporate assets.

Indeed, since the purpose of a limited partnership is to encourage "persons with capital to become partners with those having skill" *(Riviera Congress Assocs. v Yassky, 25 AD2d 291, 295,* affd *18 NY2d 540),* thereby enabling investors to aggregate their funds "into common enterprises of considerable size" *(Matter of United States v Silverstein, 314 F2d 789, 791,* cert denied *374 U.S. 807),* a general partner's managerial role is at the very core of the Limited Partnership Act. (Partnership Law § 90 et seq.) As the New York Court of Appeals stated in *Fifth Ave. Bank v Colgate (120 NY 381),* construing the Limited Partnership Act almost 100 years ago: "The policy of this law was to bring into trade and commerce funds of those not inclined to engage in that business, who were disposed to furnish capital upon such limited liability, with a view to the share of profits which might be expected to result to them from its use. And the fact that the law has been in operation in this state for nearly seventy years, and has been adopted in most if not all the states of the union, indicates that it is deemed to have its advantages, and that it serves a purpose consistent with the public welfare. It is entitled to a reasonable construction for the protection of the special partners as well as others, that the statute in its design may be rendered effectual." (Supra, at 396.)

Thus, limited partnerships perform the identical capital accumulation function of businesses operated in the corporate form. As the trial court correctly noted, a "reasonable construction" of the Limited Partnership Act has consistently equated limited partners with corporate shareholders, since both are investors who opt for limited authority in exchange for limited liability.

The analogy between limited partnerships and corporations and the concomitant fiduciary duty imposed on their managers was clearly recognized by the Court of Appeals in *Lichtyger v Franchard Corp. (18 NY2d 528):* "There is no basis or warrant for distinguishing the fiduciary relationship of corporate director and shareholder from that of general partner and limited partner. The principle is the same—those in control of a business must deal fairly with the interests of the other investors and this is so regardless of whether the business is in corporate or partnership form." (Supra, at 536.)

The evidence here presents a clear case of a managing general partner, with total control over the partnership's assets, violating his fiduciary duty by stealing money entrusted to him. Under the limited partnership agreement herein, the limited partners provided the bulk of the funds. While defendant's capital contribution was minimal, his control of the partnership assets and of the day-to-day operation of the partnership was absolute; he had total discretion in selecting the partnership's investments. Realistically, defendant's function as general partner was that of a hired manager of the limited partners' assets, and not an owner of them.

Sound public policy and morality demand that, just as the corporate director or officer is criminally responsible for a larceny from the corporation, the general partner to whom limited partners have entrusted their assets be criminally accountable for embezzling those assets. Otherwise, a general partner would have little incentive to follow the rules since the worst he could expect would be a civil accounting, which is hardly a deterrent in view of the significant potential gain to him.

Exempting general partners from criminal liability would undermine the very purpose of limited partnerships. Investors would become reluctant to place their funds in an enterprise if the fiduciary to whom they entrust them cannot be prosecuted when he steals. Since the deterrent provided by the criminal law is essential for "the protection of the special partners" *(Fifth Ave. Bank v Colgate, supra, 120 NY, at 396),* the law should be given the "reasonable construction" (supra) which leads to that salutary result. Only an interpretation of the co-ownership exemption that excludes the general partner of a limited partnership will "promote justice and effect the objects of the [Penal] law" (Penal Law § 5.00).

Thus, under the Penal Law and the Partnership Law, only "co-owners" of property are exempted from criminal liability for theft, and those who divert partnership funds for their own purposes do not "co-own" them with their innocent victims. In any event, a general partner who manages partnership property for limited partners is not exempt from prosecution for embezzlement when he steals that property.

Affirmed.

CHAPTER REVIEW

General partnerships and limited partnerships were created in order to reduce what was considered detriments of operating a business as a sole proprietorship. The general partnership provides additional sources of funding for the business and further allows for the potential of a better business by having multiple owners, each with a different area of expertise. However, as with the sole proprietorship, the general partners still retain unlimited personal liability, but this unlimited liability is somewhat tempered by the requisite contribution from the other partners.

Limited partnerships provide a greater source of potential funding by permitting persons to invest in the business. These investors gain limited personal liability for the obligations of the business, but only because they give up the right to manage and control the business. However, in order to create a limited partnership, the parties must follow detailed and costly state requirements and may also be regulated under the state securities laws if there are a sufficient number of limited partners.

In addition to the forms discussed in this chapter, three additional forms are used by partnerships formed outside of New York that wish to do business in New York (see Exhibits 3–5, 3–6, and 3–7).

KEY TERMS

Blue sky laws
Business Certificate for Partners
Certificate of Limited Partnership
Cognovit
Contribution
Four unities
General partner
General partnership
Joint and several liability
Joint liability
Joint tenancy
Joint tenant
Limited partner

Limited partnership
Limited partnership agreement
Limited partnership share
Partnership rights or interests
Revised Uniform Limited Partnership Act
    (RULPA)
Statute of Frauds
Tenancy in common
Tenancy in partnership
Tenant in common
Uniform Limited Partnership Act (ULPA)
Uniform Partnership Act (UPA)

EXERCISES

1. Why would the same person wish to be a general and a limited partner in the same limited partnership? Discuss in terms of financing, liability, marketing, and operating the business.

2. Why are limited partnerships regulated whereas general partnerships are not? Explain.

3. Go to the library and find two examples of a limited partnership agreement. Compare the samples and create a limited partnership agreement for your files.

4. Go to the library and find two examples of a general partnership agreement. Compare the samples and create a general partnership agreement for your files.

5. What factors would be important to use in determining whether a business should be organized as a general partnership or as a limited partnership? Discuss.

FACTUAL PROBLEM

A dress designer is hired by a general partnership to design a clothing line for the business. The designer is well-liked by the owners and is treated just like a partner. The designer refers to the owners as "his partners." The owners fail to pay withholding taxes and the tax department comes after the designer for the business taxes. Discuss the designer's potential liability.

Business Certificate for Partners

The undersigned do hereby certify that they are conducting or transacting business as members of a partnership under the name or designation of

at

in the County of _____ , *State of New York, and do further certify that the full names of all the persons conducting or transacting such partnership including the full names of all the partners with the residence address of each such person, and the age of any who may be infants, are as follows:*

NAME Specify which are infants and state ages.   *RESIDENCE*

....

....

....

....

....

....

WE DO FURTHER CERTIFY that we are the successors in interest to

the person or persons heretofore using such name or names to carry on or conduct or transact business.

In Witness Whereof, *We have this* _____ *day of* _____ *made and signed this certificate.*

....

....

....

....

....

State of New York, County of _____   SS.: ACKNOWLEDGMENT RPL309-a (Do not use outside New York State)

On _____ before me, the undersigned, personally appeared _____

personally known to me or proved to me on the basis of satisfactory evidence to be the individual(s) whose name(s) is (are) subscribed to the within instrument and acknowledged to me that he/she/they executed the same in his/her/their capacity(ies), and that by his/her/their signature(s) on the instrument, the individual(s), or the person upon behalf of which the individual(s) acted, executed the instrument.

_____
(signature and office of individual taking acknowledgment)

Exhibit 3–1

Business Certificate for Partners *(Forms may be purchased from BlumbergExcelsior, Inc. or any of its dealers. Reproduction prohibited.)*

For office use only

New York State Department of Taxation and Finance

Partnership Return

2000

IT-204

For calendar year 2000 or fiscal year beginning 0 0 and ending .

Read the instructions before completing this return.

▼ Employer identification number

Print or type

Legal name

Principal business activity

Trade name of business if different from legal name above

Principal product or service

Address *(number and street or rural route)*

NAICS business code number *(see instructions)* | Date business started

City, village or post office   State   ZIP code

If you do not need forms mailed to you next year, check box ....

A Check the box that applies to your entity:
  Regular partnership   Limited liability partnership (LLP)
  Limited liability company (LLC - including limited liability investment company and a limited liability trust company)

B If the income from the partnership is all from New York sources, check the box☐. **Do not** complete Schedule B, Part III.

C If your entity is an LLC or LLP, did the entity have any business activity in New York State during 2000? .... **C** ■ Yes ☐ ■ No ☐

D Check applicable box(es): ▶☐ Change of address ▶☐ Initial return ▶☐ Amended return ■ Final return *(attach explanation)*

E Is this return the result of federal audit changes? .... **E** ☐ Yes ■ No ☐
  If *Yes:* 1) Enter date of final federal determination **E1**
    2) Do you concede the federal audit changes? *(See instructions for amended return or federal changes)* ... **E2** ☐ Yes ■ No ☐

F Did you file a New York State partnership return for: .... 1998 Yes ☐ No ☐ .... 1999 Yes ☐ No ☐
  If *No,* state reason: _____

G Total number of partners in the partnership *(see instructions)* .... **G** ■

H Does the partnership currently have tax accounts with New York State for the following taxes?
    1. Sales and use tax ■ Yes ☐ ■ No ☐   If *Yes,* enter ID number **H1**
    2. Withholding tax ■ Yes ☐ ■ No ☐   **H2**

Schedule A

Part I — List all places, both in and out of New York State, where the partnership carries on business
  (Attach additional sheets if necessary)

Street address	City and state	Description *(see instructions)*

Part II — Formula basis allocation of income if books do not reflect income earned in New York

Items used as factors	A Totals - in and out of New York State Dollars	B New York State amounts Dollars	C Percent column B is of column A
Property percentage *(see instructions)*			
1 Real property owned .... ■ 1		■ 1	
2 Real property rented from others .... ■ 2		■ 2	
3 Tangible personal property owned ..... ■ 3		■ 3	
4 **Property percentage** *(add lines 1, 2, and 3; see inst.)* 4		4	4 . %
5 **Payroll percentage** *(see inst.)* .... ■ 5		■ 5	5 . %
6 **Gross income percentage** *(see inst.)* ... ■ 6		■ 6	6 . %
7 Total of percentages *(add column C, lines 4, 5, and 6)*			7 . %
8 **Business allocation percentage** *(divide line 7 by three or by actual number of percentages if less than three)* .... ■ 8			8 . %

Paid preparer's use only	Preparer's signature	Date	Mark an "X" if self-employed ☐	**Sign here**	Signature of general partner
	Firm's name *(or yours, if self-employed)*	Preparer's SSN or PTIN			Date	Daytime phone number (optional) ( )
	Address	Employer identification number			

Partnership must attach federal Form 1065 or Form 1065-B and all schedules to this Form IT-204 *(see instructions for* Penalties).
Mail your return to: **STATE PROCESSING CENTER, PO BOX 61000, ALBANY, NY 12261-0001.**

311094   **This is a scannable form: please file this original return with the Tax Department.**   IT-204 2000

Exhibit 3–2
IT-204 Partnership Return *(Courtesy of the New York State Department of Taxation and Finance.)*

IT-204 (2000) (back)

Schedule B — Partners' New York modifications, credits, etc.

Part I — Partners' New York modifications to federal items Total

9	New York State additions *(attach schedule; see instructions)*	9	
10	New York State subtractions *(attach schedule; see instructions)*	10	
11	Additions to federal itemized deductions	11	
12	Subtractions from federal itemized deductions	12	
13	Amount of interest expense incurred to carry tax-exempt obligations	13	
14	New York adjustments to federal tax preference items *(see instructions)*	14	

Part II — Partners' credit information

15	Manufacturing and production, retail enterprise, waste treatment and pollution control property - investment credit *(attach Form IT-212)*	15	Total
16	Research and development property - investment credit *(attach Form IT-212)*	16	
17	Add-back of investment credit on early dispositions *(attach Form IT-212)*	17	
18	Investment credit for the financial services industry *(attach Form IT-252)*	18	
19	Add-back of investment credit on early dispositions for the financial services industry *(attach Form IT-252)*	19	
20	Credit for employment of persons with disabilities *(attach Form IT-251)*	20	
21	Alternative fuels credit *(attach Form IT-253)*	21	
22	Add-back of alternative fuels credit on early dispositions *(attach Form IT-253)*	22	
23	Industrial or manufacturing business (IMB) credit *(attach Form DTF-623)*	23	

Empire zone (EZ) and qualified emerging technology company (QETC) tax credits

24	EZ wage tax credit *(attach Form DTF-601)*	24	
25	ZEA wage tax credit *(attach Form DTF-601.1)*	25	
26	EZ capital tax credit *(attach Form DTF-602)*	26	
27	EZ investment tax credit and EZ employment incentive credit *(attach Form DTF-603)*	27	
28	EZ investment tax credit and EZ employment incentive credit for the financial services industry *(attach Form DTF-605)*	28	
29	Add-back of EZ capital tax credit, EZ investment tax credit, and EZ employment incentive credit *(attach Forms DTF-602 and DTF-603)*	29	
30	Add-back of EZ investment tax credit and EZ employment incentive credit for the financial services industry *(attach Form DTF-605)*	30	
31	QETC employment credit *(attach Form DTF-621)*	31	
32	QETC capital tax credit *(attach Form DTF-622)*	32	
33	Add-back of QETC capital tax credit on early dispositions *(attach Form DTF-622)*	33	

Farmers' school tax credit

34	Total acres of qualified agricultural property	34	
35	Total amount of eligible taxes paid	35	
36	Total acres of qualified agricultural property converted to nonqualified use	36	

Part III — Income and deductions allocated to New York *(Partnerships whose income is all from New York sources, do not complete Part III)* Allocated New York amounts

37	Ordinary income (loss) from trade or business activities	37	
38	Net income or loss from New York rental real estate activities	38	
39	Net income or loss from other rental activities	39	
40	Portfolio income (loss)	40	
41	Guaranteed payments to partners	41	
42	Net gain (loss) under IRC section 1231 *(other than due to casualty or theft)*	42	
43	Other income	43	
44	Expense deduction for property under IRC section 179	44	
45	Deductions related to portfolio income *(do not include investment interest expense)*	45	
46	Other deductions *(see instructions)*	46	
47	Tax preference items for minimum tax *(see instructions)*	47	
48	New York adjustments to federal tax preference items *(see instructions)*	48	
49	Investment interest expense *(see instructions)*	49	
50	Other items not included above that are required to be reported separately to partners	50	

312094 This is a scannable form; please file this original return with the Tax Department. IT-204 2000

Exhibit 3–2

Continued *(Courtesy of the New York State Department of Taxation and Finance.)*

Certificate of Limited Partnership

1. The name of the limited partnership is _____
(the "Limited Partnership").

2. The office of the Limited Partnership is to be located in
_____ County.

3. The Secretary of State is designated as the agent of the Limited Partnership
on whom process against it may be served. The post office address to which
the Secretary of State shall mail a copy of any process served on him against
the Limited Partnership is _____ .

4. The name and street address of each general partner is:

_____   _____

_____   _____

5. The latest date on which the Limited Partnership is to dissolve is
_____ . The Limited Partnership may be terminated
sooner in accordance with the Limited Partnership Agreement.

6. The effective date of the Limited Partnership shall be _____ .

IN WITNESS WHEREOF, the undersigned has executed this Certificate of
Limited Partnership this _____ day of
_____ , and affirms the statments contained herein
as true under penalties of perjury.

_____
General Partner

Exhibit 3–3
Certificate of Limited Partnership

T 224—Amended Business Certificate
For Individual or Partners. 11-98

Blumbergs
Law Products

BlumbergExcelsior, Inc.
PUBLISHER NYC 10013

Amended Business Certificate

The undersigned hereby certify that a certificate of doing business under the assumed name

for the conduct of business at

*was filed in the office of the County Clerk   County, State of New York, on the
            day of   under index number   ; that the
last amended certificate was filed on the   day of   in the
office of the said County Clerk under index number*
         *It is hereby further certified that this amended certificate is made for the purpose of more accu-
rately setting forth the facts recited in the original certificate or the last amended certificate and to set
forth the following changes in such facts;*

In Witness Whereof, *the undersigned have this   day of*
made and signed this certificate.

_____

_____

_____

_____

State of New York, County of   **SS.: ACKNOWLEDGMENT RPL309-a (Do not use outside New York State)**

On   before me, the undersigned, personally appeared

personally known to me or proved to me on the basis of satisfactory evidence to be the individual(s) whose
name(s) is (are) subscribed to the within instrument and acknowledged to me that he/she/they executed the
same in his/her/their capacity(ies), and that by his/her/their signature(s) on the instrument, the individual(s),
or the person upon behalf of which the individual(s) acted, executed the instrument.

_____
(signature and office of individual taking acknowledgment)

* Set forth the residence address of each new partner, if any.

Exhibit 3–4
Amended Business Certificate *(Forms may be purchased from BlumbergExcelsior, Inc. or any of its dealers.
Reproduction prohibited.)*

Certificate of Adoption

1. The name of the limited partnership is _____ (the "Limited Partnership").

2. The original Certificate of the Limited Partnership was filed on _____ in _____ County. The name under which the Limited Partnership was formed was _____ .

3. The office of the Limited Partnership is to be located in _____ County.

4. The Secretary of State is designated as the agent of the Limited Partnership on whom process against it may be served. The post office address to which the Secretary of State shall mail a copy of any process served on him against the Limited Partnership is _____ .

5. The name and street address of each general partner is:

   _____   _____

   _____   _____

6. The latest date on which the Limited Partnership is to dissolve is _____ .

   IN WITNESS WHEREOF, the undersigned has executed this Certificate this _____ day of _____ , and affirms the statements contained herein as true under penalties of perjury.

   _____
   General Partner

Exhibit 3–5
Certificate of Adoption

Application of Authority

1. The name of the limited partnership is _____ (the "Limited Partnership").

2. The jurisdiction of the Limited Partnership is _____ , and the Limited Partnership was formed on _____ .

3. The office of the Limited Partnership in New York State is to be located in _____ County.

4. The Secretary of State is designated as the agent of the Limited Partnership on whom process against it may be served. The post office address to which the Secretary of State shall mail a copy of any process served on him against the Limited Partnership is _____ .

5. The address of the Limted Partnership in the jurisdiction of its organization is

    _____ .

6. The name and street address of each general partner is:

    _____   _____

    _____   _____

7. A copy of the Certificate of Limited Partnership is available at _____ . The Limited Partnership shall provide, upon request, a copy of its Certificate of Limted Partnership and all amendments. The request shall be made to _____ .

    IN WITNESS WHEREOF, the undersigned has executed this Application for Authority this _____ day of _____ , and affirms the statements contained herein as true under penalties of perjury.

    _____
    General Partner

Exhibit 3–6
Application for Authority

Certificate of Surrender of Authority

1. The name of the limited partnership as it appears on the index of names of existing domestic and authorized foreign limited partnerships of any type or kind in the Department of State is _____
(the "Limited Partnership"), and the fictitious name which the Partnership has agreed to use in New York State pursuant to § 121-902 of the Partnership law is _____ .

2. The Limited Partnership was formed in _____ .

3. The Limited Partnership was authorized to do business in New York State on
_____ .

4. The Limited Partnership hereby surrenders its authority to do business in New York State.

5. The Limited Partnership consents that process against it in any action or special proceeding based on any liability or obligation incurred by it within New York State before filing this Certificate of Surrender may be served on the Secretary of State in the manner set forth in § 121-109 of the Partnership Law.

6. The Secretary of State shall mail a copy of any process served on him against the Limited Partnership to _____ .

   IN WITNESS WHEREOF, the undersigned has executed this Certificate of Surrender this _____ day of
_____ , and affirms the statements contained herein as true under penalties of perjury.

_____
General Partner

Exhibit 3–7
Certificate of Surrender of Authority

Chapter 4

Miscellaneous Business Formats

INTRODUCTION

Prior to the creation of the most recent business formats, the corporation and the limited liability company, several entities were employed by entrepreneurs to operate their businesses. These formats, the joint venture, joint stock company, and business trust, are still in use today, but to a much more limited extent than previously. However, these forms still exist and must be included in any discussion of New York business law.

JOINT VENTURE

Joint venture — partnership for a limited operation or purpose.

The term **joint venture** is legally insignificant. It represents a partnership, either general or limited, that is formed for a limited purpose or operation rather than an ongoing business. This term is typically employed when companies from different countries come together for a business operation. However, the legalities surrounding this format's creation and operation are dependent on whether it is a general or limited partnership. There is no law designed particularly for the joint venture.

Example: A New York hotel wants to open a beach resort on the island of Bali in Indonesia. The New York company and the government of Indonesia form a joint venture for the construction and operation of the new resort.

Bay Casino, LLC. v. M/V Royal Empress and Seaco Ltd.
5 F. Supp. 2d 113 S.D.N.Y. (1998)

Introduction

   This matter is currently before the Court on Defendants' application, pursuant to Rule E(4)(f) of the Supplemental Rules for Certain Admiralty and Maritime Claims

("Supplemental Rules"), to vacate the arrest and attachment of the M/V ROYAL EMPRESS, and to allow Defendants to post a $200,000 bond instead.

I. Joint Ventures and Maritime Liens

Under well-established maritime law, one who is a joint venturer does not have a maritime lien, and cannot enforce one against his co-venturer. *Sasportes v. M/V Sol de Copacabana, 581 F.2d 1204, 1208 (5th Cir. 1978)*. A co-venturer may only entertain an in personam action against the vessel owner for claims arising out of their mutual joint venture. A co-venturer may not lawfully have a maritime lien against the ship itself. *Sasportes, 581 F.2d at 1208–9*.

The rationale for this established doctrine is that a co-venturer is not a "stranger to the vessel," and therefore relies not upon the credit of the ship, but rather upon the credit of the owner for payments, claims, and reimbursement. *Vera, Inc. v. The Tug Dakota, 769 F. Supp. 451, 457 (E.D.N.Y. 1991)*.

In New York, in order to form a joint venture, all of the following elements must be met: (1) two or more persons must enter into a specific agreement to carry on an enterprise for profit; (2) their agreement must evidence their intent to be joint venturers; (3) each must make a contribution of property, financing, skill, knowledge, or effort; (4) each must have some degree of joint control over the venture; and (5) there must be a provision for the sharing of both profits and losses. *Itel Containers International Corp., v. Atlanttrafik Express Service Ltd., 909 F.2d 698, 701 (2d Cir. 1990); Independent Energy Corp. v. Trigen Energy Corp., 944 F. Supp. 1184, 1201 (S.D.N.Y. 1996)*.

"The ultimate inquiry [in determining whether a joint venture exists] is whether the parties have so joined their property, interest, skills and risks that for the purposes of the particular adventure their respective contributions have become as one and the commingled property and interests of the parties have thereby been made subject to each of the associates on the trust and inducement that each would act for their joint benefit." *Independent Energy Corp v. Trigen Energy Corp., 944 F. Supp. 1184 (S.D.N.Y. 1996)*.

The finding of a joint venture is predicated on an examination of the entire relationship between the parties; no one factor is considered decisive. *Fulcher's Point Pride Seafood, 935 F.2d 208, 211–12; Sasportes, 581 F.2d at 1207*.

In this case, the Court finds that the parties had a owner-charterer relationship under the Bare Boat Agreement, and not a joint-venture as Defendants argue. First, all five elements required to be in existence under New York law in order to find a joint venture have not been shown to exist in the parties' Charter. First, although there was sharing of profits under the Agreement, there was no sharing of losses. Second, although under the agreement SeaCo was to contribute skills, knowledge, and financing, the Bare Boat Agreement did not evidence a mutual intent to be joint venturers as the second element requires. The Agreement is entitled "'Bare Boat Charter Party" and in numerous places refers to SeaCo as "Owner" and to Bay Casino as "Charterer." Not withstanding Levy's claims in his February 2 letter to Kornblum that the Agreement was "not only a charter for hire, but also a joint venture arrangement," Levy signed the Agreement on February 10, 1998 without the changes he had requested to reflect a joint venture arrangement. In addition, just approximately one month earlier Levy had signed an agreement between CGG and Belair which established SeaCo as a joint venture with its purpose as the purchase of the M/V Royal Empress. Plaintiff's Hearing Exhibit 1. In comparing the two documents, many differences are apparent. Unlike the Bare Boat Charter Agreement, the agreement between CGG and Belair is entitled and referenced throughout as a "Joint Venture Agreement." Furthermore, it refers to the parties throughout the document as the "parties" and as "joint venturers," and not as "owner" or "charterer" as SeaCo and Bay Casino are described in the Bare Boat

Charter. Furthermore, there is an explicit provision for the sharing of both profits and losses. Id. at P 2.2. Finally, the Bare Boat Charter required Bay Casino to post a visible notice stating that the Vessel was owned by SeaCo and was under a demise charter to Bay Casino. For these reasons, the Court holds that Plaintiff and Defendants did not have a joint venture agreement.

CONCLUSION

For the reasons stated above, Defendants' motion to vacate the Rule C arrest of the Vessel and the Rule B attachment of the Vessel is DENIED.

In re Roxy Roller Rink Joint Venture
67 B.R. 479 (1986)

Whether the Bankruptcy Judge erred in holding that Roxy Roller Rink Joint Venture is not a corporation as defined in Section 101(8) of the Bankruptcy Code [*11 U.S.C. § 101*(8) (1982 & Supp. III 1985)] but a partnership against which an involuntary petition could be filed by one of the co-venturers pursuant to Section 303 (b)(3)(A) of the Code [*11 U.S.C. § 303* (b)(3)(1982 & Supp. III 1985)]?

Bankruptcy Code § 303(b) provides in relevant part:

> (b) An involuntary case against a person is commenced by the filing with the bankruptcy court of a petition under Chapter 7 or 11 of this title— . . . .
>
> (3) if such person is a partnership—
>
> (A) by fewer than all of the general partners in such partnership. . . .

On October 17, 1984, Natoma Roxy Corp. ("Natoma"), proceeding under § 303(b), filed an involuntary Chapter 11 petition against Roxy Roller Rink Joint Venture ("Roxy"). In the involuntary petition, Natoma alleged that it is one of the general partners of Roxy. Natoma also alleged that the other general partner of Roxy is Twins Roller Corp. ("Twins").

In its answer to the involuntary petition, Twins denied that either Natoma or Twins were general partners of Roxy. Moreover, Twins alleged as an affirmative defense to the petition that Roxy "has the attributes of a Corporation as defined under Section 101(8) of the Bankruptcy Code." Therefore, according to Twins, "the filing of the petition by [Natoma] against [Roxy] is not provided for in the Code."

Natoma moved before the Bankruptcy Court for summary judgment dismissing Twins' affirmative defense. In its Decision and Order dated May 3, 1985, the Bankruptcy Court concluded that Roxy is a "species of partnership," that Natoma is a general partner of Roxy, and that Natoma therefore has standing to file an involuntary petition against Roxy pursuant to § 303 (b)(3)(A). However, the Bankruptcy Court did not enter an order for relief under Chapter 11 at that time due to an issue of fact with respect to whether Roxy was generally paying its debts as they became due. In its June 4, 1985 opinion the Bankruptcy Court granted a final order for relief under Chapter 11 to Roxy.

As noted supra, the only issue raised by appellant on these appeals is whether Roxy is a corporation within the meaning of § 101(8) and therefore not subject to the provisions of § 303(b). The Court agrees with the Bankruptcy Court that the August 24, 1981 agreement between Natoma and Twins, which formed Roxy, clearly establishes that Roxy is a joint venture and not a corporation.

The August 24th agreement expressly states that the parties intend to form a joint venture. According to the agreement, Twins has a 57% ownership interest and Natoma has a 43% interest in the venture. The agreement also provides for minimum capital contributions by each venturer, see id. at paras. 9(a), (b), for distributions of earnings in proportion to the venturers' ownership interests after the initial capital contributions are recouped, see id. at paras. 10, 11, and for contribution and indemnification between the venturers. Paragraph 9(c) of the agreement provides that:

> each party shall be liable for, and agrees to pay into the Venture promptly when due, his ownership interest percentage share of all costs and expenses of what-soever kind or nature incurred by the Venture in connection with its operation of business affairs, to the extent said costs or expenses are not covered by the income and available cash reserves of the Venture. . . .

Significantly, the agreement does not limit either joint venturer's liability to the extent of their capital contribution. Moreover, the agreement provides that its terms are to be construed in accordance with the laws of New York and that the "laws relating to general partnership shall govern this Venture, unless expressly indicated otherwise herein."

In determining whether a joint venture exists the Court must consider the intent of the parties, whether there was joint control and management of the business, whether there was a sharing of the profits and the losses, and whether there was a combination of property, skill, or knowledge. The express terms of the joint venture agreement, as described above, clearly establish that Roxy is a joint venture.

Moreover, a joint venture is generally treated as a partnership and not a corporation, the only significant difference between a joint venture and a partnership being that joint ventures are organized for a limited time and purpose. Thus, although neither party has raised the issue, it appears that a partnership within the meaning of § 303(b) includes joint ventures. In any event, where, as here, the parties' agreement expressly states that laws relating to general partnerships govern the venture, § 303(b) clearly is applicable.

Appellant's argument in support of its contention that Roxy is a corporation within the meaning of § 101(8) is as follows: Natoma and Twins are both corporations formed for the sole purpose of entering into the Roxy joint venture. By entering into the joint venture agreement as corporations, appellant asserts that the venturers' shareholders and promoters intended to and succeeded in limiting their personal liability to "whatever capital contributions the individuals wished or agreed to make to their respective corporations to fund the operation of" Roxy. See Appellant's Brief at 7. Since the liability of the shareholders of both corporate joint venturers is limited by their capital contribution to the corporations, appellant contends that the joint venture itself must be considered a corporation.

The Court agrees with the Bankruptcy Court that this argument is unpersuasive. Appellant is incorrect in assuming that the difference between a corporation and a partnership turns solely on whether the participants in the venture have limited personal liability. As noted above, the determination of whether an entity is a partnership (or a joint venture) turns on a variety of factors, only one of which is whether the parties share losses.

Moreover, assuming arguendo that a limitation on the liability of the participants in a joint venture is a crucial factor in determining whether the entity is a partnership or a corporation for the purposes of the Bankruptcy Code, the Court notes that the joint venture agreement does not limit the liability of either joint venturer. The agreement provides that both Twins and Natoma are fully liable for Roxy's debts on a pro rata basis. Where, as here, any limitation on the liability of the participants in a joint venture flows solely from the corporate status of the joint venturers, the joint venture does not thereby become a corporation. Indeed, the liability of natural persons who form a partnership can never exceed their assets. The situation is no different where its partners are corporations. Thus, as the Bankruptcy Court correctly noted, while a joint venture may not be carried on by individuals through a corporate form, corporations clearly may be parties to a joint venture agreement.

CONCLUSION

For the reasons set forth supra, the Court concludes that Roxy is not a corporation but instead is a partnership against which an involuntary petition could be filed by Natoma pursuant to § 303(b).

JOINT STOCK COMPANY

Joint stock company — business format that operates like a corporation but without retaining unlimited liability for its owners.

Although not in much use at the present time, the law governing a joint stock company can be found under New York's General Associations Law. A **joint stock company** is a general partnership with a very large number of partners, so many partners that in order to operate it acquires some of the attributes of a corporation (Chapter 5). The most notable characteristics of a joint stock company are:

1. The owners of the company are identified by holding transferable shares of stock in the company pursuant to an underlying agreement. This means that partners may come and go simply by alienating their shares according to the provisions of the joint stock company agreement.

2. To form a joint stock company, the parties must enter into a formal written agreement similar to the one mandated for limited partnerships.

Board of managers — persons who manage a joint stock company.

3. Because there are such a large number of partners, the business is managed by a **board of managers,** stockholders who purchase shares designated as management shares. In this fashion, the joint stock company operates under a centralized management similar to a corporate board of directors (Chapter 5).

4. Unlike the previous business formats discussed in earlier chapters, a joint stock company may have perpetual life if so specified in the joint stock company agreement.

5. The joint stock company is considered to be a separate entity from its shareholders for the purpose of income taxation. The company itself reports and pays taxes on its income, whereas the shareholder only reports the income that is attributable to them according to their proportionate interest in the company.

6. The business may hold property in a business (assumed) name and may sue and be sued in that name.

7. The stockholders retain unlimited personal liability for the obligations of the business.

Joint stock companies were one of the favored business formats during the period of exploration during the sixteenth and seventeenth centuries, but as other formats developed, the joint stock company was viewed as a less desirable business form. In recent times, one of the most notable existent examples of a joint stock company is Lloyd's of London, the insurance company. However, when Lloyd's suffered great losses due to several catastrophes in the 1990s, many stockholders became bankrupt because their personal assets were reachable by creditors of Lloyd's to satisfy claims.

Mason v. American Express Company
334 F.2d 392 (2d Cir. 1964)

This appeal presents the important question of whether an unincorporated joint stock association, organized and existing under the laws of the State of New York, should, like a corporate body which has been incorporated there, be deemed a citizen of New York for the purpose of determining whether the diversity of citizenship requirements of Article III, Section 2 of the United States Constitution and *28 U.S.C. § 1332* have been met; or whether such an association is incapable of possessing citizenship for diversity purposes, so that the citizenship of its member shareholders must be looked to in order to determine the existence or absence of the requisite diversity of citizenship. We hold such an association to be a citizen of New York for the purposes of federal diversity jurisdiction.

Under New York law an unincorporated joint stock association, such as this defendant, is created pursuant to written articles of association which must be filed, like a certificate of incorporation, as a public record. New York General Associations Law, §§ 2–4. The association may, like this defendant which has more than 20,000 shareholders, have capital stock divided into shares, and provision may be made in the articles of association that upon the death of a shareholder or the transfer of his shares no dissolution is to be worked on the association. New York General Associations Law, §§ 2, 3, 5. A dissolution may take place, however, as it may with a corporation, through group shareholder action or judicial order. Compare New York General Associations Law, 5 with New York Business Corporation Law, §§ 1001–02, 1101–04. Powers of management over the association's affairs may be concentrated in the sole hands of directors, who may number as few as three. New York General Associations Law, § 3. The association may purchase, take, hold, and convey real property in the name of its president under a variety of circumstances, New York General Associations Law § 6, and an action may be maintained by or against such an association in the name of its president or treasurer, without joining as parties the shareholder members. New York Constitution, art. 10, § 4; New York General Associations Law, §§ 12, 13. Moreover, shareholder members of a joint stock company may themselves bring suit against the association. Shareholders of a joint stock association are personally liable for the debts of the association, but once an action has been brought against the association the individual shareholders may not be sued on the same cause unless a final judgment against the association has been returned wholly or partially unsatisfied. New York General Associations Law, 16. On the basis of these and similar statutory provisions, New York's decisional law has for many years consistently recognized the corporate characteristics of joint stock associations. In *Hibbs v. Brown,* New York's leading case on the nature of the joint stock association, the Court of Appeals, holding that, despite the individual liability of shareholder members, a bond issued upon a joint stock association's general credit was not made nonnegotiable as containing only a promise to pay out of a particular fund, noted, after reviewing a joint stock association's basic characteristics, 'the complete and separate existence of the association as between it and the individual members' and stated that 'based upon such statutory provisions, decisions have been made and opinions written emphasizing their corporate character as distinguished from the ordinary partnership, wherein the individual relationship and liability of the members is universally recognized and of importance.' *190 N.Y. at 177–78, 82 N.E. at 1111.*

We think it clear that, under the reasoning of *Puerto Rico v. Russell & Co., [previously cited]* these essential characteristics of a New York joint stock association such as this defendant sufficiently invest it with a legal personality apart from its individual members, so that it is just and sensible to regard it as a separate entity for purposes of diversity of citizenship jurisdiction. Indeed, a comparison between the New York joint stock association and the sociedad which was deemed a citizen in *Puerto Rico v. Russell & Co.* indicates not only that the joint stock association is as much like a true corporate body as the sociedad, but also that the important characteristics of the sociedad and the joint stock association are almost identical.

While the joint stock association does differ from an ordinary corporation because of the individual liability of the former's shareholders, we think that there exist a number of compelling reasons for refusing to permit this single difference amid so many similarities to cause us to hold the joint stock association incapable of possessing separate citizenship. First, the individual liability of the shareholder members of a New York joint stock association, operative, when the association has been sued, only after a judgment against it has been returned unsatisfied, is almost indistinguishable from the contingent individual liability which the shareholder members of the sociedad had in *Puerto Rico v. Russell & Co.* The Court in that case said of that liability: 'Although the members whose participation is unlimited are made contingently liable for the debts of the sociedad in the event that its assets are insufficient to satisfy them * * * this liability is of no more consequence for present purposes than that imposed on corporate stockholders by the statutes of some states.' *288 U.S. at 480, 53 S.Ct. at 448.* Moreover, the individual liability of shareholders in a New York joint stock association has been deemed by New York's highest court, in the leading New York case on the subject of joint stock associations, 'practically unimportant,' *Hibbs v. Brown, supra, at 177* of *190 N.Y., 82 N.E. 1108,* and one New York court has even reasoned that the contingent nature of this liability indicates 'the legislative intent to treat associations in some respects as a corporation sole.' In addition, personal liability of individual shareholders, even as to certain corporations, is a type of liability not completely absent from New York law. See New York Banking Law, § 113-a (making shareholders in a banking or trust company corporation individually responsible for debts of their corporation to the extent of the par value of their stock holdings, over and above the amount invested in the shares of stock); New York Business Corporation Law, § 630 (making the ten largest shareholders of a corporation whose shares are not nationally quoted or listed liable for unpaid debts and wages owing by the corporation to its employees). Finally, from a purely practical standpoint we note in passing that the extent of the business operations and financial resources of this particular joint stock association, a giant nationwide express company, makes the possibility of the theoretical liability of individual shareholders actually becoming operative, a liability contingent and somewhat remote to begin with, highly unlikely. Thus, we hold this defendant joint stock company, though not a corporation but an unincorporated joint stock company, a citizen of the state of its creation, New York, for purposes of federal diversity jurisdiction.

The justice in this approach to federal diversity jurisdiction is clear to us. Persons dealing with an unincorporated joint stock association such as this defendant deal with a cohesive entity, not a mere aggregation of individuals, and, apart from what seems clearly called for by the decision in *Puerto Rico v. Russell & Co.,* all of the reasons in favor of extending citizenship to corporations for diversity purposes would seem to apply with equal force to a joint stock association. Moreover, although the court below made no express finding on this issue, the size of this association's operations and the number of its shareholders make it not unlikely that it has shareholders in all fifty states in the union, and, if so, a refusal to treat it as a legal entity would entirely foreclose access by it, as either plaintiff or defendant, to the federal courts in diversity cases.

The injustice of a rule forbidding the extension of separate status to unincorporated associations has been recognized even by courts which have felt constrained to follow such a rule; and this recognition has come in cases dealing with types of unincorporated associations which would appear to have fewer corporate attributes than New York joint stock associations. So widespread has been the discontent with the doctrine preventing treatment of unincorporated associations as citizens for diversity purposes that class suit against the members of such associations, in which the diversity of citizenship requirement need be satisfied only as to the representatives of the class, has been generally recognized as a legitimate device for circumventing the doctrine and thereby preventing a failure of justice. Section 1301(b)(2) of the proposed jurisdictional statute set forth in the American Law Institute's published Study of the Division of Jurisdiction between State and Federal Courts, Tentative Draft No. 2 (1964), provides that for diversity purposes, 'A partnership or other unincorporated association capable of suing or being sued in its common name in the State in which an action is brought shall be deemed a citizen of the State or foreign state where it has its principal place of business, and such citizenship shall be controlling in determining jurisdiction in such action, whether brought by or against such partnership or unincorporated association or by or against any person as an agent or representative thereof.' This proposed statute, which covers all types of unincorporated associations, and ordinary partnerships as well, is particularly significant, for the draft as a whole is designed to reduce the scope of federal diversity jurisdiction, yet this particular provision would significantly increase the number of cases which could meet the diversity requirements.

We do not mean to intimate, by our allusion to the criticism which has been directed toward the current doctrine dealing with unincorporated associations generally, any view as to whether separate entity treatment ought also to be accorded types of unincorporated associations other than the type now before us, for many would appear to possess fewer attributes of a separate juridical personality than does a New York joint stock association. The determination of such an issue would necessarily have to involve consideration of whether to depart from a line of decisions in this Circuit, proceeding from cases decided before the advent of *Puerto Rico v. Russell & Co., supra,* wherein we have heretofore refused to extend separate entity treatment to unincorporated associations of this sort. What we do decide is that there is no bar today to denominating a New York joint stock association a citizen for diversity purposes; and that, on the basis of the test set forth in *Puerto Rico v. Russell & Co.* such an association possesses, because of its essential characteristics under the law of its creation, a complete enough separate legal personality to be treated as a citizen for purposes of federal diversity jurisdiction.

The decision below is reversed and the cause remanded for disposition on the merits.

BUSINESS TRUST

Business trust — trust used to create a business.

During the nineteenth century and continuing until the end of World War I, the **business trust** was one of the most popular business formats used. If their histories were traced, many large corporations existing today can be found to have started their business lives as business trusts.

In order to solve the perceived detriments of the sole proprietorship and general and limited partnerships, that of unlimited personal liability of the owners, businesspersons searched to find a format that retained all of the business advantages of the existing formats but did not engender the potential unlimited liability incident to those entities. This occurred prior to the creation of the modern corporate statutes which are no more than 150 years old. In attempting to find a suitable business format, the idea of using a trust was developed.

Trust — fiduciary relationship.

Creator — person who created a trust.

Legal title — title held by a trustee.

Trustee — person who holds legal title to a trust.

Equitable or beneficial title — title held by trust beneficiary.

Beneficiary — person with equitable title to a trust.

Corpus — trust property.

Remainderman — person in whom legal and equitable titles merge.

Principal — trust property.

Certificate of beneficial interest — document identifying beneficiary.

Trust law is very ancient, having been used since early Roman times. A **trust** is a fiduciary relationship in which a person who has a transferable interest in property, known as the **creator,** transfers that property to a trust which must be created by a written instrument. In transferring his or her title, the creator divides the full title into its two component parts—legal title and equitable title. **Legal title** entitles the holder to manage the trust property, subject to any restrictions or limitations imposed by the creator. The holder of the legal title is called the **trustee** who, like agents and partners, is deemed to be a fiduciary, held to a standard of care higher than ordinary care. The **equitable or beneficial title** enables the holder to enjoy the trust property subject to any limitations and restrictions imposed by the creator. The holder of the equitable or beneficial title is called the **beneficiary.**

Typically, a creator would fund a trust with money or property to have such property, called the **corpus** of the trust, managed by one person to provide an income to another person. Private trusts, those that serve the private and personal wishes of the creator and benefit private persons, are required to terminate at a statutorily determined period of time. When the trust terminates, the legal and equitable titles merge into one person (or group of persons) known as the **remainderman.**

*Example: A mother gives $100,000 to her bank as trustee, requiring the bank to invest the funds and distribute the income from the investments equally to her two children. The trust is evidenced by a trust agreement entered into by the mother and the trust department of the bank. The mother states that the trust is to continue for 25 years, at which point any property left in the trust is to be given equally to her grandchildren then living. In this example, the mother is the creator, the bank is the trustee, the $100,000 is the corpus (in this instance called the **principal** because it is cash), the children are the beneficiaries, and the grandchildren are the remaindermen.*

Utilizing this format, a business was able to be created that gives its participants limited personal liability. The corpus of the trust is the business property. The business is managed by trustees who receive compensation for their services (always permitted under trust law). The trustees are only personally liable for a breach of any of their fiduciary obligations; they are not personally liable for the business obligations of the trust. The trust is its own legal entity, is subject to its own taxation, can sue or be sued in its own name, and is considered to be a separate entity from its trustees and beneficiaries. The beneficiaries become such by purchasing a **certificate of beneficial interest** which identifies each as beneficiaries of the trust. They receive a proportionate percentage of any profit the trust generates but are not personally liable for the trust's obligations other than what they paid to acquire their certificates. The only problem associated with operating a business in this format was the limitation on its existence. By statutory enactment, however, business trusts are permitted to exist in perpetuity. In this manner, a business may be funded, managed, and operated while maintaining limited personal liability for its owners and managers.

Business trusts remained quite popular and prevalent (note the antitrust laws of the 1890s and beyond) until the stock market boom of the 1920s when, in order to take advantage of the public interest in acquiring corporate stock, many business trusts converted to corporations. However, business trusts still exist today in two major areas:

Real Estate Investment Trust (REIT) — tax provision for real estate trust.

1. **Real Estate Investment Trust (REIT):** The Internal Revenue Service provides favorable tax treatment for trusts established exclusively for the purpose of developing real estate. Historically, the very first use of the business trust was to manage real property. Because of this tax advantage, many REITs operate today.

2. The business trust included as part of an estate plan: As discussed in Chapter 2, one of the problems associated with operating a business as a sole proprietorship concerns estate planning if the sole proprietorship is the main financial support for a family who is incapable of operating the business should the sole proprietor die. By placing the business assets in trust in the sole proprietor's will, the sole proprietor can select as trustee persons who are capable of managing the business and name the family members as the beneficiaries of the income. The trust can be designed to terminate at the point when the beneficiaries either no longer require that income or are capable of operating the business themselves.

In New York, business trusts are governed by the General Associations Law. Under Article 4 of that statute, the business trust is required to file a certificate with the New York Secretary of State, designating the Secretary of State as its agent for the service of process, stating its name, principal place of business, the location of its office in New York, and the names and addresses of its trustees. The certificate must be signed and acknowledged by the trustees.

In re Gurney's Inn Corp. Liquidating Trust
15 B.R. 659 (E.D.N.Y. 1997)

Before the Court is the motion by HAC 1, Inc. ("HAC") to dismiss the voluntary petition filed by Gurney's Inn Corp. Liquidating Trust ("Gurney's Trust") on June 23, 1997 on the ground that the Court lacks jurisdiction because Gurney's Trust is not eligible for relief under chapter 11 since it is not a "business trust." The sole issue is whether the Debtor is a business trust. If it is, it is eligible for relief under chapter 11. If not, then this Court lacks subject matter jurisdiction and the case must be dismissed. *North Fork Bank v. Abelson, 207 B.R. 382 (E.D.N.Y. 1997)* (a finding that a trust is not a business trust would deprive the bankruptcy court of subject matter jurisdiction).

DISCUSSION

The relevant facts central to a determination of the issue raised by HAC's motion are largely undisputed. See, e.g., Affidavit of Marc L. Hamroff, sworn to August 28, 1997 (the "Hamroff Aff."), and the exhibits annexed thereto; Affidavit of Paul Montemarano, sworn to October 9, 1997 ("Montemarano Aff."). The Court therefore concludes that an evidentiary hearing is not required and that the motion may be resolved based on the papers and the oral arguments of the parties presented on November 20, 1997.

It is undisputed that HAC holds a judgment (entered with the County Clerk's Office of Suffolk County on April 2, 1997) in the amount of $559,953.07, plus applicable interest, against Gurney's Trust. Hamroff Aff. P 3. The judgment arises out of the Debtor's guaranty of a $350,000 note executed by New York Resort Timeshare Management Corp. ("NY Management"). Id. HAC claims that the only asset of Gurney's Trust is a second mortgage alleged in the Debtor's petition to have a current market value of $10,500,000. Prior to the filing of the Debtor's bankruptcy petition, HAC levied on the mortgage. Id. The Debtor filed for bankruptcy protection on the eve of the anticipated sale of the mortgage by the Suffolk County Sheriff.

The Debtor claims that it owns assets in addition to the second mortgage. Primary among them is the power to appoint the members of the board of directors of Gurney's Limited. n6 Montemarano Aff. at PP 5, 6. The relationship between the Gurney's entities is explained as follows, by the Debtor:

> For approximately 60 years prior [sic] to 1982, Gurney's Inn. Corp. (["Gurney's] Corp.") owned the Gurney's Inn Resort & Spa in Montauk, New York. In 1982, Gurney's Inn Resort & Spa, Ltd. (["Gurney's] Limited") was formed as a New York State time sharing cooperative. The formation occurred pursuant to an offering plan by which 51 group time sharing interests containing 109 time share units were authorized by the New York State Attorney General to be offered for sale.
>
> Pursuant to the time share plan, [Gurney's] Limited was authorized to and did issue two classes of stock. Class A stock was issued and sold to the time share owners who own collectively 450,985 shares. Class B stock is presently held by the Debtor's nominee herein as additional security for the payment of a purchase money second mortgage in the reduced principal amount of $15,089,782.00. The mortgage encumbers the resort property. The second mortgage was originally conveyed to [Gurney's] Corp. pursuant to the time share agreement between [Gurney's] Corp. and [Gurney's] Limited. The mortgage, pursuant to the Liquidating Trust agreement, was transferred by [Gurney's] Corp. to the Debtor herein. Under the terms of the mortgage, the Debtor herein is now the owner of all of the Class B stock.
>
> By the terms of the time share offering plan, the Debtor herein is now the controlling shareholder of [Gurney's] Limited. The Debtor has the sole right to elect all directors of [Gurney's] Limited and it is [sic] the directors of Ltd. who have control over the operation of Ltd.'s business. The Debtor has selected two of the three man board of Ltd. and has allowed Class A shareholders to select one member. In affect [sic], the Debtor, through the board members of Ltd. selected by it, is operating the business of Ltd.

In addition to urging that it conducts business as a result of its authority to appoint the board members of Gurney's Limited, the Debtor claims that its assets include a lien on the unsold time share units and a mortgage on a nearby piece of property used as a tennis club.

In other words, Gurney's Corp. owned the Gurney's resort until it sold the fee to the timeshare corporation, Gurney's Limited. Upon that sale, Gurney's Corp. took back a purchase money second mortgage, ceased any further business purpose, and converted to Gurney's Trust, to which the purchase money second mortgage was transferred. See Hamroff Aff. at P 5; see also Exhibit B annexed to Hamroff Aff. at 1.

Gurney's Limited then issued Class A stock to timeshare owners. Class B stock was also issued as additional security for the payment of the purchase money second mortgage, and is presently held by Gurney's Trust's nominee.

The underlying "Agreement and Declaration of Trust, dated March 31, 1983" (the "Trust Agreement"), which established the Debtor, is annexed as Exhibit B to the moving papers. By its terms, it recites that Gurney's Corp. chose to liquidate "pursuant to *IRC Section 337*" and that a plan of liquidation was adopted by the shareholders "pursuant to which all remaining assets and liabilities of Gurney's [Corp.] are being transferred to this Liquidating Trust [i.e., the Debtor]." See Exhibit B at 1. As the recital further states:

> The shareholders of Gurney's [Corp.] have voted to dissolve Gurney's [Corp.], wind up its affairs, and distribute its assets to its shareholders, and because the

transfer of undivided interests in its assets and liabilities would be impractical (the assets of Gurney's [Corp.] are not now saleable at a fair price and are not reasonably susceptible to sale or division to shareholders) have voted to have the assets and liabilities distributed by Gurney's [Corp.] to Trustees to be held in trust for the benefit of the shareholders in order to preserve the property and collect the principal and income therefrom for the shareholders. . . .

Included among the assets transferred from Gurney's Corp. to the Trust was the purchase money mortgage made by Gurney's Limited in the principal amount of $18,249,844.37 which was subordinated to the first mortgage.

Article VI of the Trust Agreement sets forth the purpose of the Trust and the limitations placed upon its trustees. It states, in pertinent part, as follows:

> 6.1 PURPOSE OF TRUST. The sole purpose of this Trust is to receive by assignment all the assets and liabilities of Gurney's [Corp.] and to conserve and protect the Trust Estate and collect and distribute the income and proceeds to the Trust. Certificate holders after the payment of or provision for, expenses and liabilities.
>
> 6.2 LIMITATIONS ON TRUSTEES. The Trustees shall not at any time, on behalf of Trust or Trust Certificate holders, enter into or engage in any business. This limitation shall apply irrespective of whether the conduct of any such business activities is deemed by the Trustees to be necessary or proper for the conservation and protection of the Trust Estate. . . . The Trustees shall be restricted to the holding and collection of the Trust Moneys and its payment and distribution for the purposes set forth in this Agreement and to the conservation and protection of the Trust Estate and the administration thereof in accordance with the provisions of this Agreement. . . .

Exhibit B at 10–11. The Debtor does not deny the limitations enunciated in its Trust Agreement, but urges that it is nonetheless "doing more than simply holding and preserving assets." It points to the control by its trustees over Gurney's Limited, a "multi-million dollar resort," in order to ensure the largest recovery possible for its certificate holders and claims that the "business transactions in which the Trust is engaged are similar to the businesses of any corporation which is winding up its affairs." Id.

In contrast to its arguments in opposing HAC's motion to dismiss, the Debtor describes its business in its petition as the "owner of mortgage on resort property as spendthrift trust to receive and collect funds pursuant to trust agreement." See Voluntary Petition of Debtor, annexed as Exhibit D, at 1. Moreover, Exhibit A to the Debtor's Petition describes the Debtor's business purpose as having been "established as part of a time share plan and as recipient of the assets of Gurney's Inn Corp." Id. A further review of the Debtor's Petition and Schedules shows that the Debtor has no employees, no payroll or operating expenses, no executory contracts and insignificant income from "employment or operation of a business." See Id., Rule 11 Affidavit of Lola Montemarano, a trustee, sworn to on June 17, 1997; Exhibit A to Petition; and Statement of Financial Affairs. The Debtor's description of its business activities on its petition is consistent with testimony given by Nicholas Montemarano at a deposition taken in aid of HAC's enforcement of its judgment wherein he admitted that Gurney's Trust is not a business, there is no income, there is no expense. There might be expenses, but there is no business.

The Montemarano statements are also consistent with the position taken by the Debtor in the state court proceeding in which HAC and it have battled. See HAC 1, Inc. V. Gurney's Inn Restaurant Corp., Gurney's SPA Corp. d/b/a Institut De Beaute, Nicholas Montemarano as Trustee of Gurney's Inn Corp. Liquidation Trust and as Executor of the

Estate of Joyce Montemarano and Angelo Montemarano, Supreme Court of the State of New York, County of Suffolk (Index No. 95-19779) (the "State Court Action"). Throughout the State Court Action, the Debtor has maintained that its "sole purpose" is "to receive assets, conserve them, and pay out income and proceeds to the Trust's Certificate holders." Affirmation of Francis J. Donovan, at P 11 (annexed as Exhibit A to HAC's reply). Similarly, in papers filed with the Appellate Division, Second Department, the Debtor has described its Trust Agreement in the following manner:

> The first excerpt states the purpose of the Trust. The sole purpose of the Trust is to receive assets, conserve them, and pay out income and proceeds to Trust Certificate holders. The second excerpt reenforces the obligation to conserve the assets by prohibiting the Trustees from engaging in any business, "irrespective of whether the conduct of any such business activities is deemed by the Trustees to be necessary or proper for the conservation and protection of the Trust Estate."

Upon consideration of all the factual circumstances surrounding the formation and existence of Gurney's Trust, and with an eye towards "the trust documents and the totality of the circumstances," see *Secured Equip. Trust of Eastern Airlines, supra, 38 F.3d at 90–91,* the Court cannot avoid the conclusion that this Debtor is not a business trust within the meaning of section 101(9) of the Bankruptcy Code. By its own words, the Trust Agreement charges the Debtor's trustees with "conserving and protecting the Trust Estate" and expressly prohibits them from "entering into or engaging in any business." See Article VI, §§ 6.1, 6.2 (annexed as Exhibit B to Hamroff Aff.). Even those cases which have recognized that a liquidating trust may be considered a business trust, see, e.g., *In re Cooper Properties Liquidating Trust, 61 B.R. 531 (Bankr. W.D. Tenn. 1986);* but see *In re Hemex Liquidation Trust, 129 B.R. 91 (Bankr. W.D. La. 1991),* have been careful to distinguish cases in which the trust document itself rejects any construction of the trust as a business trust. See, e.g., *In re Tru Block Concrete Products, Inc., 27 B.R. 486 (Bankr. S.D. Cal. 1983).* The liquidating trust cases are therefore distinguishable, since the trust documents in the present case expressly prohibit the trustees from engaging in any business.

Nor does the Court believe that the Trust was "established to 'transact business' as that phrase is commonly interpreted." *In re Secured Equip. Trust, supra, 38 F.3d at 90.* Since its formation, the only business to which the Trust can point is its acquisition of the second mortgage (which it received at the time of its formation as a result of the dissolution of Gurney's Corp.) and its alleged authority to appoint members of the board of directors of Gurney's Limited. While it may be said that the members of the board of directors of Gurney's Limited operate the business of Gurney's Limited, the Court disagrees with the conclusion urged by the Trust that the same can be translated into the operation of a business by Gurney's Trust. In fact, the Trust's own papers acknowledge that the board of directors of Gurney's Limited are "operating the business of Ltd." See Montemarano Aff. at P 5 (emphasis supplied). Rather, the Court agrees with HAC that any of the rights and powers granted to the trustees are incidental to the purpose of the Trust, which is to protect and preserve the value of the mortgage for the Trust beneficiaries.

In addition, the structure of the transaction which resulted in the formation of the Trust in the present case differs significantly from the structure of the transaction in the typical case. Here, the shareholders of Gurney's Corp., which originally owned the resort complex, desired to convert the resort to a time-sharing entity. It therefore "conveyed its resort to a time-sharing entity formed for the purposes of selling and managing the resort as a time-share enterprise." See Debtor's Mem. at 1. The corporation sold the resort to

Gurney's Limited, and took back a mortgage, becoming a creditor. The resort, with all of its assets, operations, profit and investment potential, was transferred to an entity other than this Debtor (i.e., to Gurney's Limited). The corporation's only remaining asset, the mortgage, was then transferred to this Debtor, with instructions to "collect the principal and income therefrom" for the shareholders. This structure is telling, and precludes a finding that Gurney's Trust was formed for the purpose of carrying on the business of Gurney's Corp.

For all of the foregoing reasons, HAC's motion is granted in its entirety. This Debtor is not a "business trust" and is therefore not eligible for relief under chapter 11.

CHAPTER REVIEW

The three forms of business organizations discussed in this chapter, although available for consideration, are rarely used by the modern businessperson. However, no analysis of New York business law would be complete without mention of them.

The joint venture is merely a partnership for a limited purpose or operation.

The joint stock company is a general partnership with a very large number of partners that operates by means of a centralized management committee and is considered to be its own tax entity. This format still engenders unlimited personal liability for its owners.

The business trust, once one of the most popular forms of business, is now generally used only for real estate development and follows the legalities of general trust law.

KEY TERMS

Beneficiary
Board of managers
Business trust
Certificate of beneficial interest
Corpus
Creator
Equitable or beneficial title
Joint stock company

Joint venture
Legal title
Principal
Real Estate Investment Trust (REIT)
Remainderman
Trust
Trustee

EXERCISES

1. Under what circumstances would a person decide to operate a business as a business trust? Discuss the benefits and detriments of making this selection.

2. Indicate several benefits of operating a joint stock company.

3. Distinguish a joint venture from a general partnership, discussing all legal consequences of that decision. Why do so many international businesses operate as joint ventures?

4. Go to the library and find examples of joint stock company agreements and analyze their provisions.

5. Go to the library and find an example of a business trust agreement. Distinguish it from the provisions of a regular private trust.

FACTUAL PROBLEM

A sole proprietor is the exclusive support of his wife and three infant children. He is seeking advice about creating a business trust in his will to provide for his family's income should he die before his children become adults. Based on the discussion in the *Gurney* case, indicate how he should make sure that the trust is considered a business trust.

Chapter 5

Overview
of Corporations

INTRODUCTION

This chapter provides a general overview of one of the most common forms of business entities in New York: the corporation. In order to understand the intricacies of forming and operating a business as a corporation, it is first necessary to gain a general overview of the entity itself. This chapter is not designed to provide a complete and detailed analysis of each of the topics introduced; those details are provided in the chapters that follow. Rather, this chapter is an introduction to the corporation.

In order to understand how a corporation operates, a good starting point is the statements usually referred to as the "three great principles of corporate law":

1. A corporation is a legal entity separate and distinct from its shareholders.
2. Management of a corporation rests with its Board of Directors.
3. Ownership of a corporation vests in its shareholders.

All corporate law flows from these three simple sentences. This chapter discusses each of these concepts.

FORMING OF THE CORPORATION:
THE FIRST GREAT PRINCIPLE OF CORPORATE LAW

The concept of the corporation did not exist under the common law. Consequently, all corporate law, at least with respect to the creation of the entity, is a creature of statute. Furthermore, except for some very limited federal corporations, the overwhelming majority of corporations are creatures of state statute, and therefore, it is necessary to analyze the provisions of each state statute to determine what a corporation may and may not do.

Of all corporations formed each year, the majority are incorporated under the laws of New York, Delaware, and California, meaning that the New York statute is one of the most influential in the country. Statistically, even though the largest number of corporations are formed in Delaware because of that state's favorable corporate tax treatment, strong anti-takeover provisions, and "user-friendly" policies, the majority of corporate litigation emanates from New York, and New York still leads the country in corporate headquarters and/or offices.

Business Corporation Law (BCL) — New York's corporate statute.

The primary statute governing corporations in New York is the **Business Corporation Law (BCL).** Because corporations do not exist under the common law, all rights and obligations of New York corporations, plus all limitations on their ability to operate, come from the BCL. If the right does not appear in the statute, the right does not exist for the corporation.

Pursuant to the BCL, a New York corporation has most of the powers of a natural person: It can contract; sue and be sued; own, rent, and lease property; receive and make contributions; and so forth. A corporation may even be found guilty of a crime. All of the powers of a New York corporation appear in Article 2 of the BCL. A New York corporation is capable of having perpetual life, and as a general rule, it is responsible for its own obligations—the assets of the shareholders usually may not be reached to satisfy corporate obligations (see the following and Chapters 8 and 10).

Certificate of incorporation — document filed with the Secretary of State to form a corporation.

By-laws — document delineating the day-to-day operations of a corporation.

The requirements to form a New York corporation also appear in the BCL. To create the corporate entity, a document known as a **certificate of incorporation** must be filed with the New York Secretary of State (Chapter 6), and the corporation must adopt **by-laws**, a document detailing the day-to-day operations of the business. Once the certificate of incorporation is filed with the Department of State, the corporate existence begins.

In the certificate of incorporation, the corporation indicates which of all the potential powers permitted corporations under the BCL it will assume. Although many corporations indicate that they wish to have all of the enumerated powers, in many instances, for reasons discussed later, the corporation may wish to limit its activities. The certificate of incorporation functions to delineate the total extent of the powers the corporation may exert.

Once the corporation comes into existence, it is deemed, under the law, to be a legal entity having the attributes of an individual. Note that even though a corporation is deemed to be an individual, it is not considered to be a "citizen" for various constitutional purposes. Even though the corporation is considered to be a legal entity, an individual, it is not a natural person and may only operate by and through natural persons who act on the corporation's behalf.

OPERATING THE CORPORATION: THE SECOND GREAT PRINCIPLE OF CORPORATE LAW

Board of Directors — managers of a corporation.

Once the corporation is formed, the management function of the entity rests with its Board of Directors. The **Board of Directors** are natural persons elected by the shareholders for the purpose of managing the corporation. Because the directors are elected by the shareholders, the owners of the corporation, and may be removed by the shareholders, it is often said that the directors serve at the pleasure of the shareholders.

On February 22, 1998, the BCL was amended in several significant respects. For all corporations formed on or after that date, these new provisions apply; for corporations formed prior to that date, the earlier version of the BCL applies unless the corporation has amended its certificate of incorporation and by-laws to adopt the new provisions. Wherever there is a difference, such difference will be noted throughout the remainder of the text.

For corporations formed on or after February 22, 1998, the Board of Directors may consist of a single person. For corporations formed prior to that date, the Board of Directors must consist of at least three people, unless they have fewer than three shareholders in which instance there must be one director for each shareholder:

One shareholder, only one director is necessary.

Two shareholders, at least two directors are necessary.

Three or more shareholders, at least three directors are necessary.

Take note that there is no maximum number of directors mandated by the BCL. However, as a general rule, most corporations try to have an odd number of directors in order to avoid a management deadlock. The number of directors is fixed in either the certificate of incorporation or the by-laws and may be changed by amendment.

The directors of the corporation are deemed to be fiduciaries to the corporation and the shareholders. To this end the directors are precluded from self-dealing, must maintain accurate records and accounts, and must make all business opportunities of which they become aware available to the corporation. In managing the entity, the directors must use the business judgment of a reasonably prudent businessperson. The fiduciary standard of care for corporate directors is known as the **business judgment rule**, and provided that the directors meet this standard, the shareholders are precluded from holding the directors personally liable for any losses their decisions may cause the corporation. The application of the business judgment rule means the directors are not considered to be insurers of the corporation, guaranteeing every business decision will be profitable. It would be impossible to find anyone to serve on a Board of Directors if he or she was required to be prescient with respect to the profitability of every decision made. However, the directors may still be held personally accountable if they:

a. make a profit that should have gone to the corporation

b. act in bad faith

c. breach a statutory duty

d. act beyond their powers

Business judgment rule — fiduciary standard of care for corporate directors, using the skill of the reasonable prudent businessperson.

Wilson v. Tully
243 A.D.2d 229 (1998)

In a stockholders' derivative action based upon defendant brokerage corporation's exposure to enormous legal liability because of the sale of highly leveraged derivative securities to a municipal customer.

The complaint asserts three causes of action: (1) intentional and/or reckless breaches of the defendant directors' fiduciary duties to the Company and its shareholders, (2) indemnification, and (3) waste.

Plaintiffs allege that the defendant directors ignored or failed in their fiduciary duty to be apprised of various self-dealing factors and other "red flags" and, knowing the extent of Orange County's reliance on Merrill Lynch, defendant board knew or recklessly disregarded Merrill Lynch's fiduciary duty, as Orange County's investment advisor, not to sell it any more unsuitable securities or loan it more capital to leverage Orange County's assets in anticipation of decreasing interest rates.

The law of Delaware, the State of Merrill Lynch's incorporation, is controlling and, under Delaware law, as elsewhere, the requirement of a demand upon directors of a corporation to pursue a derivative complaint is a recognition of the inherent powers of the board to manage the affairs of the corporation, which includes making decisions about whether or not to pursue such litigation (Zapata Corp. v Maldonado, 430 A2d 779, 782 [Del]). The Delaware Supreme Court has observed that, as here, stockholders often do not make such demand, but instead bring suit, claiming that demand is excused. However, it stated: "Because such derivative suits challenge the propriety of decisions made by directors pursuant to their managerial authority, we have repeatedly held that the stockholder plaintiffs must overcome the powerful presumptions of the business judgment rule before they will be permitted to pursue the derivative claim" (Rales v Blasband, 634 A2d 927, 933 [Del] [citations omitted]).

Although no demand will be required where it would be futile, the Delaware Supreme Court has held, in Aronson v Lewis (473 A2d 805, 812 [Del]), that "the entire question of demand futility is inextricably bound to issues of business judgment and the standards of that doctrine's applicability. The business judgment rule is an acknowledgement of the managerial prerogatives of Delaware directors . . . [and] is a presumption that in making a business decision the directors of a corporation acted on an informed basis, in good faith and in the honest belief that the action taken was in the best interests of the company" (citations omitted). Proper business judgment includes both substantive due care (the terms of the transaction) and procedural due care (an informed decision) (Grobow v Perot, 539 A2d 180, 189 [Del]).

Approval of a transaction by a majority of independent, disinterested directors almost always bolsters a presumption that the business judgment rule attaches to transactions approved by a board of directors that are later attacked on grounds of lack of due care. In such cases, a heavy burden falls on a plaintiff to avoid presuit demand (Grobow v Perot, supra, at 190).

Where, as here, there is no claim that a majority of the defendant directors are not disinterested and independent, "the mere threat of personal liability for approving a questioned transaction, standing alone, is insufficient to challenge either the independence or disinterestedness of directors, although in rare cases a transaction may be so egregious on its face that board approval cannot meet the test of business judgment, and a substantial likelihood of director liability therefore exists" (Aronson v Lewis, supra, at 815).

Likewise, where the certificate of incorporation exempts directors from liability, the risk of liability does not disable them from considering a demand fairly unless particularized pleading permits the court to conclude that there is a substantial likelihood that their conduct, such as bad faith, intentional misconduct, knowing violation of law, or any other conduct for which the directors may be liable, falls outside the exemption (In re Baxter Intl., Inc. Shareholders Litig., 654 A2d 1268, 1270 [Del]).

It is also "well-settled that mere allegations of participation in the approval of a challenged transaction are insufficient to excuse a pre-suit demand" and conclusory allegations of recklessness or gross negligence are "insufficient to overcome the strong presumption of propriety afforded by the business judgment rule" (Emerald Partners v Berlin, 1993 Del Ch LEXIS 273, * 12, * 14 [Dec. 23, 1993, Hartnett, V.C.] [citations omitted]).

While the court will accept well-pleaded facts as true, it will not take as true conclusory allegations of fact or law not supported by allegations of specific fact (Grobow v Perot, supra, at 187). "A trial court need not blindly accept as true all allegations, nor must it draw all inferences from them in plaintiffs' favor unless they are reasonable inferences."

. . .

Plaintiffs' allegations support the business judgment rule presumption as much as they seek to overcome it. The complaint acknowledges that Merrill Lynch earned $35 to 40 million in commission revenues in 1992 and well in excess of $100 million in fees and commissions in 1993 and 1994 as a result of its aggressive sales to Orange County and that, by 1993, profits from Merrill Lynch's municipal financing activities had risen dramatically to constitute between 5% and 10% of the Company's entire annual revenues. They also cite press reports that, despite internal memoranda urging caution, some Merrill Lynch executives continued to aggressively seek profits from the "fast-growing business" and that Merrill Lynch undertook these sales despite unanimous agreement at the highest levels of the Company that they constituted a substantial risk to both the Company and Orange County.

However, risk is at the heart of Merrill Lynch's business, or for that matter any business, and it seems as if the risk entailed resulted, for a substantial period of time, in what plaintiffs describe as "huge fees and commissions to the company" and, presumably, financial benefit to Orange County. The further allegation that these huge fees and expenses "were at the expense of Orange County and the result of breaches of fiduciary duties owed by the Company to Orange County" is again conclusory and, therefore, insufficient to overcome the business judgment presumption that any action or inaction on the part of the defendant directors with regard to Merrill Lynch's dealings with Orange County was taken in good faith in what they thought was the best interests of the Company at that time.

That, in hindsight, such action or inaction may turn out to be controversial, unpopular or even wrong is insufficient to excuse plaintiffs' failure to make a demand upon Merrill Lynch's directors. As stated by the court in In re Caremark Intl. Inc. Derivative Litig. (698 A2d, at 967), "whether a judge or jury considering the matter after the fact, believes a decision substantively wrong, or degrees of wrong extending through 'stupid' to 'egregious' or 'irrational,' provides no ground for director liability, so long as the court determines that the process employed was either rational or employed in a good faith effort to advance corporate interests." The hard core of the business judgment doctrine is that the business outcome of an investment project that is unaffected by director self-interest or bad faith cannot itself be an occasion for director liability. (Gagliardi v Trifoods Intl., 683 A2d 1049, 1051 [Del].)

Thus, as can be seen, although the Delaware Supreme Court has refused to establish a particular "reasonable doubt" standard and each court must employ an objective analysis to determine whether a plaintiff's complaint contains the facts necessary to support a finding of reasonable doubt of director disinterest or independence, or proper business judgment. In fact, the court remarked that the theoretical exception alluded to, that some decisions may be so "'egregious'" that liability for losses they cause may follow even in the absence of conflict of interest or improper motivation, has resulted in no money judgments against corporate officers or directors in Delaware.

Applying the foregoing standards to the complaint in this action, we find that the IAS Court properly found that plaintiffs have failed to allege, with the necessary particularity, facts that would support a conclusion that any presuit demand by them would have been futile.

When utilizing the term *management* with respect to the Board of Directors, be aware of the fact that the term is not used in reference to supervising personnel. Management refers to the Board of Directors making corporate policy decisions. The business may not act unless authorized to do so by the Board. In this context, the Board of Directors act as the agent for the corporation. Furthermore, because management of the corporation rests with the Board of Directors and not with any one director, all policy decisions must be effectuated by a vote of the Board of Directors at meetings held by the Board. Once the management decision has been made, evidenced by a Board of Directors **resolution**, the actual carrying out of that decision is left to the **officers** of the corporation who are empowered with the ability to carry on the day-to-day business of the entity. In this fashion, the officers are the servants of the corporation authorized to act by the Board of Directors, the corporate agent.

> **Resolution** — document indicating Board of Directors action.
>
> **Officers** — servants of the corporation.

In addition to the general management of the corporation, the Board of Directors is required to act on the following specific items:

1. The Board is responsible for adopting the by-laws.
2. The Board selects the officers.
3. The Board determines management compensation.
4. The Board issues corporate stock and determines its value.
5. The Board declares dividends, if any.
6. The Board initiates extraordinary corporate matters (extraordinary corporate matters are generally any items that affect the structure of the corporation).

Failure to fulfill these obligations is deemed to be a breach of fiduciary duty.

Under the BCL, directors are expected to be elected annually by all of the shareholders to serve one-year terms. However, if the corporation so elects in its certificate of incorporation, it may vary this situation in the following manner:

> **Staggered Board of Directors** — Board of Directors whose members are elected at different intervals.

1. *Staggered Board of Directors.* A **staggered Board of Directors** is one in which the directors serve identical terms, but the terms end at different periods. In this respect, it is like the United States Senate. There are 100 Senators, all of whom serve six-year terms. However, one-third of the Senate is up for re-election every two years. The purpose of this "staggering" is to provide some continuity in management, ensuring there will always be some people on the Board of Directors (or in the Senate) who are aware of the history of the matter to be decided. With this type of Board of Directors, the directors may serve longer than one-year terms.

> **Classified Board of Directors** — Board of Directors whose positions are allocated to different classes of stock.

2. *Classified Board of Directors.* If the corporation in its certificate of incorporation indicates that it will have different classes of stock (Chapter 7), the corporation may allocate directorial seats to each class of stock. Once again this mimics the United States Senate: There are 100 Senators, and each state elects two. The purpose of having a **classified Board of Directors** is to ensure that one class of

shareholder will not dominate the Board of Directors to the detriment of the shareholders of the other classes.

Executive committees — groups of directors and officers who investigate matters for the full board.

Additionally, if the corporation has an unusually large number of directors, making it difficult to schedule meetings, the BCL provides that the corporation may create **executive committees**, committees composed of some of the directors and/or officers, whose function is to investigate and report on matters that must be voted on by the full Board of Directors. In certain instances, these executive committees may have some emergency powers to act on behalf of the full Board. In this fashion, the corporation can operate in an efficient and streamlined manner.

Caskie v. International Railway Company
261 N.Y. 47 (1933)

The plaintiff was an employee of the Philadelphia Rapid Transit Company. A large stockholder therein and also of the defendant dominated both corporations. He was a director of defendant and chairman of its executive committee and a managing corporation of which he was principal stockholder and president held a contract with both corporations for complete charge and supervision, "subject to the direction of the board of directors" of the properties and business of each. An oral arrangement had been made between this stockholder and the president of the defendant, whereby defendant had the right to draw upon employees of the Philadelphia organization for assistance, their salaries while so acting to be paid by defendant to the Philadelphia company upon a bill being rendered. At the request of the dominant stockholder of the two corporations the plaintiff rendered valuable services which inured to the benefit of defendant. From time to time defendant paid to the Philadelphia corporation sums of money for plaintiff's services and had paid to plaintiff a sum of money for his expenses. In this action to recover from defendant compensation for such services in addition to his salary, plaintiff cannot recover, even though it appears that such additional compensation was promised him by the dominant stockholder. The functions of the latter as chairman of the executive committee did not embrace the authority of a majority of that committee. Nor was the authority of the management corporation, of which he was president, broad enough to enable it to enter into a contract of employment, without direction or ratification by the board of directors. Plaintiff was intimately connected with the defendant's affairs, knew that the amount of his salary was charged against the defendant and there is no evidence that he based his actions upon a contract which he believed binding upon the defendant. Under such circumstances ratification by the corporation of any promise made to plaintiff is an indispensable element of recovery.

Share of stock — document evidencing ownership of a corporation.

Common stock rights — the right to vote, the right to receive dividends, and the right to the assets of the corporation on dissolution.

OWNING THE CORPORATION:
THE THIRD GREAT PRINCIPLE OF CORPORATE LAW

Ownership of the corporation vests with its shareholders. This ownership is evidenced by a document known as a **share of stock,** which entitles the holder to what are known as the **common stock rights**. In order to be lawfully formed, all New York corporations must have at least one individual who has these common stock rights:

1. The right to vote for the directors and to approve extraordinary corporate matters.

2. The right to receive dividends if declared by the Board of Directors; common shareholders have no automatic right to receive dividends.

3. The right to the assets of the corporation upon dissolution; because the shareholders are the owners of the corporation, if the corporation dissolves, after all obligations have been met, whatever is left over belongs to the shareholders. For this reason the common shareholders are often referred to as the **residual owners** of the corporation.

Residual owners — common stock owners.

In addition to the foregoing, incident to the preceding delineated common stock rights that belong to all common shareholders of every corporation in the country, New York corporate shareholders have the right to inspect the books of the company. The right to inspect the books must be asserted in writing, the inspection must take place at the corporate office during regular business hours, and the inspection must be for a lawful corporate purpose. Should the corporation refuse the inspection, the shareholder may go to court to compel the inspection if:

1. the shareholder owns at least 5% of the outstanding shares of the corporation, or

2. the shareholder's shares have a value of at least $50,000 for closely held corporations (see the following).

In the Matter of Crane Co. v. Anaconda Company
39 N.Y.2d 14 (1976)

Succinctly put, the issue here is whether a qualified stockholder may inspect the corporation's stock register to ascertain the identity of fellow stockholders for the avowed purpose of informing them directly of its exchange offer and soliciting tenders of stock? In our view this question should be answered in the affirmative. A shareholder desiring to discuss relevant aspects of a tender offer should be granted access to the shareholder list unless it is sought for a purpose inimical to the corporation or its stockholders—and the manner of communication selected should be within the judgment of the shareholder.

The significance of this appeal is evident in view of the fact that this right is the one most frequently litigated by stockholders and the fact that the tender offer is the primary method of corporate acquisition. The authority to inspect corporate books and records in general is traceable to the right given to partners to ascertain the names of other partners and the condition of the business, and is recognized both at common law. The conceptual basis for this right is derived from the shareholder's beneficial ownership of corporate assets and the concomitant right to protect his investment.

At common law, this right is qualified and can only be asserted where the shareholder is acting in good faith and has established that inspection is for a "proper purpose."

The statutory right to inspect corporate records was adopted in 1848 and has had a checkered history. The present statute (Business Corporation Law, secs. 1315, 624) was enacted in 1961 and modified the direct mandate of the Stock Corporation Law by providing that access be permitted to qualified shareholders on written demand, subject to denial if the petitioner refused to furnish an affidavit that the "inspection is not desired for a purpose * * * other than the business" of the corporation and that the petitioner has not been involved in the sale of stock lists within the last five years (Business Corporation Law, sec. 1315, subd [b]; sec. 624, subd [c]). This was deemed to work no substantive change in the law. This revision also eliminated the seldom used monetary penalty provisions and replaced them with a summary enforcement procedure in Supreme Court (Business Corporation Law, sec. 1315, subd [c]; sec. 624, subd [d]).

In an enforcement proceeding the stockholder must allege compliance with the statute. At this point the bona fides of the shareholder will be assumed and it becomes incumbent on the corporation to justify its refusal by showing an improper purpose or bad faith. Needless to say the court may exercise its discretion and deny the petition where it was not made in good faith or for unlawful purposes.

This statute should be liberally construed in favor of the stockholder whose welfare as a stockholder or the corporation's welfare may be affected. To say, as Anaconda would, that a pending tender offer involving over one-fifth of the corporation's common stock is a purpose other than the business of the corporation is myopic. Since the pendency of such an exchange offer may well affect not only the future direction of the corporation but the continued vitality of the shareholders' investment, inspection of the stock book should be allowed so that qualified shareholders may have the means to independently evaluate the situation. Nor do we consider it significant that the petitioning shareholder precipitated that which may affect the corporation or shareholders; the right adheres as one of property in the shareholder and one for the protection of that interest.

Nevertheless, Anaconda claims support of the applicable case law with special reliance on Matter of Newman v Smith (263 App Div 85, affd 289 NY 545). The appellant cites Newman for the proposition that inspection should be denied where the party seeking it is motivated primarily by a desire to solicit sales of stock. We believe this reliance is misplaced.

Newman involved a request by the owner of stock in an unincorporated stock association organized under the common-law right of contract, to examine the stock and transfer books of the association. The avowed purpose in seeking the stockholder list was to communicate an offer to purchase the association's stock at a price above market value but below book value and by that means gain control. The association refused and Newman sued to compel inspection. The Appellate Division unanimously reversed a lower court order in Newman's favor. The actual holding, the one in which all five Justices concurred, was that the petitioner had no statutory right to inspect the stock book of an unincorporated joint stock company and that mandamus would not lie to enforce a right arising out of private contract (p 88). The alternative ground, expressed by three Justices, was that even if there had been statutory authority they would have exercised their discretion to deny the request in light of the lack of benefit to either the company or its stockholders (pp 87-88). Therefore, even the Newman court recognized that the right is dependent on benefit to the corporation or its shareholders. Newman should not be read to support the proposition that an intention to solicit the sale of stock is an improper reason for inspection. The dispositive inquiry is whether the recalcitrant corporation can prove that inspection is sought for a purpose which is contrary to the best interests of the corporation or its stockholders.

The other New York cases relied on by Anaconda are inapposite either because they involved instances where the assertion of an improper motive was held not to preclude inspection if another proper purpose existed, or they rest on Newman. In Laidlaw, an application seeking examination of the stock book for the sole purpose of soliciting the sale of stock was denied. Although Newman was cited as authority, the analysis of this case stands on its own. The Laidlaw court drew a distinction between proxy contests and tender offers on the ground that the former are proper since the resultant opposition to the incumbent management may benefit the corporation. In contrast, solicitation of tender offers was considered improper since the purchase of stock with a view toward gaining control is at least an additional step removed from benefit to the corporation and "may be as consistent with the end of seeking personal gain for the purchaser as with the end of benefitting the corporation" (p 123).

Finally, it should be noted that during the pendency of this appeal, Anaconda announced a proposed merger with another corporation, Tenneco. Crane argues that the shareholder list was urgently required so it could discuss the merger with its fellow shareholders. Since our disposition was on other grounds we do not reach this question.

The order of the Appellate Division should be modified by substituting the date of February 24, 1976 for the expired February 2, 1976 date and, as so modified, affirmed.

Holder of record — shareholder who appears on the corporate books at the close of business on the record date.

Record date — day on which the shareholders who are permitted to assert specific rights are identified.

Preemptive rights — the right of a shareholder to purchase newly issued shares of his or her class of stock in the same proportion as his or her current ownership before outsiders may purchase the shares.

Authorized shares — the number of shares specified in a corporation's certificate of incorporation.

Issued shares — shares available for sale to the public.

Outstanding shares — shares held by members of the public.

In order to assert these shareholder rights, the shareholder must be the holder of record. The **holder of record** is the person who appears on the books of the corporation at the close of business on the day called the **record date.** The record date must be at least ten and no more than sixty days before the right accrues, such as the payment of a dividend or a shareholder vote, and is determined by the Board of Directors. Only the person who is listed as the holder of record may assert the right in question, even if on the actual date of the exercise of the right he or she no longer owns the stock. The purpose behind the concept of the record date is to protect the corporation from constant litigation. Because shares of stock are traded so frequently, the corporation must be able to pinpoint the shareholder who is entitled to the right to be exercised.

For corporations in existence prior to February 22, 1998, common shareholders of a corporation are entitled to **preemptive rights**, the right to purchase newly issued shares of his or her class of stock in the same percentage as his or her current ownership before outsiders may purchase the shares. For corporations formed on or after February 22, 1998, preemptive rights only attach if they are specifically provided for in the certificate of incorporation. However, preemptive rights do not attach if:

1. the new issue is made within two years of the original issue, or
2. the shares are sold for consideration other than cash or property.

In order to understand how preemptive rights work, it is necessary to understand how shares of stock are transferred from the corporation to the shareholder. In its certificate of incorporation, the corporation is required to specify the total number of shares it potentially may sell (Chapter 6). This total number is known as the corporation's **authorized shares**, the maximum number of shares it may sell.

One of the specific obligations of the Board of Directors is to issue shares of stock. **Issued shares** are shares made available for sale to the public. Only shares that have been issued may be acquired by potential shareholders. Once a shareholder acquires issued shares, the shares are referred to as **outstanding shares**, meaning they are now held by actual shareholders. It is helpful to view the process as a flow chart:

Certificate of Incorporation   Board Resolution to Sell   Purchase by Shareholder
Authorized ———————▶ Issued ———————▶ Outstanding

Preemptive rights exist to ensure that the holder of outstanding shares may maintain his or her percentage ownership of the corporation.

Example: A newly formed corporation that has provided for preemptive rights has authorized one million shares of common stock in its certificate of incorporation. The Board of Directors, in order to raise capital, resolves to offer 100,000 shares for sale. At this point, the corporation has 900,000 shares of stock authorized but unissued and 100,000 authorized and issued. The first day the stock goes on sale, 80,000 shares are sold. At this time, there are 900,000 shares authorized but unissued, 20,000 shares authorized and issued, and 80,000 shares authorized, issued, and outstanding. Eventually all the shares are sold.

A shareholder owns 10,000 of the outstanding shares. Two years later, the corporation decides to issue another 50,000 shares. The shareholder has preemptive rights to purchase 5,000 shares of this new issue before they may be offered to outsiders in order to maintain his or her percentage ownership of the company. If he or she does not exercise these preemptive rights, the shares may be sold to outsiders.

One of the primary benefits of operating a business as a corporation is the limited liability for the shareholders. As a general rule, the personal assets of the shareholders cannot be reached to satisfy the obligations of the corporation. The only assets the shareholder may lose are those that the shareholder has used to acquire the shares, the shareholder's contribution to the financing of the corporation. However, this limited liability is not absolute.

If it is determined that the shareholder has violated the first great principle of corporate law—a corporation is an entity separate from its shareholders—and has treated the corporate entity as his or her **alter ego** or as a **sham corporation**, treating the corporate assets as a mere extension of his or her own property, the court, under a doctrine known as **piercing the corporate veil**, may reach the shareholder's personal property. Note that this only occurs if the shareholder has not maintained the corporation as a separate entity.

Alter ego — a shareholder disregarding the corporate existence as a separate entity.

Sham corporation — corporate format used to attempt to shield the owner's personal liability.

Piercing the corporate veil — legal doctrine permitting the court to attach the personal assets of a shareholder to satisfy corporate obligations.

Morris v. New York State Department of Taxation and Finance
82 N.Y.2d 135 (1993)

Petitioner, a New Jersey resident who maintained a rented apartment in New York, was the president of Sunshine Developers, Inc. (Sunshine), a closely held corporation owned entirely by his brother and his nephew. Respondent New York State Department of Taxation and Finance (the Department) assessed a compensating use tax against petitioner for two cabin cruisers purchased by the corporation outside of New York and allegedly used by him on his individual business in State waters. Although owning no stock in Sunshine, petitioner assertedly controlled the corporation and his responsibility for the tax has been upheld by disregarding the separate corporate entity under the doctrine of piercing the corporate veil. Because of his leasing a New York apartment, it has been held that petitioner, although a New Jersey resident, could not claim the nonresident's exemption from the tax (see, Tax Law sec. 1118 [2]). On his appeal, the decisive question is whether the Tax Appeals Tribunal and Appellate Division properly sustained the assessment against petitioner on the theory of piercing the corporate veil. For reasons to be explained, we conclude that, on the facts in this record, that theory should not have been applied. We, therefore, reverse.

In Walkovszky v Carlton (18 N.Y.2d 414, 276 N.Y.S.2d 585, 223 N.E.2d 6), we stated the general rule that:

> "Broadly speaking, the courts will disregard the corporate form, or, to use accepted terminology, 'pierce the corporate veil,' whenever necessary 'to prevent fraud or to achieve equity.'"

The concept of piercing the corporate veil is a limitation on the accepted principles that a corporation exists independently of its owners, as a separate legal entity, that the owners are normally not liable for the debts of the corporation, and that it is perfectly legal to incorporate for the express purpose of limiting the liability of the corporate owners.

The doctrine of piercing the corporate veil is typically employed by a third party seeking to go behind the corporate existence in order to circumvent the limited liability of the owners and to hold them liable for some underlying corporate obligation. The concept is equitable in nature and assumes that the corporation itself is liable for the obligation sought to be imposed. Thus, an attempt of a third party to pierce the corporate veil does not constitute a cause of action independent of that against the corporation; rather it is an assertion of facts and circumstances which will persuade the court to impose the corporate obligation on its owners.

Because a decision whether to pierce the corporate veil in a given instance will necessarily depend on the attendant facts and equities, the New York cases may not be reduced to definitive rules governing the varying circumstances when the power may be exercised. Generally, however, piercing the corporate veil requires a showing that: (1) the owners exercised complete domination of the corporation in respect to the transaction attacked; and (2) that such domination was used to commit a fraud or wrong against the plaintiff which resulted in plaintiff's injury.

While complete domination of the corporation is the key to piercing the corporate veil, especially when the owners use the corporation as a mere device to further their personal rather than the corporate business (see, Walkovszky, supra, at 417), such domination, standing alone, is not enough; some showing of a wrongful or unjust act toward plaintiff is required. The party seeking to pierce the corporate veil must establish that the owners, through their domination, abused the privilege of doing business in the corporate form to perpetrate a wrong or injustice against that party such that a court in equity will intervene.

In deciding whether respondents have established a sufficient basis for piercing the corporate veil under these general rules, we first address the element of petitioner's control of the corporation. Because petitioner was not a stockholder of Sunshine, he argues that, as a matter of law, he was not in a position to exercise the necessary domination of the corporation. Respondents contend, nevertheless, that Joseph Morris, although not a stockholder—through his status as Sunshine's president and its only director and his close relationship with his brother and nephew, the only stockholders—was in a position to and did dominate the corporation with respect to the transactions at issue. The Appellate Division accepted this argument, holding: "we perceive that we should be concerned with 'reality and not form [and] with how the corporation operated and [petitioner's] relationship to that operation' [citation omitted]."

We have found no definitive authority on the issue of whether a nonshareholder could be personally liable under a theory of piercing the corporate veil. It is not necessary to decide the question, however, because respondents fell far short of meeting their burden on the second critical point: that petitioner, through his domination, misused the corporate form for his personal ends so as to commit a wrong or injustice on the taxing authorities of New York State. The specific finding of the ALJ that there is no indication of "fraud or wrongdoing" on the part of petitioner or the corporation, it must be noted, was not disturbed on review by either the Tax Appeals Tribunal or the Appellate Division. But, respondents maintain that there was wrongful conduct in any event and characterize the purchase of the boats by Sunshine as part of an illicit scheme to use the corporation to avoid New York taxes. We disagree.

There is no contention that there was anything improper in the formation of Sunshine for the stated purpose of purchasing, owning and leasing boats. Sunshine, it appears, in the early years after its incorporation, carried on its stated business; the very basis of the Department's successful 1982 assessment of the use tax against Sunshine for the 1978 boat was that the corporation was conducting its business within the State of New York—i.e., buying boats and chartering them to businesses for entertaining clients.

Indeed, as in the 1982 assessment, the Department initially argued that Sunshine was liable for the current assessment because of its business presence in New York. However, once the ALJ and the Tribunal determined in this proceeding that Sunshine was a nonresident corporation and not engaged in business in New York and, therefore, entitled to the nonresident exemption on the 1981 and 1984, respondents abandoned that course and took a different tack. They now claim that in doing no business during the period when the 1981 and 1984 boats were purchased, Sunshine must have operated solely as a sham to do the personal business of petitioner. They further argue that, because Sunshine was a sham, it existed solely for the purpose of avoiding taxes due on its asset.

However, there is no evidence of an intent to defraud by using the corporation as a tax shield. The corporation, not petitioner, purchased and owned the boats. There is no suggestion that any obligations of the corporation remained unpaid, including use taxes found to be due in New York. There is no reason to believe that if respondents had succeeded in their current assessment against the corporation on the 1984 boat, as they had in their 1982 assessment, Sunshine would not have paid the tax. That the Tribunal sustained the nonresident tax exemption for Sunshine on the 1984 purchase and declined to sustain it as to petitioner does not give rise to a claim of fraud or wrongdoing by petitioner.

Finally, there is a fundamental problem with respondents' claim that petitioner has somehow perverted the protective benefits of the corporate privilege to commit a wrong against respondents. This is not the usual case where a third party seeks to impose a corporate obligation on a controlling owner by penetrating the shield of limited liability. Quite the contrary. Here, there was no corporate obligation for respondents to impose. Sunshine, it has been determined, was entitled to the nonresident exemption for the 1984 boat and owes nothing. Thus, the claim against petitioner cannot be for what the corporation owed. Respondents, nevertheless, seek to collect the tax directly from petitioner because, unlike Sunshine, he maintained a rental apartment in New York and assertedly was deprived of his nonresident exemption. But, to pursue petitioner under the doctrine of piercing the corporate veil presupposes that "the corporation is liable." To hold petitioner liable by piercing the corporate veil for a debt Sunshine does not owe, we think, would be inconsistent with the essential theory of the doctrine.

We are not persuaded by respondents' argument that we should disregard the corporate entity and sustain the tax against petitioner under the theory articulated in Federal tax cases. In general, in matters relating to revenue a corporation will be recognized as having a separate taxable identity unless it is shown to have had no legitimate business purpose either in its formation or its subsequent existence or that it was a sham or set up for tax avoidance. First, of course, we are dealing here not with Federal law but with New York decisional law and a New York sales and use tax. But, even applying the rule of the Federal cases the result would be the same, for it appears that Sunshine had a legitimate business purpose in its formation and carried on its business of owning and chartering boats thereafter. There is no showing that it was set up as a sham or for the purpose of tax avoidance.

In view of the foregoing, we need not address petitioner's further contention that he was improperly denied a nonresident's exemption under Tax Law sec. 1118 (2).

The judgment of the Appellate Division should be reversed.

TAXATION OF THE CORPORATION

As legal entities, corporations are subject to income taxation on the income they generate. However, the Internal Revenue Service provides for two special tax treatments for qualifying corporations.

Subchapter S Corporation

Subchapter S refers to Subchapter S of the Internal Revenue Code. In order to qualify as a **Subchapter S corporation**, the corporation must meet the following requirements:

1. It must be a domestic U.S. corporation.

2. It cannot have more than 75 shareholders.

3. It cannot have a shareholder who is not an individual.

4. It cannot have a nonresident alien shareholder.

5. It can only have one class of stock.

If the corporation qualifies, it may elect to be treated as a Subchapter S corporation, meaning the corporation is not liable for income taxes on its revenue. All taxes become the personal responsibility of the shareholders of the qualifying corporation. Furthermore, any losses the corporation suffers may be passed through to the shareholders. In this manner, a Subchapter S corporation, for tax purposes only, operates in a manner similar to a general or limited partnership (Chapter 3). The advantages or disadvantages of the election are dependent on the personal tax obligations of the individual shareholders, which is why its provisions are only applicable to small business corporations.

Subchapter S corporation — tax election for qualifying small businesses.

Gitlitz v. Commissioner of Internal Revenue
182 F.3d 1143 (2d Cir. 1999)

The Commissioner of Internal Revenue assessed tax deficiencies against David and Louise Gitlitz and Philip and Eleanor Winn after determining the taxpayers improperly utilized excluded discharge of indebtedness income to adjust their subchapter S corporate bases. The United States Tax Court upheld the Commissioner's deficiency determinations and taxpayers now appeal. We exercise jurisdiction pursuant to 26 U.S.C. sec. 7482(a)(1) and affirm.

. . .

Subchapter S Corporations

Subchapter S of the Internal Revenue Code, 26 U.S.C. secs. 1361-1379, permits certain corporations to elect to be taxed in a similar, but not identical, fashion as partnerships. See 3 Boris I. Bittker and Lawrence Lokken, Federal Taxation of Income,

Estates and Gifts P 95.6.1 (2d ed. 1991) (highlighting major distinctions). A subchapter S corporation generally does not pay taxes as an entity. 26 U.S.C. sec. 1363(a). Instead, the corporation's profits and losses pass through directly to its shareholders on a pro rata basis and are then reported on the shareholders' individual tax returns. 26 U.S.C. sec. 1366(a). This conduit approach allows shareholders to avoid double taxation on corporate earnings. Tax integrity, meanwhile, is preserved by requiring shareholders to treat all income and deductions as if "realized directly from the source from which realized by the corporation, or incurred in the same manner as incurred by the corporation." 26 U.S.C. sec. 1366(b). In other words, "the items attain no greater dignity from being passed through the corporation." Boris I. Bittker and James S. Eustice, Federal Income Taxation of Corporations and Shareholders, P 6.06[2][c] (6th ed. 1998).

To further prevent double taxation of subchapter S corporate income upon distribution to shareholders, sec. 1367(a) normally requires shareholders to adjust their corporate bases by the items identified in sec. 1366(a). In particular, basis must be increased by, inter alia, the items of income delineated in sec. 1366(a)(1)(A). Basis must be decreased by, inter alia, the items of loss and deduction set forth in sec. 1366(a)(1)(A), as well as corporate distributions previously excluded from shareholders' income pursuant to 26 U.S.C. sec. 1368(b). Section 1368(b) provides that distributions of a subchapter S corporation having no earnings and profits (as is the case with PDW&A) are treated as follows:

(1) Amount applied against basis. — The distribution shall not be included in gross income to the extent that it does not exceed the adjusted basis of the stock.

(2) Amount in excess of basis. — If the amount of the distribution exceeds the adjusted basis of the stock, such excess shall be treated as gain from the sale or exchange of property.

Two examples help explain how this statutory scheme operates. Assume the sole shareholder of a subchapter S corporation has a basis of $100 in the corporation's stock. The corporation realizes $200 in taxable income. At the end of the tax year, the shareholder pays tax on the $200 of income under the "pass through" principles described above. The corporation distributes the $200 to the shareholder the following year. In the absence of an upward basis adjustment, the shareholder would be liable for additional tax upon the distribution pursuant to sec. 1368(b)(2) because the amount of the distribution ($200) exceeds his preexisting basis in the stock. Sections 1366 and 1367 prevent this double taxation by mandating a $200 basis increase when the corporation first realizes the income and a $200 basis decrease upon the corporation's distribution of the income.

A second example illustrates how the character of tax-exempt income is preserved under the subchapter S framework. Assume the same subchapter S corporation realizes $200 in tax-exempt income. Although a "pass through" technically occurs, the shareholder pays no tax on the income because, under sec. 1366(b), the income after "pass through" has the same character as if it was realized by the corporation. The corporation distributes the income to its shareholder the next year. Without the requisite basis adjustment, the shareholder would be forced to pay tax on the distribution under sec. 1368(b)(2) because the amount of the distribution exceeds his preexisting basis in the stock. Once again, sec. 1366 and 1367 prevent such a result by dictating a $200 basis increase when the corporation first realizes the income and a $200 basis decrease upon the corporation's distribution of the income. As a result, the shareholder pays no taxes on the income.

. . .

Section 1244 Stock

Section 1244 of the Internal Revenue Code provides for special tax treatment for small business corporations that qualify and elect to have their stock classified under this provision as **Section 1244 Stock**. In order to qualify, the corporation must qualify as a small business corporation (same as a Subchapter S corporation), it must issue shares for money or other property (not services), and it must have generated gross receipts (more than 50%) for the previous five years from the active operation of a business and not from passive income such as rents, royalties, dividends, interest, and so forth. If the corporation qualifies and so elects, should the corporation become bankrupt, the shareholders are permitted to take their losses as ordinary losses rather than capital losses. This means that the shareholder may offset this corporate loss against his or her ordinary income and may carry the losses forward to successive years if the corporate losses exceed his or her ordinary income. If the losses are taken as a capital loss, it can only be offset against capital gains, not ordinary income. This election is usually used by only very risky businesses in order to entice potential investors.

Section 1244 stock — tax election for qualifying small businesses.

HYBRID CORPORATIONS

In addition to the general business corporations discussed previously, New York law also provides for several special, or hybrid, types of corporate entities.

Close Corporation

A **close** or **closely held corporation** is a regular corporation except that it is owned by a small number of shareholders, meaning that the stock is not publicly traded. What number constitutes "small" has never been statutorily or judicially determined. If an entity operates as a close corporation, although in all other respects it is a regular corporation, for purposes of management, the law permits the shareholders and directors to manage the business in a manner similar to a general partnership. This means that shareholders are permitted more direct control in the decision-making process. Note that a Subchapter S corporation and a close corporation are not necessarily the same.

Close or closely held corporation — corporation whose shares are not publicly traded and are held by a small number of shareholders.

Professional Corporation

Until the mid-1960s, the professions were precluded from incorporating for fear they would use the protection of the corporate entity to shield themselves from personal liability for malpractice. However, due to the lobbying effort of several professional associations, states began enacting professional corporation laws to permit professionals certain corporate advantages. In order to incorporate as a **professional corporation** under the New York Professional Corporation Law, the following requirements must be met:

Professional corporation — corporation formed to provide professional services.

1. The corporation must be formed to provide professional services as defined under the New York Education Law.
2. All shareholders of the corporation must be professionals licensed by New York to provide the professional services for which the corporation was formed.
3. The corporation must include the words "professional corporation" or the initials "P.C." in its name to alert the public to its special character.

By incorporating under the statute, the professional may take advantage of certain benefits such as receiving life and health insurance as an employee benefit. However, whereas the professional may use the corporate entity to shield his or her personal assets from attachment for the regular business obligations of the corporation, the professional still retains unlimited personal liability for any malpractice.

See Exhibit 5–1 for the Certificate of Incorporation used by professional corporations.

We're Associates Company v. Cohen, Stracher & Bloom, P.C.
65 N.Y.2d 148 (1985)

The issue presented on this appeal, here by leave of our court, is whether the shareholders of a professional service corporation organized under article 15 of the Business Corporation Law may be held liable in their individual capacities for rents due under a lease naming only the professional service corporation as tenant.

Defendant Cohen, Stracher & Bloom, P.C., a professional service corporation engaged in the practice of law, whose sole officers, directors and shareholders are the individual defendants, entered into a lease agreement with plaintiff. The lease recited that it was between "We're Associates Company * * * as 'Landlord' and Cohen, Stracher & Bloom, P.C. * * * as 'Tenant'". It was signed in the name of the corporate defendant by one of the individual defendants.

The amended complaint alleged, in its first cause of action, that "Defendant CS & B failed to perform its obligations under the Lease, breached the terms thereof and defaulted thereunder, that defendant CS & B failed and refused to pay rent and additional rent in the sum of $13,333.69, as of June 1, 1983, although payment thereof was duly demanded." The second cause of action repeated the allegations of the first, including the corporate defendant's default, and further alleged: "By reason of the foregoing, [the individual] defendants Cohen, Stracher and Bloom are jointly, severally and personally liable to plaintiff in the sum of not less than $13,333.69."

The individual defendants moved to have their names stricken as parties pursuant to CPLR 1003, stating that the corporate defendant was the acknowledged tenant and that the demised premises "were occupied by the corporation and that at no time did any of the individuals act in any other capacity other than as officers and directors of the corporation," which plaintiff never denied. Special Term granted the motion, and the Appellate Division affirmed, noting in essence that the Legislature, in enacting article 15 of the Business Corporation Law, did not intend to abrogate the traditional limited liability afforded corporate shareholders except as specifically provided in that article.

Plaintiff contends the statute should be liberally construed to apply to debts incurred ancillary to the rendering of professional services; that the rationale underlying the limitation of shareholder liability, i.e., the inability of shareholders to participate in the management of the corporation, does not apply to professional service corporations, which are run by their shareholders; and that affording limited liability to the shareholders of a legal professional services corporation would contravene the Code of Professional Responsibility. Finding none of these contentions meritorious, we affirm.

The only specific provision relating to shareholder liability in article 15 of the Business Corporation Law (the article permitting the formation of domestic professional service corporations) is section 1505 (a), which states: "Each shareholder, employee or agent of a professional service corporation shall be personally and fully liable and accountable for any negligent or wrongful act or misconduct committed by him or by any person under his direct supervision and control while rendering professional services on behalf of such corporation."

The plain words of the statute, imposing personal liability only in connection with the rendition of professional services on behalf of the professional service corporation, cannot be defeated by a liberal construction which would include ordinary business debts within the definition of professional services. Words of ordinary import in a statute are to be given their usual and commonly understood meaning, unless it is clear from the statutory language that a different meaning was intended. Especially is this so in the present case where strict, not liberal, construction is required because the statute carves out a limited exception to a rule of broad and general application and imposes liability unknown at common law. The available legislative history and commentary on article 15 and section 1505 (a) support this interpretation.

The foregoing analysis also disposes of plaintiff's second contention, that the inability of the shareholders to participate in management is not a characteristic of professional service corporations. Plaintiff cites South High Dev. v Weiner, Lippe & Cromley Co. L.P.A. (4 Ohio St 3d 1, 445 NE2d 1106), in which, under similar circumstances to the case at bar, individual shareholders of an incorporated law firm were held in as parties to an action to recover rents allegedly due under a lease executed solely by the corporate entity as tenant. However, the court's decision in that case was premised on a court rule which specifically provided: "The participation by an individual as a shareholder of a legal professional association shall be on the condition that such individual shall, and by such participation does, guarantee the financial responsibility of the association for its breach of any duty, whether or not arising from the attorney-client relationship." That rule is diametrically opposed to Business Corporation Law sec. 1505 (a).

The contrary Ohio rule notwithstanding, the rationale that shareholders of a professional service corporation should be held personally liable for ordinary business debts of the corporation because they are "closer" to the management of such corporation than are shareholders of an ordinary business corporation has not prevailed in our State over the general policy of allowing corporations to be formed for the express purpose of limiting liability. Even single-person businesses are allowed to incorporate, and, so long as no fraud is committed and the corporate form is respected, no individual liability will result. If shareholders of a conventional business corporation may enjoy limited liability under such circumstances, so may those of a professional service corporation except as limited by Business Corporation Law sec. 1505 (a).

The Code of Professional Responsibility provides no basis for the imposition of personal liability in this case. Plaintiff does not suggest, and indeed no authority has been brought to our attention which has held, that an attorney may be held personally liable for the debts of any business corporation of which he is a shareholder simply because he is an attorney and is thus subject to the strictures of the code.

In light of our holding, based on what we discern to be the clear command of New York law, it is unnecessary to determine whether the Federal tax laws would have precluded our reaching a contrary conclusion. The order of the Appellate Division should be affirmed.

Not-for-Profit Corporation

Not-for-profit corporation — corporation organized for charitable purposes.

New York law permits charitable organizations to incorporate under its Not-for-Profit Corporation Law. The purpose of this statute is to provide a legal format under which a charitable organization may operate. A **not-for-profit corporation** is precluded from declaring dividends, and the shareholders simply vote for the directors who will manage the charity. These corporations are exempt from New York State income taxation, but the organizations are not necessarily exempt from federal income taxation, nor are they necessarily permitted to accept tax deductible contributions. (See Exhibit 5–2 for the certificate of incorporation used by not-for-profit corporations.)

CHAPTER REVIEW

The corporation is probably the most widely used business format in New York. The New York statute that governs the organization and operation of corporations is the Business Corporation Law (BCL), and all rights and obligations of New York corporations emanate from this statute.

Corporations, once validly formed, are considered to be legal entities, separate and distinct from their shareholders. In this respect, corporations are responsible for all their own liabilities, and the assets of the owners generally cannot be reached to satisfy claims against the corporation.

Corporations are managed by a Board of Directors, persons who are elected by the shareholders to act as agents and fiduciaries for the corporation. The Board of Directors is responsible for enacting all corporate policy.

Ownership of the corporation vests in the shareholders. One of the primary reasons a person wishes to operate a business as a corporation is the limited liability afforded corporate owners. As a general rule, shareholders can only lose the consideration they have given the corporation to become owners; their personal assets cannot be attached.

All corporations are required to issue at least one security that has the common stock rights: the right to vote, the right to receive dividends, and the right to the assets of the corporation on dissolution.

In addition to the general business corporation, New York permits certain hybrid situations: close corporations for businesses whose shares are not publicly traded and are owned by a small group of people; professional corporations, for persons providing professional services; and not-for-profit corporations for charitable organizations.

KEY TERMS

Alter ego
Authorized shares
Board of Directors
Business Corporation Law (BCL)
Business judgment rule
By-laws
Certificate of incorporation
Classified Board of Directors
Close or closely held corporation
Common stock rights
Executive committees
Holder of record
Issued shares
Not-for-profit corporation

Officers
Outstanding shares
Piercing the corporate veil
Preemptive rights
Professional corporation
Record date
Residual owners
Resolution
Section 1244 stock
Sham corporation
Share of stock
Staggered Board of Directors
Subchapter S corporation

EXERCISES

1. Discuss why a person might wish to operate a business as a corporation.
2. Discuss three disadvantages of operating a business as a corporation.
3. How does a corporation differ from a limited partnership?
4. Under what circumstances would a close corporation not qualify as a Subchapter S corporation?
5. What is your opinion of permitting professionals to incorporate? Discuss.

FACTUAL PROBLEM

A husband and wife wish to go into business together. The husband is a licensed attorney, and the wife is a CPA. They would like to use the format of a professional corporation to limit their liability. Can they do this under New York law? If not, can they so incorporate in another jurisdiction and then operate in New York? Explain your conclusions.

T 635—Certificate of Incorporation: Professional
Corporation: Article 15, BCL: 1-87

© 1970 BY JULIUS BLUMBERG, INC.,
PUBLISHER, NYC 10013

Certificate of Incorporation of

under Article 15 of the Business Corporation Law

IT IS HEREBY CERTIFIED THAT:

(1) The name of the proposed corporation is

(2) The purpose for which the corporation is formed is to practice the profession of

The corporation, in furtherance of its corporate purposes set forth above, shall have all of the powers conferred by the Business Corporation Law upon corporations formed thereunder, subject to any limitations contained in Article 15 of the Business Corporation Law or in accordance with any other provisions of any other statute of the State of New York.

(3) The name, residence address, profession, professional license or certificate number and office to be held of all individuals who are to be the original shareholders, directors and officers of the corporation, are as follows:

Attached hereto is a certificate or certificates issued by the licensing authority certifying that each of the proposed shareholders, directors and officers is authorized by law to practice the profession which the corporation is being organized to practice.

Exhibit 5–1

Certificate of Incorporation for Professional Corporation *(Forms may be purchased from BlumbergExcelsior, Inc. or any of its dealers. Reproduction prohibited.)*

(4) The office of the corporation is to be located in the county of State of New York.

(5) The aggregate number of shares which the corporation is authorized to issue is

(6) The Secretary of State is designated as the agent of the corporation upon whom process against it may be served. The post office address to which the Secretary of State shall mail a copy of any process against the corporation served upon him is

IN WITNESS WHEREOF, *the undersigned incorporator(s), being 18 years of age, subscribe this certificate and affirm(s) that the statements made herein are true under the penalties of perjury.*

Dated

Type Name	**Signature**
Address	
Type Name	**Signature**
Address	
Type Name	**Signature**
Address	

Exhibit 5–1

Continued *(Forms may be purchased from BlumbergExcelsior, Inc. or any of its dealers. Reproduction prohibited.)*

Certificate of Incorporation

of

under section 402 of the Not-for-Profit Corporation Law

IT IS HEREBY CERTIFIED THAT:

(1) The name of the corporation is

(2) The corporation is a corporation as defined in subparagraph (a)(5) of section 102 (Definitions) of the Not-for-Profit Corporation Law.

(3) The purpose or purposes for which the corporation is formed are as follows:

The corporation, in furtherance of its corporate purposes above set forth, shall have all the powers enumerated in section 202 of the Not-for-Profit Corporation Law, subject to any limitations provided in the Not-for-Profit Corporation Law or any other statute of the State of New York. Nothing herein shall authorize this corporation, directly or indirectly, to engage in, or include among its purposes, any of the activities mentioned in Not-for-Profit Corporation Law, section 404 (b)-(u).

Exhibit 5–2
Certificate of Incorporation for Not-for-Profit Corporation *(Forms may be purchased from BlumbergExcelsior, Inc. or any of its dealers. Reproduction prohibited.)*

(4) *The corporation shall be a Type* corpora*tion pursuant to section 201 of the Not-for-Profit Corpo-ration Law. (In the case of Type A, B and C corporations set forth the names and addresses of at least 3 initial directors. Type C corporation must set forth the lawful public or quasi-public objective which each business purpose will achieve.)*

(5) *The office of the corporation is to be located in the County of* **State of New York.**

(6) *The Secretary of State is designated as agent of the corporation upon whom process against it may be served. The post office address to which the Secretary of State shall mail a copy of any process against the corporation served upon him is*

Exhibit 5–2
Continued *(Forms may be purchased from BlumbergExcelsior, Inc. or any of its dealers. Reproduction prohibited.)*

(7) State and Federal exemption.

State and Federal exemption language for Type B and C corporations seeking tax exemption.

Notwithstanding any other provisions of these articles, the corporation is organized exclusively for one or more of the purposes as specified in §501(c)(3) of the Internal Revenue Code of 1954, and shall not carry on any activities not permitted to be carried on by a corporation exempt from Federal income tax under IRC §501(c)(3) or corresponding provisions of any subsequent Federal tax laws.

No part of the net earnings of the corporation shall inure to the benefit of any member, trustee, director, officer of the corporation, or any private individual (except that reasonable compensation may be paid for services rendered to or for the corporation), and no member, trustee, officer of the corporation or any private individual shall be entitled to share in the distribution of any of the corporate assets on dissolution of the corporation.

No substantial part of the activities of the corporation shall be carrying on propaganda, or otherwise attempting to influence legislation [except as otherwise provided by IRC §501(h)] or participating in, or intervening in (including the publication or distribution of statements), any political campaign on behalf of any candidates for public office.

In the event of dissolution, all of the remaining assets and property of the corporation shall, after necessary expenses thereof, be distributed to another organization exempt under IRC §501(c)(3), or corresponding provisions of any subsequent Federal tax laws, or to the Federal government, or state or local government for a public purpose, subject to the approval of a Justice of the Supreme Court of the State of New York.

In any taxable year in which the corporation is a private foundation as described in IRC §509(a), the corporation shall distribute its income for said period at such time and manner as not to subject it to tax under IRC §4942, and the corporation shall not (a) engage in any act of self-dealing as defined in IRC §4941(d), retain any excess business holdings as defined in IRC §4943(c), (b) make any investments in such manner as to subject the corporation to tax under IRC §4944, or (c) make any taxable expenditures as defined in IRC §4945(d) or corresponding provisions of any subsequent Federal tax laws.

Exhibit 5–2

Continued *(Forms may be purchased from BlumbergExcelsior, Inc. or any of its dealers. Reproduction prohibited.)*

IN WITNESS WHEREOF, the undersigned incorporator, or each of them if there are more than one, being at least eighteen years of the age, has subscribed this certificate on

_____
Type name of incorporator

_____
Address

_____
Signature

_____
Type name of incorporator

_____
Address

_____
Signature

Certificate of Incorporation

of

under Section 402 of the Not-for-Profit Corporation Law

Filed By:

Office and Post Office Address

Exhibit 5–2

Continued *(Forms may be purchased from BlumbergExcelsior, Inc. or any of its dealers. Reproduction prohibited.)*

Chapter 6

Forming
the Corporation

INTRODUCTION

Few legal professionals physically prepare and file the paperwork involved in creating a corporate entity. Most law firms utilize an incorporation service to perform the actual task of filing the necessary documents because these organizations are specifically geared to form business entities in every jurisdiction. However, it is still the function and responsibility of the law office to provide the service with the information necessary to create the entity, so all legal professionals must be familiar with the information and format of the document needed to form a New York corporation.

Under the laws of the state of New York (and all other states as well), a corporation comes into existence once its certificate of incorporation is filed with the state Secretary of State. As previously discussed, the certificate of incorporation is the creating document for corporate entities, the "birth certificate" of the corporate individual. For the general business corporation, the requirements for the certificate appear in the BCL.

Prior to the filing of the certificate of incorporation, the person desiring to create the business, referred to as the **organizer** or **promoter**, may enter into valid contractual relationships on behalf of the corporation to be formed. At this point, because the corporation does not come into existence until the certificate is filed, the organizers are acting as general partners or joint venturers (Chapters 3 and 4). As such, they are personally liable for all obligations they enter into on behalf of the business. In order to minimize or avoid such potential liability, several strategies may be utilized:

Organizer — promoter of a corporation.

Promoter — Organizer of a corporation.

Condition Precedent — factor event that must occur prior to contractual liability.

1. *Condition precedent.* Under general contract law, a **condition precedent** is an event that must occur prior to the parties being contractually liable. In the context of preincorporation contracts, this condition could take the form of the parties inserting a clause stating that they are only bound if the anticipated corporation is actually formed. If the organizers subsequently change their minds with respect to

incorporating, their contractual obligations would be avoided (absent a showing of bad faith).

Example: The organizers wish to form a corporation to manufacture men's dress shirts. Prior to incorporating, they are offered fabric at a bargain price. Not wanting to lose this opportunity, they enter into a contract with the fabric manufacturer to purchase a quantity of the fabric for delivery in several months, but with a condition that if the corporation they are planning to create is not formed within thirty days of the execution of the contract, they will not be bound thereunder.

Assignment — transfer of contract rights.

Promissee — person to whom a contract promise is owed.

Assignee — transferee of contract rights.

2. *Assignment.* An **assignment** is a transfer of contractual rights from the **promissee**, the one to whom the right is owed, to a third party, known as the **assignee**. Although legally an assignment only concerns a transfer of rights, most parties treat the assignment as a transfer of obligations as well. Most contracts are assignable, and the assignee usually becomes liable for the obligations under the contract. If the assignee does not perform, the original promissor can still go against the promissee.

Example: In the contract from the previous example, rather than inserting a condition precedent, the parties agree that the contract may be assigned to the corporation to be formed. In this manner, the organizers have not eliminated liability, but this enables them to transfer the liability to the corporation, thereby being only secondarily liable if the corporation fails to perform under the contract.

Novation — substitution of parties to a contract.

3. *Novation.* A **novation** is the substitution of parties to a contract. Unlike an assignment in which the original parties continue to remain liable, with a novation the contracting parties agree that one side may substitute a different party, thereby relinquishing all contract rights and obligations. After the novation, the contract reads as though the novated party was always the original party to the contract.

Example: In the contract from the preceding examples, the parties agree that the contract may be novated. Once the corporation is formed, the organizers effect the novation, thereby rendering the contract one between the fabric manufacturer and the corporation; the organizers are totally deleted from the contract.

Preincorporation share subscription — offer to purchase shares of a corporation yet to be formed.

Share subscription — offer by potential investor to purchase shares of stock.

Despite the potential problem of liability for the organizers when they enter into preincorporation contracts, there is one type of such agreement that is generally favored. A preincorporation agreement is known as a **preincorporation share subscription**. A regular **share subscription** is an offer from interested investors to purchase shares of a corporation for a stated price. As the name would indicate, a preincorporation subscription is an offer from interested investors to purchase shares of a corporation once the corporation is formed. Preincorporation subscriptions are permitted under the BCL with the following limitations:

1. The subscription must be in writing.
2. The preincorporation subscription is irrevocable for a period of three months.
3. The preincorporation subscription is assignable.

No liability attaches until and unless the corporation is formed and the directors of the corporation accept the subscription offer. Such agreements help in the financial planning for the corporation (Chapter 7).

This chapter focuses on the requirements to complete and file a certificate of incorporation in order to create a valid New York corporation. (See the form provided in Exhibit 6–1.)

CERTIFICATE OF INCORPORATION

Basic Requirements

The basic requirements of a New York certificate of incorporation are set out in the BCL. As with all statutes, the first article provides the definitions of the specific terms that will be used throughout the statute.

Section 102(a)(3) of the BCL defines "certificate of incorporation" not only as the document filed, but also any special act or charter of the New York legislature that may be used to form a corporate entity. Unlike other jurisdictions in which the term "Articles of Incorporation" are used, in New York the correct wording is "Certificate of Incorporation" which encompasses more than just a document filed.

Domestic corporation — corporation formed under the laws of New York.

Foreign corporation — corporation formed under the laws of a state other than New York.

Alien corporation — corporation formed under the laws of a foreign nation.

Application for Certificate of Authority — document filed by a foreign corporation that regularly conducts business in New York.

Also, under this Article, the term **domestic corporation** is defined as any corporation organized and created under the laws of the state of New York. A **foreign corporation** is defined as a corporation formed under the law of any state other than New York, and an **alien corporation** is a corporation formed under the laws of a foreign nation. All three types of corporations may operate within the state, but the rights and obligations may vary, depending on whether the entity is a domestic, foreign, or alien corporation.

All foreign and alien corporations that regularly conduct business in New York are required to file an **Application for Certificate of Authority** to do business in New York as a foreign corporation (BCL Article 13). Once authorized, the foreign corporation is entitled to all rights and obligations of a domestic corporation. When a foreign corporation no longer wishes to conduct business in New York, it must surrender its authority to the Secretary of State after obtaining the approval of the New York State Tax Commission.

Marine Midland Realty Credit Corporation v. Welbilt Corporation
145 A.D.2d 84 (1989)

At issue on this appeal is whether personal jurisdiction was obtained over defendant, a foreign corporation authorized to do business in this State, by service of process in accordance with Business Corporation Law sec. 307, which provides the appropriate method of service on the Secretary of State on behalf of an unauthorized foreign corporation, rather than Business Corporation Law sec. 306, which provides the appropriate method for service on the Secretary of State in the case of a corporation authorized to do business in this State. Plaintiff, as the holder of mortgages on certain real property in the Town of Esopus, Ulster County, commenced a foreclosure action in 1977. At that time, defendant had a judgment lien against the property which was apparently junior and inferior to plaintiff's mortgages. Seeking to join defendant in its foreclosure action, plaintiff served a summons and complaint on the Secretary of State and sent notice of service on the Secretary of

State and a copy of the process to defendant, by registered mail with return receipt requested, which defendant received. The method of service used by plaintiff was that specified in Business Corporation Law sec. 307, which provides for service on an unauthorized foreign corporation. In attempting to serve process on defendant in the foreclosure action, plaintiff made two mistakes: it used the method of service appropriate for an unauthorized foreign corporation when, in fact, defendant was authorized to do business in this State; and plaintiff erroneously referred to defendant as Welbut Corporation, instead of Welbilt Corporation. Defendant never answered or appeared in the foreclosure action. A judgment of foreclosure and sale was entered in favor of plaintiff in March 1980.

. . .

Business Corporation Law sec.sec. 306 and 307 contain additional requirements as to the manner of service of process when the Secretary of State is served on behalf of a corporation with the former statute containing the applicable provisions in the case of a domestic or authorized foreign corporation and the latter statute containing the applicable provisions in the case of an unauthorized foreign corporation. Both statutes provide that delivery of process to the Secretary of State or his deputy or his designated agent must occur at the office of the Department of State in the City of Albany. Pursuant to section 306, duplicate copies must be served and service is complete when the Secretary of State is so served (Business Corporation Law sec. 306 [b]). Pursuant to section 307, only one copy of process has to be served on the Secretary of State and a second copy, together with notice of service on the Secretary of State, must be personally delivered to the foreign corporation or sent to it by registered mail with return receipt requested; service is complete 10 days after an affidavit of compliance, together with certain other papers, is filed with the clerk of the court in which the action is pending (Business Corporation Law sec. 307 [b], [c]). We conclude that while the persons and place designated for service on the Secretary of State in these two statutes may be viewed as jurisdictional requirements with which there must be strict compliance (Meyer v Volkswagen of Am., 92 AD2d 488), mistakes or omissions with respect to the other requirements should be viewed as mere irregularities that, in the absence of prejudice to the defendant corporation, do not deprive the court of jurisdiction over the defendant and can be disregarded, pursuant to CPLR 2001 (Orzechowski v Warner-Lambert Co., 91 AD2d 681; Hoerning v Stihl Am., 70 AD2d 696). We reach this conclusion based largely upon the purpose of CPLR 311 (1), which necessarily extends to its companion statutes in the Business Corporation Law, to give the corporation notice of the commencement of the suit (Fashion Page v Zurich Ins. Co., 50 NY2d 265, 271, supra).

In the case at bar, process was delivered to a proper person and at the proper place for service on the Secretary of State, and defendant received a copy of the process via registered mail with return receipt requested. To deprive the court of jurisdiction over defendant merely because the wrong person (plaintiff's process server instead of the Secretary of State) actually placed defendant's copy of the process in the mail would exalt form over substance and impose the type of narrow and technical statutory construction criticized by the Court of Appeals in Fashion Page v Zurich Ins. Co. (supra). In this regard, we note that, although Business Corporation Law sec. 306 (b) requires the Secretary of State to send one of the duplicate copies of process to the authorized foreign corporation, the failure to do so is not a jurisdictional defect (Micarelli v Regal Apparel, 52 AD2d 524). We also note that a foreign corporation that has obtained authorization to do business in this State might reasonably expect that when an action is commenced against it by service on the Secretary of State, process will be forwarded to it by the Secretary of State, but we see no prejudice to defendant herein which received not only a copy of the process, but also notice of service on the Secretary of State. We hold, therefore, that service on defendant, a foreign corporation authorized to do business in this State, in accordance with the provisions of Business Corporation Law sec. 307, which is applicable in the case of an unauthorized foreign corporation, was sufficient to provide personal jurisdiction over defendant pursuant to CPLR 311 (1).

As to plaintiff's misstatement of defendant's name in the summons and complaint, such a misnomer is a mere irregularity which in no way affects jurisdiction.

In the Matter of Shigoto International Corporation
101 Misc. 2d 646 (1978)

In this article 78 proceeding, petitioners Shigoto International Corp., Shigoto Industries, Ltd., and Sekai Manufacturing Co., Inc., seek a judgment directing the respondent Secretary of State to strike the names Shigoto Far East Importers, Ltd., and Sekai Far East Importers, Ltd., from the index of authorized foreign corporations.

The court finds that the Secretary of State has abused his discretion by allowing the challenged names to be placed in the index of foreign corporations authorized to do business in the State of New York.

Section 301 (subd [a], par [2]) of the Business Corporation Law provides that: "Except as otherwise provided in this chapter, the name of a domestic or foreign corporation * * * Shall not be the same as the name of a corporation of any type or kind, as such name appears on the index of names existing domestic and authorized foreign corporations of any type or kind in the department of state, division or corporation, or a name the right to which is reserved, or a name so similar to any such name as to tend to confuse or deceive." (Emphasis supplied.)

The Department of State has wide discretion as to whether a name is so similar as to tend to confuse or deceive. However, if the choice of the name is so wanting in logical premise as to be violative of good sense and reason, the choice will be deemed to be an abuse of discretion (American Auto Accessories Stores v Lomenzo, 69 Misc 2d 972).

The respondent had previously disallowed the names Shigoto Far East Ltd. and Sekai Far East Ltd., but had permitted the indexing upon the addition of the word "Importers" to each name.

It is clear that the challenged names, either with or without "Importers" added thereto, tend to confuse and deceive the public, as would the use of the name "Chrysler Importers, Ltd." as opposed to "Chrysler Corporation" or "Sears Roebuck Importers, Ltd." as opposed to "Sears, Roebuck & Co., Inc."

Furthermore, out of the myriad of names that could have been used, the choice of the names Shigoto Far East (Importers) Ltd. and Sekai Far East (Importers) Ltd., could only have been made with the "intent to deceive." The court has made this determination even though the requirement of such intent is no longer necessary under section 301 (subd [a], par [2]) of the Business Corporation Law.

Although not relevant to the determination made herein, the court notes that petitioners' counsel has conceded, at the oral argument of this motion, that petitioner corporations are not in business at this time.

The petition is granted.

Pursuant to section 102(a)(10), the official office of the corporation is the address that appears in the corporation's certificate of incorporation. This is important to note, especially if the corporation is being sued and papers must be served on the corporate entity. In many instances, the location at which the corporate activities are carried out are not in the official "office" of the corporation.

> *Example: A New Jersey resident wishes to form a New York corporation for a business she is planning to start. At the present time, she has no address in New York, and so the law office puts its address on the certificate of incorporation for convenience. If the certificate is never amended (Chapter 11), the address of the law office remains the "office" for the corporation.*

Section 104 specifies certain requirements with respect to the certificate of incorporation:

1. The certificate must be written in English, except for the corporate name (see following).
2. The certificate must give a complete address for the corporation.
3. The certificate must be signed by the incorporator, subscribers for shares, a majority of the prospective directors, or a potential officer.
4. The certificate must be filed with the Department of State.

There is a fee that must be paid when filing the certificate of incorporation, and the complete schedule of fees for all corporate filings appears in section 104-A.

Section 109 of the BCL provides that the state Attorney General is authorized to bring an ex parte action against any person or entity who violates the provisions of the BCL, known as quo warranto proceedings (see following).

Corporate Purposes and Powers

As discussed in Chapter 5, corporations are creatures of state statutes, and therefore, in New York corporations may only have such purposes and powers as are permitted under the BCL. The purposes for which a corporation may be formed in New York are the powers that appear in Article 2 of the BCL.

Section 201 specifies that a New York corporation may be formed for "any lawful purpose." This is an extremely broad grant of authority, and most corporations so specify in their certificates of incorporation. However, a corporation may decide to assume more limited powers, and if it so wishes, it must specify the exact power it wishes to have in its certificate. However, if a corporation limits its purposes and a corporate opportunity presents itself in an area not so authorized, the corporation may not engage in the activity unless it amends its certificate to include that purpose.

> *Example: A corporation is formed to manufacture building supplies. After several years in the business, the corporation becomes aware of several opportunities to purchase undeveloped land and construct buildings on its own. Because the corporation had limited its purposes, it cannot take advantage of this business opportunity. It would be beyond the scope of its specific purposes.*

Section 202 lists all of the powers a New York corporation may have. The list is quite far-reaching; as a general concept in New York, corporations have the same legal powers as a natural person. As with the corporate purposes, if it so wishes, a corporation may elect to limit its powers by so specifying in its certificate of incorporation. However, as with the corporate purposes, if the corporation limits its powers, it may not engage in any activity that requires powers it has not assumed.

> *Example: A New York corporation may grant loans to its directors (Chapter 8). A corporation, in its certificate, decided not to accept such powers. Two years after its formation, one of the directors needs money, and the corporation is in a position to lend it to him. However, if the corporation goes ahead with the loan, it has violated its certificate of incorporation.*

Ultra vires — beyond the scope.

If a corporation or its directors enters into activities that go beyond the purpose and powers permitted in the BCL or assumed by the corporation in its certificate of incorporation or violates any other law, such corporate activity is deemed to be **ultra vires**, beyond the scope. In such instances, any injured party may sue the corporation or the directors for injuries suffered. The injured party may be a shareholder who may seek an injunction to stop the ultra vires action or damages from the directors or officers who perpetrated the actions that injure the corporation, or the state Attorney General who may bring suit against the corporation for violating the provisions of the BCL. Such actions by the Attorney General are called **quo warranto** proceedings, authorized by section 109, which are ex parte proceedings brought to revoke the corporate charter because the corporation engaged in ultra vires activities. These lawsuits by both the shareholder and the Attorney General are specified in section 203 of the BCL.

Quo warranto — action by Attorney General to revoke a corporate charter.

Corporate Name and Service of Process

Section 301 of the BCL mandates that all New York corporations have as part of their names the words "corporation," "incorporated," "limited," "corp.," "inc.," or "ltd." This requirement is imposed in order to alert members of the public who deal with the entity that they are dealing with a corporation. As a corollary, no other business entity is permitted to use those designations in their names.

The name of the corporation must be in English, but if it is in a different alphabet, it may be transliterated in to the Latin alphabet. Furthermore, corporations are precluded from using certain terms (which appear in the statute) that may mislead the public into believing that the corporation is a governmental subdivision or a charitable enterprise.

Name reservation form — document used to reserve a company name.

Every New York corporation must have a name that is unique to New York corporations. Section 303 of the BCL permits an organization to reserve a name prior to incorporation by filing a **name reservation form** (see Exhibit 6–2). This form must indicate:

a. the name of the person reserving the corporate name

b. the address of the person reserving the corporate name

c. the corporate name to be reserved

d. the reason for which the name reservation is sought

The form is sent to the Secretary of State, and a moderate fee is charged. Once granted, the name is reserved for a sixty-day period, and this period may be renewed. During this period, no other person may incorporate with the reserved name in New York. If a certificate of incorporation is filed with a name already in use, the certificate will be rejected by the Secretary of State and returned to the incorporator.

N. J. Henry Mfg. Co., Inc. v. Henry Screen Mfg. Co., Inc.
204 A.D. 27 (1922)

The action is brought to enjoin the use by defendant of its corporate name in connection with the business of manufacturing and selling screens and weather strips. Plaintiff also asked that the defendant be restrained from in any manner representing that it is the plaintiff or making any representations liable to lead the public to believe that it is the plaintiff. Some incidental relief was granted the plaintiff, the defendant being restrained from using a picture of a "Fly" and the words "The Original" upon its letterheads, literature, etc. Neither party appeals from this portion of the decree.

The plaintiff was incorporated October 28, 1918, to engage in the business of manufacturing window, door and porch screens and all kinds of weather strips, and ever since has been and now is engaged in that business with a salesroom and a factory in the borough of Brooklyn, city of New York. The object of the business is to sell direct to the individual householders desiring to install screens and weather strips in their homes, and to secure such business the plaintiff employs solicitors and resorts to advertising by descriptive circulars and has spent large sums of money therefor. The plaintiff has so conducted its business as to acquire a valuable reputation for integrity and efficient service. The business as established is very extensive and plaintiff's product has been widely advertised and is very well and favorably known; there has been and is a great demand therefor and it has secured a large number of customers in the borough of Brooklyn.

The defendant was organized August 15, 1921, to engage in the same business, and is now engaged in that business in the borough of Brooklyn. The defendant was incorporated and its name selected with full knowledge by all its stockholders and directors of all these facts. These facts are admitted by the pleadings and found by the court. In addition, the plaintiff proved by exhibits admitted in evidence and the court has found: "That the defendant, by doing business by means of the use or issuance of any letters, circulars, envelopes or other advertising descriptive, illustrative or printed matter imitative of or in any form similar to those used or issued by the plaintiff, and more particularly by using or issuing such of the defendant's letterheads, envelopes and circulars, advertising letters, as contain the pictures of the 'Fly' and the words 'The Original,' is liable to confuse the customers of the plaintiff under the belief by such customers that they are dealing with the plaintiff." N. J. Henry was one of the incorporators of the plaintiff and is still a stockholder therein. He is also one of the organizers of the defendant, a stockholder therein and the president thereof, his name appearing in that capacity on its letterheads.

The result of all the cases, as I view them, is that if the similarity of names is such that the public is likely to be deceived, then the plaintiff is entitled to the relief prayed for. A corporation cannot, by the adoption of a name so closely resembling that of another as to induce people to deal with it in the belief that they are dealing with the other, appropriate the business of the first corporation. A corporation which has established a valuable business with a valuable reputation built up by years of upright dealing and the expenditure of large sums of money for advertising cannot be deprived of that business by a corporation which adopts a name which so closely resembles the former as to deceive the public by leading it to believe that it is dealing with the former when dealing with the latter. The first corporation is the N. J. Henry Mfg. Co., Inc. It manufactures screens. It sets forth upon its letterheads (none of its literature was introduced in evidence) that its business is "Window, Door and Porch Screens," making it clear that screens are the principal feature of its business. The defendant's name as printed on its letterheads) is the "Henry Screen Mfg. Co., Inc." It is engaged in exactly the same business. It seems reasonably clear that many eople would think of and know the first corporation as the Henry Screen Company. It would be the natural and ordinary way to speak of it. Can it be doubted that as a practical matter this similarity of names is likely to deceive? It seems clear that it was intended to deceive. The defendant not only adopted a name so closely resembling plaintiff's, but it also adopted letterheads and envelopes that, except for the slight difference in names, street addresses and telephone calls, are duplicates of the plaintiff's.

The pictorial effect is the same. The plaintiff adorned its letterheads, etc., with pictures of several flies; the defendant did the same and placed them in exactly the same places on the paper and envelopes. The defendant also advertised as "The Original" above its name. These acts of the defendant have been restrained and properly so, but they serve to show defendant's intention and also to show that it thought the names so similar that one might be mistaken for the other, as it falsely stated it was "The Original." If there was no danger of mistake, this designation was unnecessary. Its purpose and its necessity are as clear as its falsity.

This confusion is rendered "worse confounded" by the fact that N. J. Henry, who was one of the incorporators of plaintiff and whose name forms a part of its corporate name, is now the president of the defendant and his name as such appears on its letterheads. Therefore, any one receiving a communication from defendant has every distinguishing feature of plaintiff's name presented to him on defendant's letterhead. It would take a very retentive and analytical memory to carry in mind the fact that the "Henry Screen Mfg. Co., Inc.," of which N. J. Henry is president, is not the same as the "N. J. Henry Mfg. Co., Inc.," which manufactures screens. This use of the name of N. J. Henry on defendant's letterheads cannot be restrained. The defendant has the right to elect him its president and to advertise that fact. That is a legitimate use of an individual name. (Meneely v. Meneely, 62 N. Y. 427; Higgins Co. v. Higgins Soap Co., 144 id. 463.) Those cases, however, clearly indicate that defendant's right to its corporate name is in no wise affected by the fact that one of its incorporators bears the name of Henry. The defendant derives no immunity from the fact that the name of "Henry" is in its corporate name. (Higgins Co. v. Higgins Soap Co., supra.)

I think it is reasonably clear that under the circumstances here disclosed the name of the defendant is so similar to that of the plaintiff as to cause confusion and to mislead and deceive plaintiff's customers and would-be customers.

The judgment in so far as appealed from should be reversed upon the law, with costs, and judgment directed in favor of the plaintiff restraining the defendant from using the name of "Henry Screen Mfg. Co., Inc.," or any corporate name in imitation of the name of the plaintiff, with costs.

A corporation, just like every other business entity in New York, may operate under a name different than its official name by the filing of a DBA form. (See Exhibit 6–3 for a Certificate of Assumed Name form.) Although similar to the DBA forms used by partnerships and sole proprietorships, this form is sent by the Secretary of State once the corporation is formed.

Section 304 of the BCL requires that all New York certificates of incorporation appoint the Secretary of State as agent for service of process on the corporation. Additionally, section 305 requires that the corporation appoint a registered agent as well.

The corporation's registered agent may be any natural person who resides or works in New York or another New York corporation. The registered agent may be appointed in the certificate of incorporation or may be appointed by filing a separate document with the Department of State.

Service of process on a New York corporation must be effectuated in one of the following ways:

1. If the registered agent is served, the party suing may use any method of service permitted under New York law.
2. If the Secretary of State is served, it must be personal service and the Secretary must be served with duplicate copies of the papers.

If the Secretary of State is served, the corporation is given an extra twenty days in which to respond because the Secretary of State must forward the documents to the corporation. In any instance in which the Secretary of State is served, the corporation is precluded from alleging improper service of process.

Formation

Incorporator — natural person over eighteen years of age who files and signs the certificate of incorporation, calls the organizational meeting of the corporation, and appoints the initial Board of Directors.

Many jurisdictions use the term *incorporator* to refer to the organizers of the corporate entity. In New York, the **incorporator** is specifically defined by Article 4 of the BCL and may be a person who has nothing to do with operating the business.

In New York, the incorporator must be a natural person, eighteen years of age or older. The incorporator in New York only has four functions:

1. signing the certificate of incorporation
2. filing the certificate of incorporation
3. calling the organizational meeting of the corporation (Chapter 8)
4. appointing the initial Board of Directors (Chapter 8)

These are the only functions of the incorporators, and often these functions are provided by an employee of the corporate service the law office is using to complete and file this paperwork.

Capitalization

Par — amount below which the directors may not sell a share of stock.

No par — no minimum value for corporate stock.

Probably the most important section of the certificate of incorporation concerns the capitalization of the corporation—how it is to be financed. Article 6 of the BCL requires that the certificate of incorporation specify the total number of authorized shares of the corporation, all classes of stock it may have, and all rights and obligations incident thereto. The certificate of incorporation must indicate whether the shares will have a par value or will have no par value. **Par** is an artificial number assigned to a share of stock that represents the minimum dollar amount the directors may receive for the stock when the share is first issued (Chapter 5). After the initial issue, once the share is outstanding, par is irrelevant. **No par** means that the directors may receive any amount of consideration for the sale of the share with no minimum amount required.

Example: Acme Corporation has authorized 1,000 shares of common stock with a $10 par value. At the first issue of 100 shares, the directors receive $10 per share for each share sold. Two days later, one of the shareholders changes her mind about owning the stock and sells her one share to a neighbor for $8. This is permitted. Par only applies to the initial issue of the share by the Board of Directors.

The purpose of having a par value is to assure potential shareholders that the corporation has actually received valuable consideration for the sale of the shares, so that there is something in the corporate coffers. Also, the amount assigned to par has an effect on the filing fee charged by the Department of State when the certificate of incorporation is filed.

Frankowski v. Palermo
47 A.D.2d 579 (1975)

Order unanimously reversed, with costs, and summary judgment granted plaintiff in accordance with the following memorandum: A cash purchase of par value stock cannot be made under section 504 of the Business Corporation Law for less than par value. In determining whether full par value has been paid for the issuance of par value stock, the cancellation of a corporation debt is considered equivalent to a cash payment in the amount of the debt.

At a meeting of the board of directors on April 27, 1972 attended by defendants Palermo and Wylegala, the minutes signed by the secretary of D & M Fish Shoppe, Inc., state that a discussion was had concerning the payment of certain loans made by president Palermo to the corporation and a resolution was passed that the corporation issue to Palermo sufficient stock at the present day book value to convert Palermo's loan on the books of the corporation into a capital investment. The minutes further state that it was determined that 44 shares of the stock of the corporation be issued to Palermo and that the sum of $2,726 be added to the capital of the corporation as a capital investment of Palermo. The financial report incorporated into the minutes of the April 27 meeting lists total loans from Palermo to the corporation in the amount of $2,726.

It appears from the minutes of the April 27 meeting that 44 shares of the stock of the corporation of the par value of $100 were issued to Palermo in exchange for the cancellation of the corporate debt in the amount of $2,726. Thus the minutes recite that Palermo paid $1,674 less than the $4,400 value of the 44 par value shares issued to him.

Shares issued for less than par value are voidable at the option of other shareholders absent the intervention of third-party rights. The minutes of the board of directors' meeting stating that $2,726 of corporate debt was canceled in favor of Palermo as consideration for the issuance of 44 shares of $100 par value stock constitute prima facie evidence of the facts stated in the minutes as to the transaction (Business Corporation Law, sec. 624, subd. [g]).

Respondents Palermo et al. do not challenge such consideration as recited in the minutes and in such a circumstance they should be bound by the prima facie provisions of subdivision (g) of section 624 of the Business Corporation Law. Plaintiff is entitled to judgment directing cancellation of the shares issued to defendant Palermo at less than par value, which judgment should provide that: (1) The action of the board of directors in issuing 44 shares of $100 par value stock in D & M Fish Shoppe, Inc., in consideration of the cancellation of the corporate debt to Palermo in the amount of $2,726 be nullified. (2) The directors of the corporation be ordered to record in the books of the corporation the cancellation of the 44 shares. (3) The board of directors be directed to call a stockholders meeting forthwith and no new shares be issued by the directors prior to such meeting.

For corporations formed on or after February 22, 1998, if preemptive rights are to attach, they must be specified in the certificate of incorporation, or such rights will not exist. For corporations formed prior to February 22, 1998, the New York courts, under their equitable jurisdiction, could permit **quasi-preemptive rights** to protect shareholders, even if such rights were not specified in the certificate of incorporation.

A complete discussion of corporate finance appears in Chapter 7.

Quasi-preemptive rights
—preemptive rights granted by court action; no longer available in New York.

Other Matters

In addition to the foregoing, the certificate of incorporation may include any other item of appropriate corporate business. Some examples of such items are:

a. a directors' indemnification clause
b. number of directors
c. retaining certain corporate decisions for shareholder approval
d. certain stock rights and options
e. staggered Board of Directors

Basically, any item that would appear in the by-laws may be placed in the certificate of incorporation. The decision as to where to place the item is made based on whether the organizers wish the item to be easy or difficult to change. Corporate by-laws may be amended by a vote of the Board of Directors, whereas a certificate of incorporation may only be amended by a vote of the shareholders, meaning it is more complicated to effect. However, the certificate of incorporation may not include any matter that would be violative of general law or policy.

Lastly, the certificate of incorporation may indicate the duration of the corporate entity. New York corporations may exist in perpetuity and are assumed to be so created unless a statement to the contrary appears in the certificate.

Once the certificate is filed with the Secretary of State, the corporation comes into existence.

Haenel v. Epstein
88 A.D.2d 652 (1982)

In an action, inter alia, for a permanent injunction, plaintiff appeals (1) from an order of the Supreme Court, Nassau County (Burke, J.), dated March 23, 1981, which denied her motion for a preliminary injunction and granted "defendants'" cross motion for summary judgment, and (2) from a judgment of the same court, entered upon the order on April 13, 1981, which, inter alia, determined that defendants Epstein and Procton were entitled to indemnification by Allmetal Screw Products Company, Inc., for the expenses they incurred in defense of another action.

Prior to the instant action, plaintiff Beatrice Haenel brought a nonderivative suit against these defendants and others seeking, among other things, to enjoin a board of directors appointed by defendant Epstein pursuant to a 1969 shareholders' agreement from taking any actions and to direct Epstein to agree with her upon a board pursuant to a 1977 agreement, to which only some of the shareholders were parties. By decision dated May 20, 1980 (Spatt, J.), the 1977 agreement was held to be invalid and the complaint was dismissed. This judgment was thereafter appealed and the appeal is still pending.

Defendants Procton and Epstein, two directors of defendant Allmetal, notified Sylvan Haenel, the third director and husband of plaintiff, that a special meeting would be held on August 25, 1980 to consider the appointment of Bertram Harnett, pursuant to section 724 (subd [b], par [2]) of the Business Corporation Law, to give an opinion as to whether Procton and Epstein were entitled to indemnification pursuant to section 723 of the Business Corporation Law for their expenses incurred in defense of the initial suit. Over Mr. Haenel's objection, Harnett was appointed and plaintiff commenced this action, inter alia, for injunctive relief.

Special Term was correct in its determination that defendants Epstein and Procton had met the requirements for indemnification under subdivision (a) of section 723 of the Business Corporation Law, that is, that they had been sued as directors and had acted in good faith for the best interests of the corporation. However, the court was incorrect in its finding that, pursuant to subdivision (a) of section 724 of said law, indemnification of these defendants was "mandatory" as they had been "wholly successful."

Where the action for which indemnification is sought is pending on appeal, it cannot be said that the defendant directors have been "wholly successful." Rather, this situation is covered in subdivision (c) of section 724 of the Business Corporation Law, which provides that the corporation may pay the expenses incurred in a civil proceeding brought under section 722 or 723 of the Business Corporation Law in advance of the final disposition in the manner authorized by subdivision (b) of section 724. Under this section, payment is allowed if authorized by the board acting by a quorum of disinterested directors, or, if such quorum is not obtainable with due diligence—as here—section 724 (subd [b], par [2], cl [A]) provides that "indemnification * * * shall be made by the corporation * * * [by] the board upon the opinion in writing of independent legal counsel that indemnification is proper."

Contrary to plaintiff's contention, the appointment of Mr. Harnett was properly made. The individual defendants were not prohibited from voting on his appointment as they were not "interested" within the meaning of section 713 of the Business Corporation Law. Neither would said defendants be disabled from voting on indemnification following a favorable recommendation by the independent counsel, as section 724 (subd [b], par [2], cl [A]), by the use of the term "shall," requires the board to give its approval (see 3 White, New York Corporations [13th ed], par 724.02). We must note, as we did in Nelson v Nationwide Measuring Serv. (64 AD2d 606, 607), that the corporation should not be represented by an attorney who also represents one of the individual defendant directors.

DEFECTS IN FORMATION

There are circumstances in which a person may wish to challenge the legality of the corporate existence. This occurs when the person is seeking to attach the personal assets of the corporate owners. One of the primary advantages of the corporation is the limited liability for its owners. However, if it can be demonstrated that the corporation was not properly formed, that shield against personal liability is lost, and the owners are treated as general partners (or sole proprietors if there is only one shareholder) with unlimited personal liability.

If a corporation's status is attacked, the corporation may defend by asserting one of two claims:

De jure corporation — validly formed corporation.

1. *It is a de jure corporation.* A **de jure corporation** is one that is organized in substantial compliance with the law. In other words, complete compliance is not necessary to find that a corporation has been validly formed.

   Example: An entity completes and files its certificate of incorporation, but it forgets to appoint a registered agent. In this instance, it is most likely that it will be found to be a de jure corporation.

De facto corporation — business that has acted in good faith as a corporation so that the courts will consider it to be a corporation.

2. *It is a de facto corporation.* A **de facto corporation** is one that is treated as being a corporation even though it has not substantially complied with the provisions of the BCL. To be found a de facto corporation, the entity must prove the following:

   (a) There is a law under which it could have incorporated.

   (b) It made a good faith attempt to comply with that law.

   (c) It acted like a corporation in good faith.

The determination as to whether a corporation is de jure or de facto is made on a case by case basis.

Garzo v. Maid of the Mist Steamboat Company
303 N.Y. 516 (1952)

The General Corporation Law (sec. 45) provides that a corporation, the term of whose existence under its certificate of incorporation is about to expire, may file a certificate extending its corporate existence for a term of years or in perpetuity, by authority of a majority of its members or the holders of a majority of its stock. Under section 49 (eff. April 6, 1944) a like certificate may be filed after the stated term of existence of a corporation has expired (except where liquidation has been initiated and except in certain other circumstances listed in subdivision 11). The language of section 49 and its legislative history show that it validly applies retrospectively to a going corporation such as the one in this case, which inadvertently permitted its fifty-year term of duration to expire in 1942 and which filed a certificate of revival of existence in 1947 under section 49.

When the present corporation was organized in 1892, the predecessor of section 45 was already in existence, and became part of the corporation's charter by operation of law. Section 49, enacted in 1944, in effect permits a going corporation, which has inadvertently omitted to file a certificate under section 45, to file one after the expiration of the term set forth in its certificate of incorporation. The new section makes no organic change and violates no constitutional prohibition against the enactment of retroactive laws. The predecessor of section 45 required the consent of the holders of two thirds of the stock, and the revival in this case has been consented to by the holders of approximately three fourths of the stock. The State has reserved the power to alter corporation laws and charters. (N.Y.

Const., art. X, sec. 1; General Corporation Law, sec. 5.) A corporation whose charter has expired continues to have a de jure existence for the purpose of winding up its affairs (General Corporation Law, sec. 29). Further, where, as here, a corporation continues to carry on its business, it is a de facto corporation as well, and no one but the State may question its existence.

Section 49 does not afford objecting minority stockholders (such as plaintiffs in this action to dissolve the corporation and distribute its assets) a right to be paid the appraised cash value of their stock. It is not necessary to determine whether such a right must be provided in order to validate an organic or fundamental change. The extension after inadvertent expiration in this case was not such a fundamental change.

In the case before us, the corporation inadvertently neglected to provide for the extension of its charter during its fifty-year term. There was no thought in anyone's mind of permitting the company to expire or come to an end. Its business and its activities continued precisely as before, and—prior to the institution of this proceeding—plaintiffs continued, without protest, to enjoy their rights as stockholders in the going enterprise. Section 49 and the revival of the corporation under it only served therefore to remedy an oversight and to allow the regular continuance of the corporate enterprise in accordance with the intent and expectation of all those connected with it. A statute which thus "simply enlarges" the term of a corporation involves no "organic" change and violates no constitutional prohibition against the passage of retroactive laws.

The power reserved to the state to alter corporation laws and charters is specific and ample warrant for this legislation. The mere ending of the corporate term did not render such reserve power inoperative. Corporations whose charters may have expired continue to have a de jure existence for the purpose of winding up their affairs, and, to that end, meetings may be held, corporate property conveyed, suits brought and defended, directors elected and debts paid (General Corporation Law, sec. 29). In addition, where, as here, a corporation carries on its affairs and exercises corporate powers as before, it is a de facto corporation as well, and ordinarily no one but the state may question its corporate existence.

In point of fact, as already noted, section 49 is limited in its application to corporations which have neither determined to dissolve nor taken steps looking toward dissolution (subd. 11). The statute was not enacted to resuscitate a lifeless corpse or to operate in a vacuum; it was put into the law, and is here invoked, to deal with a truly functioning enterprise. As Judge SEARS, sitting at Special Term, sagely observed in Wilson v. Brown (107 Misc. 167, 174): "If the analogy of physical death is sought to be applied to the expiration of the term of corporate existence of an organization which the law recognizes as a person, it is easy to answer that there is no greater difficulty in considering the organization as existing after its death than before its birth. * * * Such analogies are often misleading. Physical life with birth and death is an evidence of immutable natural law. Corporate life rests upon legislative fiat, and there is no reason to apply such a doubtful analogy to such a case as this, where the same kind of acts, in so far as the corporate character of the same is concerned, were done by men similarly authorized by their associates after, as before, the limit of the term of the corporation's existence."

The courts will not fail, then, to look beyond the letter of the corporate charter and apply the legislative mandate to the practical situation which it was designed to meet. Thus, in Delaware & Hudson Co. v. Mechanicville & F.E.R.R. Co. (268 N.Y. 394), this court was asked to rule that an action could not be brought to procure a judgment "dissolving" a corporation whose charter had already expired. In holding that such an action would lie, the court declared: "We think that the Legislature so intended. We are not now concerned with legal dialectics but with practical administration of law" (p. 398). So, here, it was the legislative design that a corporation such as the one before us might be revived after expiry of the term specified in its charter. Under the state's broad reserve power, that design must be given effect.

Corporation by estoppel
—equitable doctrine precluding a challenge to a business's corporate status; not permitted in New York.

It should be noted that some jurisdictions permit an entity to defend an attack on its status by claiming that it is a **corporation by estoppel**, which acts to shield the shareholders from personal liability only against that particular challenger because that challenger knew it was not a valid corporation and now seeks to take advantage of that fact. Such defense is not available in New York.

CHAPTER REVIEW

A corporation comes into existence in New York once its certificate of incorporation has been filed with the Secretary of State. The requirements for the certificate of incorporation appear in the BCL and may be summarized as follows:

1. The certificate must be in English (except for the name).
2. The certificate must be signed.
3. The name of the corporation must be unique to corporations in New York and must include the words "corporation," "incorporation," "limited," "corp.," "inc.," or "ltd."
4. The certificate must indicate an office with a complete address.
5. The certificate must appoint the Secretary of State as agent for service of process.
6. The certificate must indicate the purpose for which the corporation is formed.
7. The certificate must indicate all of the powers the corporation wishes to assume.
8. The certificate must specify all information with respect to the corporate shares.
9. The certificate must indicate the corporation's duration if it is not to be perpetual.
10. The certificate may indicate any other appropriate corporate matters.

If the corporation's status is challenged, the corporation may defend by asserting that it is either legally (de jure) or factually (de facto) formed.

KEY TERMS

Alien corporation	Domestic corporation
Application for Certificate of Authority	Foreign corporation
Assignee	Incorporator
Assignment	Name reservation form
Corporation by estoppel	No par
De facto corporation	Novation
De jure corporation	Organizer

Par
Preincorporation share subscription
Promissee
Promoter

Quasi-preemptive rights
Quo warranto
Share subscription
Ultra vires

EXERCISES

1. Check the appropriate section of the BCL to determine which terms are prohibited for use in a corporate name.
2. What would be the long-term effect of a court finding an entity to be a de facto corporation? Explain.
3. Locate the names and addresses of three corporate services in your area and find out their fees.
4. Why are quo warranto proceedings ex parte? Explain.
5. Indicate some reasons why a corporation might wish to limit its corporate purposes.

FACTUAL PROBLEM

A family business has been operating in New York for the past fifty years as a corporation manufacturing jewelry findings. Recently the company has undergone financial reverses, and several suppliers are suing for breach of contract. The suppliers discover that the business never in fact incorporated. The family thought they had incorporated, but the founder of the company has been dead for ten years and no records exist. The company has paid corporate income taxes every year it has operated. Argue the rights and obligations of both sides.

Certificate of Incorporation of

under Section 402 of the Business Corporation Law

IT IS HEREBY CERTIFIED THAT:

(1) The name of the corporation is

(2) The purpose or purposes for which this corporation is formed, are as follows, to wit:
To engage in any lawful act or activity for which corporations may be organized under the Business Corporation Law. The corporation is not formed to engage in any act or activity requiring the consent or approval of any state official, department, board, agency or other body.*

The corporation, in furtherance of its corporate purposes above set forth, shall have all of the powers enumerated in Section 202 of the Business Corporation Law, subject to any limitations provided in the Business Corporation Law or any other statute of the State of New York.

*If specific consent or approval is required delete this paragraph, insert specific purposes and obtain consent or approval prior to filing.

Exhibit 6–1

Certificate of Incorporation *(Forms may be purchased from BlumbergExcelsior, Inc. or any of its dealers. Reproduction prohibited.)*

(3)   The office of the corporation is to be located in the County of
State of New York.

(4)   The aggregate number of shares which the corporation shall have the authority to issue and a statement of the par value of each share or a statement that the shares are without par value are

Exhibit 6–1

Certificate of Incorporation *(Forms may be purchased from BlumbergExcelsior, Inc. or any of its dealers. Reproduction prohibited.)*

(5) The Secretary of State is designated as agent of the corporation upon whom process against it may be served. The post office address to which the Secretary of State shall mail a copy of any process against the corporation served upon the Secretary of State is

(6) A director of the corporation shall not be liable to the corporation or its shareholders for damages for any breach of duty in such capacity except for

(i) liability if a judgment or other final adjudication adverse to a director establishes that his or her acts or omissions were in bad faith or involved intentional misconduct or a knowing violation of law or that the director personally gained in fact a financial profit or other advantage to which he or she was not legally entitled or that the director's acts violated BCL § 719, or

(ii) liability for any act or omission prior to the adoption of this provision.

The undersigned incorporator, or each of them if there are more than one, is of the age of eighteen years or over.

IN WITNESS WHEREOF, this certificate has been subscribed on   by the undersigned incorporator(s).

Type name of incorporator   Signature

Address

Type name of incorporator   Signature

Address

Type name of incorporator   Signature

Address

*Publisher's Note: If you wish to grant preemptive rights to shareholders, you may type the following in the blank space:

(7) The holders of any of the corporation's equity shares shall be entitled to preemptive rights in accordance with the provisions of BCL § 622.

Exhibit 6–1
Certificate of Incorporation *(Forms may be purchased from BlumbergExcelsior, Inc. or any of its dealers. Reproduction prohibited.)*

T284— Application for Reservation of
Corporate Name, BCL & N-PCL, 8-97

© 1997 **Blumberg**Excelsior Inc.
PUBLISHER, ALBANY, NY

Department of State
Division of Corporations
41 State Street
Albany, New York 12231

Sirs:

Application is hereby made to reserve a corporate name and the following is set forth in support of the application. This application is made pursuant to the ☐ Business Corporation Law
☐ Not-for-Profit Corporation Law.

(1) Applicant's name and address—

(2) Name to be reserved—

(3) The basis for the reservation is—

☐ Applicant intends to form a domestic corporation.

☐ Applicant, a domestic corporation, intends to change its name.

☐ Applicant a foreign corporation, intends to make application for authority to do business in this state.

☐ Applicant, an authorized foreign corporation, intends to change its name.

☐ Applicant intends to incorporate a foreign corporation under the laws of the state of
and have said foreign corporation apply for authority to do business in this state.

☐ Applicant is a foreign corporation. It intends to use a fictitious name because its name (in its original jurisdiction) is not available in New York State.

☐ Applicant, an authorized foreign corporation, intends to change its fictitious name.

(4) The nature of the business to be conducted.

(5) The location of the principal office will be in the county of

(6) Accompanying this application is a certified check for $
Business Corporation $20.
Not-for-Profit Corporation $10.
Additional for expedited service $25.

Very truly yours,

_____
Type name of applicant

by _____
Signature

Certificate of reservation to be sent to:

☐ Applicant at above address

☐ Agent _____

address _____

_____

☐ Attorney _____

address _____

_____

Exhibit 6–2

Application for Reservation of Corporate Name *(Forms may be purchased from BlumbergExcelsior, Inc. or any of its dealers. Reproduction prohibited.)*

DEPARTMENT OF STATE, DIVISION OF CORPORATIONS   Re: _____
41 State Street, Albany, N.Y. 12231-0001

_____
Entity name

_____
Assumed name

Please file the enclosed Certificate of Assumed Name for the above entity. Fees* for filing of $ _____ are enclosed.

☐ Please forward _____ certified copy(ies) of the original certificate. Fees* of $ _____ for certified copy(ies) are enclosed.

Our* _____ check for $ _____ to cover the cost of filing and the certified copy(ies) is enclosed. Send the receipt(s) and certified copy(ies) to _____

_____

Print or type name _____   Signature _____   Tel. No. _____
*See reverse for fees, methods of payment and instructions.

Separate at perforation before mailing.   © 1998 by **Blumberg**Excelsior, Inc.

Certificate of Assumed Name *Pursuant to General Business Law, §130*

1. Name of entity

2. Business formed under (check one):
   ☐ Business Corporation Law   ☐ Insurance Law   ☐ Not-for-Profit Corporation Law
   ☐ Education Law   ☐ Limited Liability Company Law   ☐ Revised Limited Partnership Act
   ☐ Other (specify law): _____

3. Assumed name

4. Principal place of business in New York State (must be number and street. If none, insert out-of-state address)

5. Counties in which business will be conducted under assumed name
   ☐ ALL COUNTIES (if not, circle county[ies] below)

Albany	Clinton	Genesee	Monroe	Orleans	Saratoga	Tompkins
Allegany	Columbia	Greene	Montgomery	Oswego	Schenectady	Ulster
Bronx	Cortland	Hamilton	Nassau	Otsego	Schoharie	Warren
Broome	Delaware	Herkimer	New York	Putnam	Schuyler	Washington
Cattaraugus	Dutchess	Jefferson	Niagara	Queens	Seneca	Wayne
Cayuga	Erie	Kings	Oneida	Rensselaer	Steuben	Westchester
Chautauqua	Essex	Lewis	Onondaga	Richmond	Suffolk	Wyoming
Chemung	Franklin	Livingston	Ontario	Rockland	Sullivan	Yates
Chenango	Fulton	Madison	Orange	St. Lawrence	Tioga	

6. Number and street address(es) and county of each business location within New York State
   (Use continuation sheet, if needed)   ☐ No New York State Business Location

INSTRUCTIONS FOR SIGNATURE: If corporation, by an officer or director; if limited partnership, by a general partner; if limited liability company, by a member or manager; or authorized person, or attorney-in-fact for such corporation, limited partnership, or limited liability company.

Type or print name	Capacity in which signed	Signature

Filer's name _____   Date filed _____
                                                                For Department of State Only

Filer's address _____
                No. and Street   City   State   Zip Code

Blumberg Law Products   * **T 339**—Certificate of assumed name, corporation: 11-98   **Blumberg**Excelsior, Inc., NYC 10013

Exhibit 6–3
Certificate of Assumed Name *(Forms may be purchased from BlumbergExcelsior, Inc. or any of its dealers. Reproduction prohibited.)*

Chapter 7

Financing the Corporation

INTRODUCTION

As is apparent from the preceding chapter, for the most part the process of incorporation is a fairly rote procedure. However, there is one section of the certificate of incorporation that does require planning and forethought: the capitalization of the corporation.

Most new businesses fail because they have been inadequately or inappropriately financed. Corporate capital is obtained principally from investors and creditors who exchange money, property, or services for securities issued by the corporate entity. The term **security** is defined as a contractual, proprietary obligation that exists between a business enterprise and an investor. For corporations, securities fall into two broad categories: debt and equity.

Debt security refers to securities issued by the business enterprise representing a long-term loan. The person who acquires the debt security becomes a creditor of the corporation. **Equity security** refers to the shares of stock issued by the corporation to persons who wish to become owners of the enterprise. In order to have a corporation, or any business for that matter, properly financed, the organizer must determine initially what will be the optimum debt-equity ratio for the business.

The **debt-equity ratio** refers to the percentage of capital raised by borrowing funds in relation to the percentage of capital raised by selling an ownership interest in the business. Few, if any, businesses are financed wholly by either debt or equity; rather, each industry has certain average debt-equity ratios that have been developed over the years to reflect the perceived optimum debt-equity mix for the industry. For the organizer of the corporation, ascertaining this optimum mix for the industry in which it will incorporate is crucial. People will neither loan funds to nor invest funds in a business whose financial structure varies greatly from the industry norm. Even though the certificate of incorporation is only concerned with the equity portion of the equation, the organizer must have made appropriate financial decisions prior to indicating the number and types of authorized shares that will appear in the certificate.

Security — proprietory interest in a business.

Debt security — bonds and debentures.

Equity security — stock.

Debt-equity ratio — proportion of capitalization that is derived from loans as opposed to ownership.

This chapter details the financial decisions that must be made prior to filing the certificate of incorporation and discusses the various financing strategies the organizer may employ.

DEBT SECURITIES

Even though the debt securities do not appear in the certificate of incorporation, the percentage of funds the corporation intends to raise by means of debt must be determined prior to the decision as to the quality and quantity of equity securities the organizers will authorize to raise funds by means of selling ownership interests.

Debt securities fall into two broad categories: bonds and debentures. A **bond** is a long-term loan issued by a business (or the government) that is secured by some property. This security, or **collateral**, is available to the creditors, known as **bondholders**, in case the corporation defaults on the loan, and no other corporate creditor can attach that collateral before the bondholder. The most frequently used collateral for a corporate bond is cash held in a trust account known as a **sinking fund.** The percentage of the total loan kept in this account will vary, but it is usually no more than 10 percent of the total bond. A **debenture** operates in the same fashion as a bond, but it is not secured. For simplicity, the term *bond* is used to detail the operation of these securities unless a specific difference must be noted.

A bond is a long-term loan made to the business; the average life of a bond is 20 to 30 years, although bonds may be issued for longer or shorter periods. The amount that the bondholder pays (loans) for the bond is indicated on the bond and is known as the **face value.** This is the amount the debtor will return to the bondholder when the bond "matures," that is, becomes due, known as the **maturity date** which also appears on the face of the bond.

In exchange for receiving the funds, the debtor agrees not only to repay the loan, but also to pay the bondholder for the use of the funds. The amount the bondholder receives is known as the **interest rate**, which represents the bondholder's return on his or her investment. The amount of interest the debtor must pay depends on the risk incident in the investment: the greater the risk, the higher the interest rate. The appropriate interest rate ranges between the rate of interest the federal government pays on its bonds for a like period of time (government securities have a **risk free interest rate** because the obligation is backed by the full faith and credit of the United States) to whatever the market will bear for risky investments. When the interest rate is determined, it is also printed on the face of the bond.

The issuer (debtor) typically agrees to distribute the interest periodically, usually twice per year. At maturity, the bondholder receives the face value back from the issuer.

> *Example: Acme Corporation decides to raise capital by issuing a bond. It creates a 20-year bond for a face value of $100,000 with an interest rate of 8% per annum, payable in two distributions per year. The person who acquires the instrument will pay $100,000 for the bond. Every year for twenty years she will receive $4,000 in interest every six months. At the maturity date, she will have the $100,000 returned, and the obligation will be discharged.*

The preceding example indicates how a bond generally operates. However, time and market fluctuations may vary this scenario. For example, assume that on the day the bond goes to the printer, the 8% interest rate was reasonable. By the time the bond comes back

Bond — secured debt security.

Collateral — security for a debt.

Bondholders — owners of a secured debt.

Sinking fund — account maintained as security for bondholders.

Debenture — unsecured debt security.

Face value — amount appearing on debt security representing amount debtor will pay on maturity.

Maturity date — day when debt security must be repaid.

Interest rate — return on investment for a creditor.

Risk free interest rate — interest rate paid by government backed securities.

from the printer, interest rates have gone up. At this point, a 9% interest rate would be more appropriate. Now investors will look for a 9% rate of return on an investment with similar risk factors. In order to sell this bond with the 8% interest rate printed on it, the bond will have to be sold at a discount. A **discount** means the creditor pays less than the face value for the instrument. This increases the actual rate of return the bondholder receives.

Discount — purchasing a debt security at less than face value to increase the actual rate of return.

> *Example: Using the numbers from the preceding example, the bondholder pays $95,000 for the bond. Every year she still receives $8,000 in interest because that is printed on the bond (8% of $100,000). However, $8,000 is more than an 8% rate of interest on a $95,000 investment. Furthermore, at the maturity date the bondholder will receive the face value printed on the bond—$100,000. All of this increases the bondholder's actual rate of return.*

Assume the opposite situation. Now the interest rates have fallen, and the 8% rate appearing on the bond is now a very good rate of return, higher than the issuer would have to pay if the bond were printed at this moment. Now the bond will probably be sold at a **premium**, an amount over the face value of the bond that works to reduce the bondholder's actual rate of return.

Premium — paying more than the face value for a debt security to reduce the actual rate of return.

> *Example: Using the same figures from the preceding examples, now the appropriate interest rate for the bond would be 7%. The bondholder purchases the bond for $105,000, the $5,000 reflecting the change in interest rates. The bondholder still receives $8,000 per year, but that is less than an 8% rate of return on an investment of $105,000. Additionally, at maturity the bondholder will only receive the face value from the corporation—$100,000—all of which acts to reduce his or her actual rate of return.*

Determining the appropriate rate of return is crucial to the marketability of the bond and the amount of capital that the issuer will likely receive.

The preceding example describes the most typical type of bond known as a coupon bond. A **coupon bond** is a secured debt that makes periodic distributions of interest to the creditor. Historically (before computers), bonds actually had coupons attached to them, and at each interest distribution date, the bondholder would clip the coupon from the bond and turn it in to the issuer to receive the interest payment. When there were no more coupons left, the bond matured.

Coupon bond — bond that makes periodic distributions of interest.

Over the past several decades, a variation of this type of bond has become popular. This bond known as a zero coupon bond. A **zero coupon bond** is a bond that makes no periodic distribution of income but accumulates the interest until maturity. Zero coupon bonds are sold at very deep discounts so that the price the bondholder pays plus the accumulated interest (which itself generates interest) will equal the face value at the maturity date. An example of a zero coupon bond is the U.S. government Series E Savings Bond.

Zero coupon bond — bonds that make no periodic distribution of interest.

During the 1980s, a period of tremendous corporate expansion, a term came into common parlance to describe bonds issued by very risky issuers: junk bonds. A **junk bond** is an ordinary bond whose underlying issuer is in serious financial difficulty, meaning that it is more probable than not that the issuer will default. In order to attract bondholders, the issuer would have to offer an extraordinarily high interest rate to reflect the degree of risk

Junk bond — bond issued by a financially risky issuer.

associated with the issuer's business. The term *junk bond* became a marketing tool, but legally the junk bond is no different than any other type of corporate debt security.

Promissory note — short-term loan.

Corporations may also acquire capital by taking out a short-term loan known as a **promissory note.** Although these loans affect the debt-equity ratio, because they are short-term they are usually excluded from the concept of a debt security. The short duration of the loan goes against the definition of "security" as a proprietary interest in the issuer. The person who holds a three-year promissory note does not have the proprietary interest in the debtor that a bondholder of a thirty-year bond has. Most financial professionals exclude promissory notes of less than five or ten years duration from the concept of a debt security.

Law Research Service, Inc. v. Franklin Corporation
26 A.D.2d 478 (1966)

Pursuant to an agreement between the parties dated March 15, 1965, plaintiff issued and sold to defendant at par $125,000 principal amount of 8% debentures, due April 1, 1972, $78,750 thereof being convertible at defendant's option into shares of plaintiff's common stock. Section 9.10 of the agreement provides in pertinent part as follows: "In the event that any or all of the Convertible Debentures shall be prepaid, in part or in whole, prior to April 1, 1972, the holder thereof shall nevertheless have and continue to have, through April 1, 1972, the right to purchase from the Company, for cash, at a price equal to the Conversion Price from time to time, the number of shares of Common Stock issuable upon conversion of Debentures into which the principal amount so prepaid would, in the absence of such prepayment, have been convertible under the provisions of this Section 9 at the time of such purchase." All of the debentures have been paid, in the circumstances related below. Whether they were "prepaid" within the meaning of section 9.10 is the issue in dispute.

By letter to plaintiff dated July 6, 1965, and acting under provisions of the agreement permitting acceleration of the stated maturity of the debentures upon the occurrence of defined "Events of Default" defendant declared all of the debentures due and payable by reason of default in payment of the July 1, 1965 interest installment. Plaintiff contended it had made timely tender of the installment, but this was denied by defendant. On July 7, 1965 plaintiff tendered the amount of the installment, but it was rejected. Further declarations that the debentures were due and payable were made by defendant later in July for asserted failure of plaintiff to obtain insurance on the life of its president and to furnish defendant with certain financial statements. On October 11, 1965 plaintiff commenced an action for a declaration that it was not in default under the March 15, 1965 agreement. Counterclaims interposed by defendant alleged that the debentures had been declared due and payable by reason of "Events of Default" and demanded judgment for the principal amount of the debentures, together with interest and attorneys' fees. On or about January 26, 1966 (1) plaintiff paid defendant $125,000, together with an amount equal to interest thereon at the rate of 8% per annum for the period April 1, 1965 to July 7, 1965, and at the rate of 6% per annum for the period July 8, 1965 to January 26, 1966; (2) plaintiff paid defendant's attorneys an agreed fee; (3) a stipulation was executed discontinuing the action, including the counterclaims, with prejudice; and (4) the debentures were surrendered to plaintiff stamped "Paid."

Plaintiff's common stock is traded in the over-the-counter market. The bid price per share was quoted at $2.375 on July 1, 1965; $2 on October 11, 1965; and $12.50 on January 26, 1966. On March 2, 1966, when the bid price was $28.25, defendant tendered plaintiff a check for $78,750 and notified plaintiff that it was exercising its right under section 9.10 of the debenture agreement to purchase 25,000 shares at the price of $3.15 a share, a figure computed as provided in the section. Plaintiff, however, deeming the section inapplicable, rejected the tender and brought the present action for a declaration that defendant has no rights under the section. Defendant counterclaimed for specific performance or, if not decreed, for damages in the amount of $627,500 (the difference between $28.25 and $3.15 applied to 25,000 shares). Both parties appeal from an order denying their respective motions for summary judgment.

We think the debentures were not "prepaid" within the contemplation of section 9.10. Grouped in section 5 of the debenture agreement are a number of provisions relating to "prepayments, optional or required." Section 5.1 requires plaintiff to "make prepayments of the Debentures * * * at par, without premium" in the amount of $6,250 quarterly commencing July 1, 1967. Subdivision (a) of section 5.2 provides that plaintiff "may, from time to time, apply to the prepayment of the Debentures * * * at par and without penalty, on any prepayment date specified in Section 5.1, a sum which, together with all other prepayments made under this Section 5.2(a) in the same fiscal year of the Company, will not exceed $25,000 in the aggregate." Subdivision (b) of section 5.2 provides that "in addition to the optional prepayments permitted under Section 5.2(a), the Company may, at its option, upon not less than 10 days' prior written notice to the holders of the Debentures, at any time and from time to time, after April 1, 1966, prepay the Debentures" in part or in whole at par plus a specified premium varying in amount with the 12 months period in which the "prepayment date" occurs.

Section 9.10 is not to be construed in isolation, and when read in the light of the considered delineation of the types and modes of prepayment—expressly denominated as such—in section 5, the conclusion seems inevitable that "prepaid" in section 9.10 was intended to refer to section 5 prepayments. Defendant's notices of acceleration were sent pursuant to section 10, which provides that in the event of a default "the holders of not less than 25% of the unpaid principal amount of Debentures then outstanding may at their option, by written notice to the Company, declare all of the Debentures to be due and payable, whereupon the maturity of the then unpaid balance of all of the Debentures shall be accelerated and the same, and all interest accrued thereon, shall forthwith become due and payable." We find nothing in section 10 which implies any relevant equivalence between prepayment of debentures and payment of debentures declared due by reason of default.

Defendant is an investment company federally licensed to finance "small-business concerns." The debenture agreement, a document running 60 pages in the record, was prepared by defendant and with manifest care. It is hardly conceivable that section 9.10 would have been phrased as it was had the construction defendant now espouses been intended. We are not persuaded by the argument that unless that construction is adopted it would have lain within plaintiff's power to destroy defendant's rights under section 9.10 by committing an intentional default. The argument would base contract interpretation on the assumption that the parties will act in bad faith and it underestimates the ability of courts to frustrate acts of bad faith should one occur.

The order appealed from should be modified, on the law, to the extent of granting plaintiff's motion for summary judgment, and, as so modified, affirmed, with costs and disbursements to plaintiff.

EQUITY SECURITIES

Equity securities, like debt securities, fall into two broad categories: common stock and preferred stock.

Common Stock

Equity securities refer to ownership interests that an investor acquires by exchanging money, property, or services for corporate shares. The authority for a corporation to issue shares appears in Article 5 of the BCL, which states that a corporation may issue all manner of shares and classes of stock *provided* that at least one security entitles the holder to the common stock rights. The common stock rights, as discussed in Chapter 5, are the right to vote, the right to receive dividends if declared by the Board of Directors, and the right to the assets of the corporation on dissolution. The actual **share** itself represents to the **shareholder**, or **stockholder**, a property interest in the corporation that arises when the corporation accepts the consideration offered by the investor for the share. Section 504 of the BCL authorizes the corporation to accept money, tangible or intangible property, or labor or services in exchange for its shares. The only caveat is that the corporation may not issue shares in exchange for promises of future payments or services.

Share — stock.

Shareholder — owner of a corporation represented by owning a share of stock.

Stockholder — another term for "shareholder."

> *Example: A law office provides professional services to the organizers of a corporation with respect to forming the company. Instead of receiving a cash payment, the law office accepts shares of stock in the new entity. Because the services for which the shares were issued have already been performed, the issue is permitted under section 504 of the BCL.*

Lewis v. Dansker
357 F. Supp. 636 (S.D. N.Y. 1973)

This is a stockholder's derivative action brought under The Securities Exchange Act of 1934 ("the Act"). Plaintiff alleges that defendants procured shareholder approval at a special meeting of the stockholders for various corporate acts through the use of a proxy statement that was materially false and misleading, in violation of sec. 14(a) of the Act and S.E.C. Rules.

THE COMPLAINT

Plaintiff Harry Lewis owned Class A stock of Investors Funding Corporation of New York ("IFC") at the time of the alleged wrongs. The defendants, other than the corporate defendant, are alleged to have been officers and directors of IFC during the period complained of. Defendants Jerome, Norman and Raphael Dansker ("the Danskers") were the principal officers and directors, owning 90% of IFC's Class B stock. Defendant IFC is a New York corporation, which invests in, purchases and sells real estate.

The complaint charges that the defendants, by means of a materially false and misleading proxy statement, procured stockholder approval for three corporate acts:

(1) an employee stock option plan of which the Danskers would be principal beneficiaries; (Complaint Par. 12); [omitted]
(2) issuance of a total of 30,000 stock warrants of Class A stock to the Danskers at $15. per share; [omitted]
(3) sale of 15,000 Class A shares to the Danskers at $15. per share, payable by them over twenty quarters by non-interest bearing notes.

Plaintiff contends that the issuance and sale of 15,000 IFC shares to the Danskers for their promissory notes violated sec. 504 of the New York Business Corporation Law, McKinney's Consol. Laws c. 4. (Complaint Par. 16.)

. . .

Here plaintiff moves for summary judgment on the ground that the third corporate proposal—the outright sale of 15,000 IFC shares to the Danskers evidenced by a series of non-interest bearing promissory notes—is violative of sec. 504 of the New York Business Corporation Law. We agree.

Section 504(b) states in pertinent part:

"(b) Neither obligations of the subscriber for future payments nor future services shall constitute payment or part payment for shares of a corporation."

It is clear the prohibition of section (b) was violated since the promissory notes constitute "obligations of the subscriber for future payments." If there were any doubt about this construction of the statute it is quickly dispelled by an examination of the legislative background of sec. 504 (as set forth in 6 McKinney's Consolidated Laws of New York). It is indicated there that Paragraph (b) is derived from Model Business Corporation Act sec. 18 (sic sec. 19) and is consistent with the old Penal Law sec. 664(3). Section 19 of the Model Act states:

"Neither promissory notes nor future services shall constitute payment or part payment for the issuance of shares of a corporation." (emphasis supplied)

And, sec. 664(3) of the Penal Law made it a misdemeanor for a director to authorize the corporation. . . .

"To discount or receive any note or other evidence of debt in payment of an installment of capital stock actually called in, and required to be paid, or with intent to provide the means of making such payment;" (emphasis supplied)

See also 2 White on New York Corporations 504.03 (1972) ("A mere promise to pay money in the future, such as a promissory note . . . does not constitute payment or part payment for shares of a corporation although it may otherwise constitute good consideration to sustain a contract at common law.") Since the promissory notes were not secured or otherwise collateralized, we need not decide whether a collateralized agreement to pay would remove it from the reach of paragraph (b) of sec. 504 as suggested by the defendants in reliance on American Radiator and Standard v. U.S., 295 F.2d 939, 155 Ct. Cl. 515 (1961).

The Danskers would have us limit the prohibition of sec. 504 to newly formed corporations which, they argue, are more in danger of becoming insolvent than established businesses. No authority or legislative material is cited to support this interpretation. [On the contrary, the broad reach of the statute suggests that creditors, the public and other stockholders were to be protected at all times during the life of the corporation.]

Defendant Grunebaum argues there was no violation of sec. 504 because the stockholders ratified the proposal. However, it is hornbook law that stockholders may only ratify and render valid acts done or authorized by the board of directors, but which were beyond the powers of the directors, if the stockholders themselves could have authorized such acts. See Fletcher on Corporations, sec. 764 Vol. 2. Since the sale of the stock here was expressly prohibited by sec. 504 the "ratification" was, therefore, ineffective. Furthermore, since the statute is designed, in part, to protect creditors of the corporation, it would defeat its purposes to allow the stockholders to ratify the proposal.

The cases cited by defendant Grunebaum, Kimmel Sales Corp. v. Lauster, 167 Misc. 514, 4 N.Y.S. 2d 88 (Sup. Ct., Monroe Co. 1938) and Usher v. Schenectady Mason Supply Corp., 278 App. Div. 610, 102 N.Y.S. 2d 93 (3d Dept. 1951), though running counter to the principle referred to above, presented exceptional circumstances not here present. In Kimmel the plaintiff, a stockholder, sought to cancel shares of issuance of stock to the defendants on the ground that the shares were transferred for inadequate consideration, in violation of sec. 69 of the Stock Corporation Law, the predecessor statute to sec. 504. The court did not disturb the transaction "[inasmuch] as [the payments of monies paid out of the corporate treasury] represented personal liabilities of [Kimmel's] own and were acquiesced in by all of the stockholders of the corporation and no rights of creditors [were] involved . . ." Kimmel, supra 4 N.Y.S. 2d at 93. Here the picture is altogether different. Although the record does not indicate whether IFC had creditors, it can safely be assumed it does since it is a large public corporation. Moreover, defendants have admitted that there were dissenting shareholders. See Dansker Affidavit, par. 6.

Again, the Usher case involved another close corporation where the issuance of stock for no consideration was ratified "by men who were not only officers of the corporation, but its only stockholders . . ." Usher, supra 102 N.Y.S. 2d at 94. The question of creditors was not considered by the court.

In summary:

. . .

Plaintiff's motion for summary judgment that defendants have violated Section 504(b) of the New York Business Corporation Law is granted.

Watered stock — stock sold for consideration not even nominally equivalent to its par value.

Treasury shares — outstanding shares reacquired by the corporation and maintained on its books with no dividend or voting rights.

Stated capital — account representing the consideration the corporation has received for the sale of its shares.

The purpose of section 504 is to ensure that the corporation receives something of legal value in exchange for its shares. If the directors accept consideration not even nominally equivalent to the share's par value (or actual value for no par stock, see Chapter 5), it is considered to be a breach of the directors' fiduciary duties. The directors will be personally liable, and the shareholder who acquired such shares may be required to pay to the corporation the true value of the shares. This type of stock sold below par is called **watered stock** and is prohibited by the BCL. The only exception is for treasury shares. **Treasury shares** are shares of stock that have been outstanding but have been reacquired directly by the corporation. When a corporation reacquires its own shares, it may either cancel those shares permanently, meaning that they may never be reissued, or retain the shares as treasury shares. Treasury shares receive no dividends, are not entitled to vote, and are not subject to preemptive rights, but they may be reissued by the corporation at a later date for any value authorized by the Board of Directors.

Example: In order to avoid a takeover, a corporation decides to buy back its shares from the public. The shares have a par value of $1, and the company reacquires them for $2 per share. Once reacquired, the Board of Directors declares them to be treasury shares. Later, when the takeover has been avoided, the directors may reissue the shares for any amount they consider adequate—they are no longer bound by the $1 par value.

The consideration the corporation receives from the sale of its shares appears on its books in an account called **stated capital.** If none of the shares has a par value, the entire amount of the consideration is placed in this one account. If the shares have a par value, the

Capital Surplus — surplus other than earned surplus.

Paid-in surplus — amount above par paid for stock with a par value.

consideration is subdivided under the stated capital account into a par account and a **capital surplus** or **paid-in surplus** account to indicate the amount above par that the Board of Directors received for the sale of the shares.

> *Example: A corporation issues 100 shares of stock with a $1 par value for $10 per share for a total price of $1,000. Under its Stated Capital account, there are two subaccounts: The Par Account contains $100, and the Capital Surplus account contains $900, to reflect a total in Stated Capital of $1,000.*

Scrip — document representing a fraction of a share of stock.

Section 509 of the BCL permits a corporation to issue **scrip**, a document that represents a fraction of a share; however, many corporations, because of bookkeeping costs, no longer issue scrip. Most corporations indicate in their certificates of incorporation that if a shareholder acquires a fraction of a share, the corporation will pay the shareholder the market value of that portion of the share.

> *Example: A woman owns 100 shares of Acme stock. For their birthday, she gives her triplet nieces the shares. Each niece acquires 33 1/3 shares. The one-third interest would be represented by a piece of paper called scrip, unless the corporation has indicated that it will not issue scrip but will pay the holder the market value of this one-third share of stock.*

Preferred Stock

Preferred stock — share with rights different from common stock.

In addition to common stock, section 502 of the BCL permits a corporation to issue **preferred stock,** shares that have some rights different or superior to the common stock shares. Automatically by law, preferred shares have a priority over the common shares to the assets of the corporation in dissolution and with respect to receiving dividends. The preferred shareholders must receive their dividend before dividends can be paid to the common shareholders. In exchange for these priorities, as a general rule, preferred shareholders do not have the right to vote.

Strout v. Cross, Austin & Ireland Lumber Company
283 N.Y. 406 (1940)

Defendant, a corporation organized under the laws of the State of New York, issued in addition to classes of junior stock, first preferred seven per cent cumulative stock of $100 par value, of which plaintiff holds 515 shares. Payment of dividends on such stock was suspended from May 1, 1932, to July 31, 1935. On April 16, 1937, the defendant's board of directors declared a dividend of $22.75 per share on such preferred stock, being the accumulated arrears of dividends unpaid, and provided that payment should be made by distributing to the preferred stockholders for each share owned $2.75 in cash and $20 face amount of fifty-year income notes issued by the defendant's subsidiaries and theretofore held by the defendant. In accordance therewith plaintiff, who resides in a foreign State and had no notice of such dividend action, received a circular letter inclosing a check for a sum equal to $2.75 for each share of preferred stock held by her, together with two fifty-year income notes of subsidiaries of the defendant, issued and registered in plaintiff's name, in amount sufficient together to equal the difference between the amount paid plaintiff in cash and the amount due to her for arrears in dividends. Plaintiff, after notifying the defendant that she had not consented to receive income notes in payment of dividends, returned the notes but retained the portion of the dividends paid in cash. In this action in equity to compel the defendant to cancel the notes of its subsidiaries issued and registered in the name of the plaintiff, without her consent, a dismissal of the complaint was error. The defendant's obligation to plaintiff as an owner of its first preferred stock may not legally be satisfied by transfer to her of income notes of its subsidiaries in the absence of her consent to such action. Defendant, as owner of such notes, having carried through the formalities necessary to issue and register in her name the two notes forwarded to plaintiff, she is entitled to relief in this action in equity, requiring the defendant, as owner, to carry through formalities necessary to cancel the registration of said notes in her name and to amend its illegal action in relation to them. (Hastings v. International Paper Co., 187 App. Div. 404, distinguished.)

Relief in equity may not be withheld from the plaintiff because she has retained that portion of the dividend declared by defendant which was paid in cash. She is under no duty to return that which she is entitled to receive in any event. If the action of the board of directors was a declaration of a dividend generally, the plaintiff is entitled to retain what she regards as part payment in cash. If it was a declaration of a cash and income note dividend, the cash dividend is severable from the dividend of income notes, and plaintiff may keep the cash.

Unlike common stock, which is issued by every corporation in the country, preferred shares are not statutorily required, and only a small percentage of corporations issue such securities. Preferred shares are usually individually negotiated with the potential investor, and unlike common stock whose rights are identical to all common shares, preferred shares usually differ depending on the requirements of the corporation and the investor. Despite this individuality, there are certain preferences that are generally encountered:

Conversion rights: This right or preference entitles the security holder to exchange his or her security for a different type of corporate security at a stated ratio, for example, to exchange one share of preferred for two shares of common.

Redemption rights: This right entitles the security holder to compel the corporation to repurchase the shares at a set price. This type of preference usually requires the corporation to maintain a sinking fund to assure the security holder that funds will be available should the right be exercised.

Participation rights: This right enables the preferred shareholder to receive not only the dividend declared for the preferred share, but also to receive an additional dividend by participating with the common shareholders in their dividend.

Cumulative dividend rights: This right entitles the preferred shareholder to a minimum set dividend, and if in any given quarter the corporation fails to declare the dividend, the amount of that dividend will accumulate for the shareholder until a dividend is actually declared and distributed. If the preferred shareholder does not have the right to accumulate dividends, it is called **noncumulative dividend rights.**

Example: A preferred shareholder has cumulative dividend rights with a guaranteed dividend of $1 per share per quarter. For the first two quarters of the year, the Board of Directors does not declare a dividend because it does not have sufficient funds available. When a dividend is finally declared in the third quarter, the shareholder will receive $3 per share, the $1 dividend for the current quarter plus the $2 accumulated from the previous two quarters.

Conversion rights — preference giving the security holder the ability to exchange one type of security for another at a set ratio.

Redemption rights — the right to compel the corporation to repurchase shares of stock.

Participation rights — preference giving the shareholder the right to receive both a preferred and a common stock dividend.

Cumulative dividend rights — stock preference giving the holder the right to have undeclared dividends accumulated for him until a dividend is eventually declared.

Noncumulative dividend rights — undeclared dividend does not accumulate for the shareholder.

Warrants — long-term options to purchase shares of stock at a stated price.

Warrants: They may appear separately or as part of a preferred issue. A warrant entitles the holder to purchase a set amount of shares for a specified period of time at a predetermined price per share. If the right must be exercised within nine months, it is usually referred to as an *option;* warrants last for a longer period of time. The warrant holder may exercise the right, sell the warrant because it is a separate instrument, or simply let the right lapse.

Pinnacle Consultants, Ltd. v. Leucadia National Corporation
94 N.Y.2d 426 (2000)

At the heart of this factually complex commercial case are two legal issues: first, whether a claim has been stated for breach of fiduciary duty and waste, and second, whether Business Corporation Law sec. 612 was violated in connection with a merger effectuated by the corporate defendant. Concluding that there was neither, we affirm the Appellate Division order dismissing the complaint.

Analysis

On appeal to this Court, Pinnacle urges first, that, as officers and directors of Leucadia, the individually named defendants breached their fiduciary duty and committed corporate waste by issuing the warrants to Cumming and Steinberg, and second, that under Business Corporation Law sec. 612 TLC should have been precluded from voting its shares in favor of the merger.

Pinnacle's claims concerning the warrants are barred by collateral estoppel. Collateral estoppel, or issue preclusion, prevents a party from "relitigating in a subsequent action or proceeding an issue clearly raised in a prior action or proceeding and decided against that party." The doctrine applies if the issue in the second action was "raised, necessarily decided and material in the first action," and if the party "had a full and fair opportunity to litigate the issue in the earlier action."

Here, Pinnacle's claims that defendants breached their fiduciary duty and committed corporate waste by issuing the warrants to Cumming and Steinberg were raised and necessarily decided in the Federal court action. As predicate acts for its RICO claim, Pinnacle alleged that Leucadia's Board of Directors illegally authorized the warrants and that they were not supported by valid consideration (see, Business Corporation Law sec. 505[a][1]). The Second Circuit rejected Pinnacle's argument, holding that the warrants had been validly issued in order to reward Cumming and Steinberg for Leucadia's "dramatic turnaround"; that there was "no fraud shown in the issuance of the warrants"; and that "the Directors' business judgment is conclusive that valid consideration was received for the warrants" (101 F.3d at 905). Thus, the court concluded that the warrants were properly issued and that their issuance was economically justified as compensation for Cumming and Steinberg's service to Leucadia.

From this decision, it follows necessarily that issuance of the warrants was not corporate waste and not a breach of fiduciary duty. Indeed, the premise of Pinnacle's corporate waste and breach of fiduciary duty claims is that, in authorizing the warrants, the directors improvidently exercised their business judgment. That, however, was the very issue decided by the Second Circuit against Pinnacle.

Further, it is of no moment that, after dismissing Pinnacle's RICO claim, the Second Circuit dismissed its State law waste and fiduciary duty claims for lack of Federal jurisdiction rather than on the merits. Indeed, in view of the RICO dismissal, the Federal court lacked subject matter jurisdiction to determine the merits of the pendent State law claims. Nevertheless, since, as noted, the Federal court's dismissal of the RICO claim necessarily determined the same issues raised by the corporate waste and breach of fiduciary duty claims, the State law claims are barred by collateral estoppel (see, id. applying collateral estoppel even though, in dismissing RICO claim, Federal court never assumed jurisdiction over State law claims]).

Moreover, Business Corporation Law sec. 505(h) states that "in the absence of fraud in the transaction, the judgment of the board shall be conclusive as to the adequacy of the consideration * * * for the issue of rights or options for the purchase from the corporation of its shares." As the Appellate Division recognized, since the Second Circuit found "no fraud shown in the issuance of the warrants" (101 F.3d at 905), plaintiff's challenge cannot stand.

We next turn to Pinnacle's argument that Business Corporation Law sec. 612(b) barred TLC from voting its shares in favor of the merger. At the outset, defendants contend—as the Appellate Division held—that Pinnacle lacks standing, and is estopped from bringing this claim, because it failed to vote its shares against the merger. In support of this argument, defendants rely on the general principle that a shareholder who participated in an activity may not subsequently challenge its legality in a derivative suit. In addition, defendants cite cases finding estoppel where shareholders in closely-held corporations did not oppose the challenged actions.

While it might be reasonable to expect a shareholder in a close corporation to object affirmatively to an action before bringing suit, the dynamics are quite different in a publicly-traded corporation. To be sure, a shareholder in a publicly-held corporation who votes in favor of a merger—and thus participates in the challenged activity—might be deemed to have acquiesced to it. But that does not also mean that the shareholder who abstains from voting must be estopped from later bringing suit. This is especially true where, as here, a predetermined number of affirmative votes are required to approve the merger, thus making abstention the equivalent of a negative vote.

TLC was not, in any event, barred by Business Corporation Law sec. 612 from voting its shares in favor of the merger. Section 612(b) states:

"Treasury shares and shares held by another domestic or foreign corporation of any type or kind, if a majority of the shares entitled to vote in the election of directors of such other corporation is held by the corporation, shall not be shares entitled to vote or to be counted in determining the total number of outstanding shares."

This section states that a subsidiary—that is, a corporation a majority of whose voting shares are owned by the parent corporation—may not vote shares held in the parent corporation. The reason for this rule is that, "if cross-ownership and cross-voting of stock between parents and subsidiaries were unregulated, officers and directors could easily entrench themselves by exchanging a sufficient number of shares to block any challenge to their autonomy."

Pinnacle argues that TLC was, in effect, a subsidiary of Leucadia, because Leucadia owned a controlling interest (56%) in MIC, and MIC, in turn, owned a controlling interest (54%) in TLC. Indeed, as noted, Cumming and Steinberg served as directors of all three companies, which supports Pinnacle's argument that TLC was in fact under Leucadia's control. Thus, Pinnacle contends that section 612(b) barred TLC from voting its shares in favor of the merger.

Regardless, however, of whether TLC was effectively controlled by Leucadia, section 612(b) does not apply in this case, because that section explicitly applies only to corporations, and TLC was a partnership. Section 612(b) is very articular: it applies only to shares held by a "domestic or foreign corporation of any type or kind" (emphasis added). In fact, section 612(b) uses the term "corporation" no less than three times to define its scope. As the Appellate Division, trial court and the United States District Court concluded, this statute applies only to corporations—not to partnerships. We must respect the legislative judgment that the prohibition on cross-voting between parents and subsidiaries applies only to corporations.

Accordingly, the order of the Appellate Division should be affirmed, with costs.

All rights that attach to all classes of shares, both common and preferred, must be specified in the certificate of incorporation and must also appear on the face of the share certificate itself (see Section 508 of the BCL).

REGISTERING AND SELLING SECURITIES

Once the corporation has authorized its securities, in order to raise the capital, the securities must be sold. To arrange for the sale, the corporation may either attempt to issue the securities directly, if it knows of potential investors, or employ the services of an underwriter.

An **underwriter** is the person or institution who arranges for the sale of a security for a corporate issuer to initial security holders. The underwriter may either attempt a **private placement**, in which all of the shares are sold to one or a small group of investors, for closely held corporations, or a **public offering** to attract a wide spectrum of shareholders. There are two methods of acquiring the services of an underwriter: best efforts and firm commitment.

Best efforts underwriting refers to the situation in which the underwriter merely agrees to use its best efforts to arrange the sale of the securities and receives a **commission**, or fee, for each share actually sold. With **firm commitment underwriting**, the underwriter actually buys the securities itself, usually at a quantity discount, thereby becoming the initial shareholder. At a later date, the underwriter will sell the shares, presumably at a profit. With best efforts underwriting, the risk remains with the issuer because the shares may never be sold; with firm commitment underwriting, the risks are transferred to the underwriter who may acquire shares that turn out to be worthless.

The sale of securities is regulated by both the state and federal governments. The state laws, known as "blue sky laws," require that all security issuers file disclosure statements with the state government prior to selling the shares. In New York, issuers with fewer than forty investors are exempt from this requirement.

Under federal law, the sale of securities is regulated by the **Securities Act of 1933** which mandates that corporate securities may not be sold until the issuer files a **Registration Statement** with the **Securities and Exchange Commission (SEC)**. The federal regulation only applies to companies whose shares are sold on a national exchange, such as the New York Stock Exchange, or that have a minimum number of shareholders and assets exceeding a minimum amount. Pursuant to judicial interpretation of the statute, "security" has been defined as "any scheme that involves the investment of money in a common enterprise with profits to come solely from the efforts of others." *SEC v. W.J. Holvey Co.,* 327 U.S. 773 (1945). For corporations who come within the purview of the act, prior to issuance the corporation must file the Registration Statement with the SEC that discloses all factors which may affect the fairness of the issue and the financial status of the corporation. The statute imposes civil and criminal penalties for a material misrepresentation on a Registration Statement, and the SEC requires yearly updates.

Under writing — the process of arranging the sale of securities to the public.

Private placement — arranging for the sale of a security to a small group of investors.

Public offering — sale of securities to the general public.

Best efforts underwriting — method of compensating underwriters by paying them a commission on each share sold.

Commission — fee paid to seller of a security.

Firm commitment underwriting — underwriting in which the underwriter purchases the securities outright at a discount.

Securities Act of 1933 — federal securities law.

Registration Statement — document required to be filed with the SEC.

Securities and Exchange Commission (SEC) — government agency regulating securities.

Recall from Chapter 5 that one of the obligations of the Board of Directors is to issue shares and determine its value. If a shareholder believes that the Board of Directors has issued shares for inadequate consideration, the shareholder may sue the directors for breach of a fiduciary obligation.

In determining whether or not the Board of Directors did in fact accept inadequate consideration, the courts have formulated two tests:

True value test — test used to determine the adequacy of the consideration the directors accepted for shares of closely held corporations with no quantifiable assets.

1. The **true value test**, which is used for publicly traded companies or closely held corporations with quantifiable assets. For public corporations, the court looks at the price at which the shares were trading on the exchange on the date in question, and if the Board of Directors accepted consideration roughly equivalent to that amount, the Board of Directors will be exonerated. For closely held companies with quantifiable assets, the court will take the value of the assets and divide it by the number of shares to determine a price per share.

Absence of fraud test — test used by the courts to ascertain whether the directors have received adequate consideration for the sale of the corporate shares.

2. The **absence of fraud test** is used for corporations that are not publicly traded nor have quantifiable assets. In this case, the court looks to see if there was any fraud involved in the sale.

CHAPTER REVIEW

In order to complete its certificate of incorporation, the corporation must determine the total number of shares of stock, of all classes and types, it wishes to authorize. The BCL requires that the number of authorized shares, including all rights incident thereto, must be specified in the certificate of incorporation. To make this determination, the organizers must analyze their optimum debt-equity ratio to see how their capital will be acquired.

Debt securities refer to bonds and debentures (and infrequently promissory notes) that represent long-term indebtedness acquired by the corporation in order to raise capital. The amount of the debt securities represents a liability of the company that must be fully repaid at a specified time. During the period of the loan, the corporation is obligated to pay for the use of these funds by paying the security holder interest on his or her loan.

Equity securities refer to ownership interests in the corporation. The holders of equity securities, either common or preferred shareholders, own the company, and the consideration they have given to acquire this interest belongs to the corporation outright. It does not have to be repaid. The shareholder makes a return on the investment by having the Board of Directors declare dividends from its operating profits.

The sale of securities to the public is regulated by both state and federal laws, and the issuer is required to disclose to potential investors all material information that would affect the investor's decision with respect to investing in the security. The Board of Directors is required to receive adequate consideration for sale of its shares and, to this end, often utilizes the services of underwriters to arrange for

Senior securities — bonds and preferred stock.

the public sale of its corporate securities.

Because of their priority in liquidation, bonds and preferred stock are often referred to as **senior securities.**

KEY TERMS

Absence of fraud test

Best efforts underwriting

Bond

Bondholders

Capital surplus

Collateral

Commission

Conversion rights

Coupon bond

Cumulative dividend rights

Debenture

Debt-equity ratio

Debt security

Discount

Equity security

Face value

Firm commitment underwriting

Interest rate

Junk bond

Maturity date

Noncumulative dividend rights

Paid-in surplus

Participation rights

Preferred stock

Premium

Private placement

Promissory note

Public offering

Redemption rights

Registration Statement

Risk free interest rate

Scrip

Securities Act of 1933

Securities and Exchange Commission (SEC)

Security

Senior securities

Share

Shareholder

Sinking fund

Stated capital

Stockholder

Treasury shares

True value test

Underwriter

Warrants

Watered stock

Zero coupon bond

EXERCISES

1. Discuss the benefits and detriments of each type of preference discussed in the chapter. Under what circumstances would a corporation wish to issue shares with each type of preference?

2. Acquire a stock certificate and analyze the rights and obligations that attach to it as they appear on the face of the certificate.

3. Under what circumstances would an underwriter use firm commitment underwriting? Discuss.

4. Acquire a Registration Statement from the SEC and analyze its provisions.

5. Discuss the significance of the debt-equity ratio to corporate finance.

FACTUAL PROBLEM

A company has been operating a retail establishment for five years. It has done well and now wishes to expand by opening up three new locations. The company does not have the cash to finance the new stores. What are the possibilities for the company to finance the new operation? Assume that the corporation has decent assets (good location, excellent merchandise, and skilled employees) but little operating capital.

Chapter 8

Managing
the Corporation

INTRODUCTION

This chapter focuses on the corporate cast of characters: the individuals who actually operate the corporation. Because a corporation is an artificial entity with no hands, arms, or legs, the only way it can function is by means of natural persons who act on its behalf. There are three distinct groups of persons who act in this capacity for the corporation: the Board of Directors, the officers, and the shareholders.

In analyzing the roles played by these three groups of individuals with respect to running the corporation, it is important to understand that, although the same person may be performing two or more functions for the corporation, it is the role rather than the role player that is legally significant. What a person may do as a shareholder he or she may not do as a director. Consequently, the focus is always on the legal function the person is performing rather than on the person who is performing the function.

As discussed in Chapter 5, management of a corporation rests with the Board of Directors. These persons are authorized by the BCL to formulate the management policy for the corporation. Actions taken that are not authorized by either the Board of Directors or the provisions of the BCL are deemed to be *ultra vires* and may engender personal liability for the individuals who participated in such action.

The day-to-day operations of the corporation are the responsibility of the corporate officers. These persons are appointed by the Board of Directors to carry out the policy decisions the Board has authorized. In the general scheme of corporate hierarchy, these persons are the upper echelon employees of the company.

Ownership of the corporation vests in the shareholders, the persons for whom the directors and officers are working. The shareholders are responsible for electing (and removing) the directors, who serve at the shareholdersí pleasure. The shareholders enjoy the rights and benefits of ownership without, in most instances, the detriment of personal liability.

The rights and obligations of each of these three categories of individuals are analyzed in this chapter. It is important to remember that it is the role being performed rather than the actor that has the legal significance.

BOARD OF DIRECTORS

General

Legally, the Board of Directors acts as the agent for the corporation, and as such the directors are fiduciaries to the corporation and the shareholders. As stated previously, it is the entire Board of Directors that acts as the agent; the individual directors (unless the Board consists of only one person) do not have the authority to bind the corporation without the assent of the other directors. However, this authority of the Board may be restricted or transferred to one or more persons, including the shareholders or an Executive Committee of a closely held corporation (Chapter 5), if:

a. such transfer of authority is specified in the certificate of incorporation,

b. *all* of the incorporators or shareholders of record have authorized the transfer,

c. all subsequent shareholders have notice of the transfer and agree to it in writing, and

d. the shares are not traded on an exchange.

The only specific requirement with respect to the qualifications for being a director of a corporation under the BCL is that the person must be at least eighteen years of age. For corporations formed on or after February 22, 1998, the Board of Directors may consist of only one director; no maximum number of directors is specified in the BCL. The number of directors on the Board of Directors may be changed by amendment of the by-laws, shareholder vote, or by specific action of the Board of Directors if such action is provided for in the by-laws.

Vacancies on the Board of Directors may be filled by vote of the existing directors until the next annual meeting of the shareholders, at which time the shareholders will exercise the right to elect the directors. However, if a vacancy arises because a director has been removed without cause, such vacancy may be filled only by vote of the shareholders unless such authority has been granted to the Board of Directors in the by-laws or certificate of incorporation. Only shareholders may remove a director without cause; directors may be removed for cause by the shareholders or the Board of Directors if the Board has been given such authority, except that directors elected by class or cumulative voting may not be removed by the Board. A director may be removed by judicial authority if a proceeding for removal is brought by the New York Attorney General or by holders of 10 percent of the outstanding shares.

Meetings of the Board of Directors

Because corporate management decisions may be effectuated only by Board action, in order to manage the corporation, the directors must hold meetings to decide corporate policy. The BCL specifies three types of directorial meetings:

1. organizational meeting of the Board
2. regular meetings of the Board
3. special meetings of the Board

Organizational meeting — first meeting of the corporation.

Initial Board of Directors — first Board of Directors appointed by the incorporators.

1. *Organizational meeting.* The **organizational meeting** is the very first meeting of the corporation held after the certificate of incorporation has been filed with the Secretary of State. This meeting is called by the incorporators, whose first and only function at the organizational meeting is to elect the **initial Board of Directors,** if such persons have not been indicated in the certificate of incorporation. If the certificate of incorporation named initial directors, these are the persons who call the organizational meeting.

As its name would imply, the purpose of this initial meeting is to establish the organizational structure of the corporation. The following items of business are accomplished at this time:

a. The by-laws are adopted.

b. The corporate seal is adopted.

c. The Board adopts the form of the share certificates.

Bank resolution — document used to establish a depository for corporate funds.

d. A **bank resolution** is adopted to authorize the corporation to have a depository for corporate funds.

e. Preincorporation share subscriptions, if any, are accepted.

f. The officers of the corporation are appointed.

g. Certain tax elections, such as Subchapter S status and Section 1244 stock will be made.

h. If the corporation elects to operate in a jurisdiction outside of New York, the Board of Directors must resolve to do business as a foreign corporation in that state and authorize the officers to see that the appropriate papers are filed.

i. Preincorporation contracts are assigned.

j. A registered agent is appointed.

k. If the corporation elects to operate under an assumed name, such name will be chosen and the paperwork completed.

l. All other general business necessary to establish the corporation as a functioning business will be decided.

Corporate minutes — record of what occurs at corporate meetings.

Corporate books — where corporate minutes are kept.

Regular meeting — corporate meetings required by statute.

The records of this and all subsequent meetings of the Board of Directors and shareholders are kept by the secretary of the corporation as the **corporate minutes** and are maintained in the official **corporate books.**

2. *Regular meetings.* All Board action is required to take place at a **regular meeting** of the Board, and the directors may participate either in person or by means of a conference or telephone call that permits all directors to hear each other at the same

time. BCL § 708 (c). Action by the Board of Directors may only take place without a meeting if the directors unanimously consent in writing to such action, unless such written approval is prohibited by the certificate of incorporation. BCL § 708(b). Without this formal agreement, action taken on behalf of the corporation without a meeting may be valid only if it can be shown that the directors ratified or acquiesced to that action.

The requirements for providing notice of the meetings are detailed in sections 710 and 711 of the BCL. Generally, Board of Directors meetings may be held either in or outside of New York, and the time and place of such meetings are established in the by-laws or, if not in the by-laws, by action of the Board. If the time and place of the meetings are fixed, no notice of the meeting is required; if the time and place of the meeting is not fixed, notice must be sent. Unless required by the by-laws, the purpose for the meeting need not be included in the notice. A director may waive notice either by:

a. signing a written waiver
b. attending the meeting without protesting the lack of notice

If notice is required and no notice is given, any action taken at such meeting is void unless subsequently ratified by the directors.

Quorum — minimum number necessary to have a valid meeting.

The **quorum** requirement, the minimum number of persons who must attend in order to constitute a valid meeting, is a simple majority under the BCL unless the by-laws call for a greater number. Board action may be approved by a majority of the directors present at the meeting, except for Board action to change the number of directors, which requires approval of a majority of the entire Board of Directors.

For corporations formed on or after February 22, 1998, only a simple majority is needed to amend the certificate of incorporation or effect a structural change (Chapter 11); for corporations formed prior to that date, a two-thirds vote of the Board of Directors is necessary for such action.

Because voting is a fiduciary obligation of the directors, the directors may not vote by proxy.

Special meetings — corporate meetings called for a particular purpose.

3. *Special meetings.* **Special meetings** of the Board of Directors may be called for emergency matters that cannot wait until the next regularly scheduled meeting of the Board. All of the rules indicated previously with respect to notice and quorum requirements apply to special meetings as well.

The actions approved by the Board of Directors are called *resolutions,* and the Board, once a resolution has been approved, authorizes the officers to carry out the resolution.

Fiduciary Obligations

The directors are fiduciaries of the corporation and therefore owe special obligations to the corporation and the shareholders:

Duty of care. Directors of a corporation are held to a fiduciary standard of care that requires them to use the care and skill that would be exercised by a reasonably prudent businessperson. This standard is called the "business judgment rule" (discussed in Chapter 5). If a director does not exercise such care, the director may be held personally liable for any loss proximately caused by such action.

Duty of loyalty. Directors of a corporation must exercise their authority in good faith. In this context, as a general principle, a corporate director may not benefit personally from the business decisions made on behalf of the corporation. This means that the directors must avoid any conflict of interest with the corporation and avoid any personal benefit. However, under section 713 of the BCL, New York has listed the circumstances in which a corporation may enter into transactions with interested directors without breaching a fiduciary obligation. The corporation may enter into such agreements if the transaction is fair and reasonable to the corporation, or if the transaction has been approved by the Board of Directors (excluding the vote of the interested director) or the shareholders, provided that the interested director has made full disclosure of his or her interest prior to such approval.

Corporate opportunity doctrine — requirement that directors offer all business opportunities to the corporation and not take advantage of them personally.

Insider trading — buying or selling stock based on nonpublic information that was acquired by reason of being a fiduciary of the corporation.

A director (as well as an officer or a controlling shareholder) may not divert to himself or herself any business opportunity that should go to the corporation. This is known as the **corporate opportunity doctrine.** Any benefit such director acquires may be held in a constructive trust for the corporation which has the legal ability to force the director to disgorge such benefit. Furthermore, a director may not benefit from his or her own knowledge of the inner workings of the company by engaging in **insider trading**, buying or selling shares of stock based on the director's private information that he or she has acquired because of his or her status as a director. Such activity not only violates fiduciary obligations, but is also prohibited by federal securities laws.

Wolff v. Wolff
67 N.Y.2d 638 (1986)

The order of the Appellate Division should be modified by reversing so much thereof as affirmed the injunction against plaintiff and any corporation of which he is a shareholder and, except as so modified, the order should be affirmed, with costs to plaintiff.

Plaintiff and his three siblings (the individual defendants) charged wrongdoing and misappropriation against each other in connection with their food and game vending machine business, Hot Coffee Vending Service, Inc. The court after trial rejected plaintiff's claims of oppression, waste and breach of fiduciary duty by defendants, and instead concluded that plaintiff himself had breached his fiduciary duties as a corporate officer, misappropriated Hot Coffee's property and diverted its business opportunities. In particular, the court found that, while a Hot Coffee officer, plaintiff had surreptitiously organized Top Score Fun 'N Food in his own name and for his own benefit, and had thereby diverted business opportunities and property from Hot Coffee. The court specifically identified as lost business opportunities the Top Score facilities at Hunter College and the Madison Square Garden Bowling Center, as well as relations with the College of the City of New York. While plaintiff contended at trial that he had acted at the direction of defendant Bernard Wolff in operating these businesses for himself only after he had been wrongfully frozen out of the corporation, the affirmed findings of the trial court rejecting this as well as additional arguments tendered by appellant have support in the record and are therefore beyond our review (see, Humphrey v State of New York, 60 NY2d 742).

Plaintiff now contends that it was error for the courts below to impose an injunction against competition by him (or any corporation of which he is a shareholder) with the business of Hot Coffee, and specifically against doing business at the Madison Square Garden Bowling Center, arguing that such an injunction—unbounded by time or geography—in effect deprives him of an opportunity to earn a livelihood. Indeed, the purpose of an injunction being remedial and not punitive (see, May's Furs & Ready-to-Wear v Bauer, 282 NY 331, 343), we agree that the courts below abused their discretion in enjoining plaintiff's legitimate competition with Hot Coffee. Even an otherwise valid covenant not to compete will not be enforced if, it would be unreasonable in time, space or scope, or would operate in a harsh or oppressive manner (see, American Broadcasting Cos. v Wolf, 52 NY2d 394, 403–404).

We do not, however, find merit in plaintiff's remaining arguments. First, while he urges that the business was not a corporation but a family joint venture, and that corporate fiduciary standards are inapplicable, the conclusions below regarding corporate status are amply supported by the record, including plaintiff's own admissions. Second, Hot Coffee being a corporation, we agree with the Appellate Division that property found to have been misappropriated by respondent Bernard Wolff should be returned to the corporation rather than to its shareholders. Finally, there is no anomaly in the direction that plaintiff account to Hot Coffee for diversions of its assets, contracts and business opportunities, until the date of settlement of the account, even though his shares are to be valued as of the day prior to the date upon which his complaint was filed. This relief was imposed not for breaches of fiduciary duty committed after the date of dissolution and valuation, but for wrongs to the corporation while plaintiff served as its officer. Where, as here, an officer has been found to have diverted corporate assets and opportunities, he may be held accountable for the fruits of his wrongdoing (see, Blaustein v Pan Am. Petroleum & Transp. Co., 293 NY 281, 300; New York Trust Co. v American Realty Co., 244 NY 209, 216; Restatement [Second] of Agency @ 403).

Diamond v. Oreamuno
24 N.Y.2d 494 (1969)

Upon this appeal from an order denying a motion to dismiss the complaint as insufficient on its face, the question presented—one of first impression in this court—is whether officers and directors may be held accountable to their corporation for gains realized by them from transactions in the company's stock as a result of their use of material inside information.

The complaint was filed by a shareholder of Management Assistance, Inc. (MAI) asserting a derivative action against a number of its officers and directors to compel an accounting for profits allegedly acquired as a result of a breach of fiduciary duty. It charges that two of the defendants—Oreamuno, chairman of the board of directors, and Gonzalez, its president—had used inside information, acquired by them solely by virtue of their positions, in order to reap large personal profits from the sale of MAI shares and that these profits rightfully belong to the corporation. Other officers and directors were joined as defendants on the ground that they acquiesced in or ratified the assertedly wrongful transactions.

MAI is in the business of financing computer installations through sale and lease back arrangements with various commercial and industrial users. Under its lease provisions, MAI was required to maintain and repair the computers but, at the time of this suit, it lacked the capacity to perform this function itself and was forced to engage the manufacturer of the computers, International Business Machines (IBM), to service the machines. As a result of a sharp increase by IBM of its charges for such service, MAI's expenses for August of 1966 rose considerably and its net earnings declined from $262,253 in July to $66,233 in August, a decrease of about 75%. This information, although earlier known to the defendants, was not made public until October of 1966. Prior to the release of the information, however, Oreamuno and Gonzalez sold off a total of 56,500 shares of their MAI stock at the then current market price of $28 a share.

After the information concerning the drop in earnings was made available to the public, the value of a share of MAI stock immediately fell from the $28 realized by the defendants to $11. Thus, the plaintiff alleges, by taking advantage of their privileged position and their access to confidential information, Oreamuno and Gonzalez were able to realize $800,000 more for their securities than they would have had this inside information not been available to them. Stating that the defendants were "forbidden to use [such] information * * * for their own personal profit or gain," the plaintiff brought this derivative action seeking to have the defendants account to the corporation for this difference. A motion by the defendants to dismiss the complaint—pursuant to CPLR 3211 (subd. [a], par. 7)—for failure to state a cause of action was granted by the court at Special Term. The Appellate Division, with one dissent, modified Special Term's order by reinstating the complaint as to the defendants Oreamuno and Gonzalez. The appeal is before us on a certified question.

It is well established, as a general proposition, that a person who acquires special knowledge or information by virtue of a confidential or fiduciary relationship with another is not free to exploit that knowledge or information for his own personal benefit but must account to his principal for any profits derived therefrom. This, in turn, is merely a corollary of the broader principle, inherent in the nature of the fiduciary relationship, that prohibits a trustee or agent from extracting secret profits from his position of trust.

In support of their claim that the complaint fails to state a cause of action, the defendants take the position that, although it is admittedly wrong for an officer or director to use his position to obtain trading profits for himself in the stock of his corporation, the action ascribed to them did not injure or damage MAI in any way. Accordingly, the defendants continue, the corporation should not be permitted to recover the proceeds. They acknowledge that, by virtue of the exclusive access which officers and directors have to inside information, they possess an unfair advantage over other shareholders and, particularly, the persons who had purchased the stock from them but, they contend, the corporation itself was unaffected and, for that reason, a derivative action is an inappropriate remedy.

It is true that the complaint before us does not contain any allegation of damages to the corporation but this has never been considered to be an essential requirement for a cause of action founded on a breach of fiduciary duty. This is because the function of such an action, unlike an ordinary tort or contract case, is not merely to compensate the plaintiff for wrongs committed by the defendant but, as this court declared many years ago, "to prevent them, by removing from agents and trustees all inducement to attempt dealing for their own benefit in matters which they have undertaken for others, or to which their agency or trust relates."

Just as a trustee has no right to retain for himself the profits yielded by property placed in his possession but must account to his beneficiaries, a corporate fiduciary, who is entrusted with potentially valuable information, may not appropriate that asset for his own use even though, in so doing, he causes no injury to the corporation. The primary concern, in a case such as this, is not to determine whether the corporation has been damaged but to decide, as between the corporation and the defendants, who has a higher claim to the proceeds derived from the exploitation of the information. In our opinion, there can be no justification for permitting officers and directors, such as the defendants, to retain for themselves profits which, it is alleged, they derived solely from exploiting information gained by virtue of their inside position as corporate officials.

In addition, it is pertinent to observe that, despite the lack of any specific allegation of damage, it may well be inferred that the defendants' actions might have caused some harm to the enterprise. Although the corporation may have little concern with the day-to-day transactions in its shares, it has a great interest in maintaining a reputation of integrity, an image of probity, for its management and in insuring the continued public acceptance and marketability of its stock. When officers and directors abuse their position in order to gain personal profits, the effect may be to cast a cloud on the corporation's name, injure stockholder relations and undermine public regard for the corporation's securities. As Presiding Justice Botein aptly put it, in the course of his opinion for the Appellate Division, "[the] prestige and good will of a corporation, so vital to its prosperity, may be undermined by the revelation that its chief officers had been making personal profits out of corporate events which they had not disclosed to the community of stockholders." (29 A D 2d, at p. 287.)

The defendants maintain that extending the prohibition against personal exploitation of a fiduciary relationship to officers and directors of a corporation will discourage such officials from maintaining a stake in the success of the corporate venture through share ownership, which, they urge, is an important incentive to proper performance of their duties. There is, however, a considerable difference between corporate officers who assume the same risks and obtain the same benefits as other shareholders and those who use their privileged position to gain special advantages not available to others. The sale of shares by the defendants for the reasons charged was not merely a wise investment decision which any prudent investor might have made. Rather, they were assertedly able in this case to profit solely because they had information which was not available to any one else—including the other shareholders whose interests they, as corporate fiduciaries, were bound to protect.

Accepting the truth of the complaint's allegations, there is no question but that the defendants were guilty of withholding material information from the purchasers of the shares and, indeed, the defendants acknowledge that the facts asserted constitute a violation of rule 10b-5 of the federal Securities Act. The remedies which the Federal law provides for such violation, however, are rather limited. An action could be brought, in an exceptional case, by the SEC for injunctive relief. This, in fact, is what happened in the Texas Gulf Sulphur case (401 F. 2d 833, supra). The purpose of such an action, however, would appear to be more to establish a principle than to provide a regular method of enforcement. A class action under the Federal rule might be a more effective remedy but the mechanics of such an action have, as far as we have been able to ascertain, not yet been worked out by the Federal courts and several questions relating thereto have never been resolved. These include the definition of the class entitled to bring such an action, the measure of damages, the administration of the fund which would be recovered and its distribution to the members of the class. (See Note, 54 Cornell L. Rev. 306, 309, supra.) Of course, any individual purchaser, who could prove his own injury as a result of a rule 10b-5 violation can bring an action for rescission but we have not been referred to a single case in which such an action has been successfully prosecuted where the public sale of securities is involved. The reason for this is that sales of securities, whether through a stock exchange or over-the-counter, are characteristically anonymous transactions, usually handled through brokers, and the matching of the ultimate buyer with the ultimate seller presents virtually insurmountable obstacles. Thus, unless a section 16(b) violation is also present, the Federal law does not yet provide a really effective remedy.

In view of the practical difficulties inherent in an action under the Federal law, the desirability of creating an effective common-law remedy is manifest. "Dishonest directors should not find absolution from retributive justice," Ballantine observed in his work on Corporations ([rev. ed., 1946], p. 216), "by concealing their identity from their victims under the mask of the stock exchange." There is ample room in a situation such as is here presented for a "private Attorney General" to come forward and enforce proper behavior on the part of corporate officials through the medium of the derivative action brought in the name of the corporation. Only by sanctioning such a cause of action will there be any effective method to prevent the type of abuse of corporate office complained of in this case.

There is nothing in the Federal law which indicates that it was intended to limit the power of the States to fashion additional remedies to effectuate similar purposes. Although the impact of Federal securities regulation has on occasion been said to have created a "Federal corporation law," in fact, its effect on the duties and obligations of directors and officers and their relation to the corporation and its shareholders is only occasional and peripheral. The primary source of the law in this area ever remains that of the State which created the corporation. Indeed, Congress expressly provided against any implication that it intended to pre-empt the field by declaring, in section 28(a) of the Securities Exchange Act of 1934 (48 U.S. Code 903), that "[the] rights and remedies provided by this title shall be in addition to any and all other rights and remedies that may exist at law or in equity."

The order appealed from should be affirmed, with costs, and the question certified answered in the affirmative.

The Board of Directors may authorize a personal loan to a director out of corporate funds without being in breach of a fiduciary obligation, provided such loan is approved by the shareholders, or, for corporations formed on or after February 22, 1998, by the Board provided that the Board finds the loan would result in some benefit to the corporation. Absent such approval, loans to the directors are not permitted and violate fiduciary obligations.

A director is deemed to have participated in all Board action unless his or her dissent is placed in the minutes of the meeting and is presented in writing to the secretary either before or promptly after the meeting at which the questionable action had been taken. Directors who are not present at such meetings are presumed to have consented to the action absent a written dissent.

An action may be maintained against a director for breach of fiduciary obligations by the corporation itself, a trustee in bankruptcy, a judgment creditor of the corporation, or an officer, director, or shareholder of the corporation. If the director is found liable, the court may compel an accounting, set aside the unlawful transaction, and/or enjoin a proposed unlawful transaction.

Bansbach v. Zinn
258 A.D.2d 710 (1999)

This shareholder derivative action was brought by plaintiff on behalf of Besicorp Group, Inc., a corporation engaged in the business of power production and heating technology. In May 1997, Besicorp and its then president and chair of its board of directors, defendant Michael F. Zinn (hereinafter defendant), were indicted for alleged violations of Federal campaign finance laws. The charges stemmed from a scheme allegedly concocted by defendant, whereby defendant would solicit campaign contributions from various Besicorp employees and then reimburse the employees for such contributions through falsely labeled "raises" and "bonuses," all in an effort to hide the fact that Besicorp was making the contributions in violation of applicable Federal laws. One month later, in June 1997, Besicorp and defendant each pleaded guilty to two felonies—filing a false tax return and causing a false statement to be filed with the Federal Elections Commission. It appears that defendant was sentenced to six months in prison and two years of supervised release and that Besicorp and defendant each were fined approximately $36,000.

According to plaintiff, Besicorp's subsequent filings with the Securities and Exchange Commission in July 1997 revealed that the corporation had incurred approximately $800,000 in legal fees and expenses in connection with the Federal investigation during the fiscal year ending March 31, 1997. Specifically, plaintiff asserted that a July 1997 proxy statement indicated that Besicorp had "agreed to advance indemnification payments on behalf of certain persons" involved in the campaign finance proceedings and that the "indemnification payments advanced on behalf of [defendant] as of July 25, 1997, for legal fees . . . totaled $208,250," an amount that "could vary significantly depending on the ultimate outcome of the matter." Neither filing indicated, according to plaintiff, that the corporation's board of directors, then consisting of defendant and defendants Gerald A. Habib, Harold Harris and Richard E. Rosen, had taken any action to recover damages from defendant and/or defendant Michael J. Daley, Besicorp's then vice-president, chief financial officer and corporate secretary, for the harm caused to Besicorp as a result of defendant's scheme or to obtain repayment from defendant or Daley for the sums advanced for legal fees.

Plaintiff thereafter commenced this action in August 1997 alleging, inter alia, that defendant and Daley breached their fiduciary duties to Besicorp and wasted corporate assets. Defendant and Daley moved to dismiss the complaint pursuant to CPLR 3211 (a) (7), contending, inter alia, that plaintiff had failed to comply with Business Corporation Law sec. 626 (c) by making a demand upon Besicorp's board of directors to bring the action in the corporation's name. A similar motion was filed by Besicorp, Habib, Harris and Rosen. Supreme Court granted the requested relief and this appeal by plaintiff ensued.

Although Business Corporation Law sec. 626 (a) permits shareholders to bring an action in the right of a domestic or foreign corporation and secure a judgment in its favor, Business Corporation Law sec. 626 (c) requires that the complaint in such action "set forth with particularity the efforts of the plaintiff to secure the initiation of such action by the board or the reasons for not making such effort." This "demand" requirement, or the necessity of offering a sufficient explanation for failing to make one, "derives from one of the basic principles of corporate control—that the management of the corporation is entrusted to its board of directors . . . who have primary responsibility for acting in the name of the corporation and who are often in a position to correct alleged abuses without resort to the courts" (Barr v Wackman, 36 NY2d 371, 378 [citation omitted]). Thus, the rule has developed in this State that demand will be excused because of futility when a complaint alleges with particularity that (1) a majority of the board of directors is interested in the challenged transaction; (2) the board members did not fully inform themselves of the challenged transaction to the extent reasonably appropriate under the circumstances; or (3) the challenged transaction was so egregious on its face that it could not have been the product of sound business judgment (see, Marx v Akers, 88 NY2d 189, 200–201). "Director interest," in turn, "may either be self-interest in the transaction at issue . . . or a loss of independence because a director with no direct interest in a transaction is 'controlled' by a self-interested director" (id., at 200).

On a motion to dismiss pursuant to CPLR 3211 (a) (7), this Court must, of course, assume each fact alleged in the complaint to be true and construe the complaint liberally in favor of the plaintiff (see, Barr v Wackman, supra, at 375). Accordingly, our inquiry here distills to whether plaintiff "set forth sufficient details 'from which it may be inferred that the making of a demand would indeed [have been] futile'" (Tak Shing David Tong v Hang Seng Bank, 210 AD2d 99, 100, quoting Curreri v Verni, 156 AD2d 420, 421).

A review of the underlying complaint reveals that plaintiff is relying upon the "interested director" prong of Marx v Akers (supra) by alleging that defendant so dominated and controlled Habib, Harris and Rosen that a demand upon the board would have been futile. In this regard, plaintiff alleges that Habib, Harris and Rosen, each of whom purportedly were hand-picked by defendant for service on Besicorp's board of directors, were personal friends of defendant and had business relationships with him as well. Specifically, as to the alleged business relationships, plaintiff alleges that defendant and a third party had once formed a corporation with Harris and that such corporation, in turn, did business with Besicorp. When such corporation failed to meet its obligations with Besicorp, plaintiff alleges, Besicorp "wrote off" a note payable to it in the amount of $127,500 and defendant reimbursed Harris for a $14,000 payment made to finance the failed project. As to Habib and Rosen, plaintiff alleges that each had sought to do business with Besicorp and that Habib had submitted a written marketing and business consulting services proposal to Besicorp. Although we agree that the mere allegation of personal friendships is insufficient to establish domination and control, we find the allegations of business dealings to be sufficient to permit the complaint to survive the respective motions to dismiss. Accordingly, Supreme Court's order granting defendants' respective motions to dismiss must be reversed and the complaint reinstated.

Ordered that the order is reversed, on the law, with costs, and motions denied.

The BCL permits a corporation to indemnify its officers and directors for actions instituted against them in their official capacities, provided that such indemnification is:

1. approved by a resolution of the shareholders,
2. approved by a resolution of the directors, and
3. based on an agreement to provide such indemnification.

A director may not be indemnified in the following circumstances:

1. The director acted in bad faith.
2. The director made a profit that should have gone to the corporation.
3. The director breached a statutory obligation.
4. The director was acting beyond his or her authority.

Biondi v. Beekman Hill House Apartment Corporation
94 N.Y.2d 659 (2000)

This appeal brings up for review two issues: (1) whether public policy bars a cooperative apartment corporation from indemnifying one of its directors for punitive damages imposed on the director who, in violation of various civil rights laws, denies a proposed tenant's

sublease application on the basis of race and retaliates against a shareholder for opposing the denial; and (2) whether, under the same facts, Business Corporation Law sec. 721
bars indemnification where the underlying judgment establishes that the director acted in
bad faith. We conclude that, in these circumstances, indemnification is prohibited.

Plaintiff, Nicholas Biondi, is the former president of the board of directors of defendant Beekman Hill House Apartment Corporation. In 1995, Simone Demou, a shareholder of Beekman, informed Biondi that she intended to sublease her apartment to
Gregory and Shannon Broome, a financially eligible couple. Biondi assured Demou that
he would meet with Gregory Broome and that, in keeping with the usual practice, a full
board interview would not be required. Nevertheless, after Biondi's meeting with Gregory
Broome, Beekman's managing agent advised the Broomes that a full Board meeting was
necessary. Prior to that meeting, Biondi informed another board member that Gregory
Broome was African-American, and told yet another board member that he felt "uneasy"
about him. The Board unanimously denied the Broomes' application and issued a notice
of default against Demou for "objectionable conduct" arising from her accusations of
racism against Biondi and the Board.

On January 30, 1996, Biondi, represented by Beekman's counsel, commenced a
defamation action against Demou in Supreme Court. On February 2, 1996, the Broomes
filed a lawsuit in the United States District Court for the Southern District of New York,
alleging that Beekman and its directors ("the Beekman defendants"), including Biondi,
violated various State and Federal civil rights laws by denying their sublease application
based on Gregory Broome's race. The Beekman defendants counterclaimed against the
Broomes and brought a third-party action against Demou for injurious falsehoods.
Demou removed Biondi's defamation action to Federal court, consolidated it with the
Broomes' Federal action and asserted counterclaims against the Beekman defendants
for retaliation.

After trial, the jury found that the Beekman defendants, including Biondi both personally and in his official capacity, violated the Federal Fair Housing Act, 42 U.S.C. secs.
1981 and 1982, and New York Human Rights Law sec. 296(5). The jury awarded the
Broomes $230,000 in compensatory damages and $410,000 in punitive damages,
$125,000 of which was assessed individually against Biondi. As to Demou, the jury found
that Biondi and the Beekman defendants violated her rights under the Federal Fair
Housing Act and the New York Human Rights Law, breached their fiduciary duties to her
and tortiously interfered with her sublease agreement with the Broomes. The jury
awarded Demou a total of $107,000 in compensatory damages and $57,000 in punitive
damages, $29,000 of which was assessed individually against Biondi.

Following the verdict, the Beekman defendants moved, in part, for a new trial. In
denying the motion, the Federal District Court concluded that: (1) the evidence supporting Demou's breach of fiduciary duty claim established that "the Beekman board members acted in bad faith and with a purpose that was not in the best interests of the
cooperative"; and (2) the evidence established that the Beekman defendants acted "willfully or maliciously when they rejected the Broomes' sublet application * * * and retaliated
against Demou for trying to oppose the Board's actions" (Broome v Biondi, 17 F. Supp.
2d 211, 220, 228 [SD NY]). Biondi and the Beekman defendants appealed to the United
States Court of Appeals for the Second Circuit. At a settlement conference, Biondi and
Beekman's directors agreed to limit their liability to their respective punitive damage
awards. After Biondi failed to comply with the settlement, a second conference ensued,
at which the parties agreed to reduce Biondi's punitive damage contribution to $124,000.

Biondi subsequently sued Beekman for indemnification under Article VII of its by-
laws, and Beekman moved to dismiss Biondi's complaint for failure to state a cause of

action pursuant to CPLR 3211. Supreme Court denied Beekman's motion. It held that Beekman's by-laws authorized indemnification for directors who act in good faith, and the "mere fact" that the Federal jury found Biondi liable for violating the Broomes' civil rights was not "dispositive" of that issue. It further held that the public policy prohibition against indemnification for punitive damages did not apply because the settlement agreement did not clearly identify Biondi's damages as punitive.

The Appellate Division unanimously reversed and dismissed the complaint. The court held that Biondi's settlement agreement limited his liability to punitive damages and that indemnification for punitive damages is prohibited by public policy. The court also held that Business Corporation Law sec. 721 barred indemnification, where the jury in the underlying action found that Biondi had acted in bad faith toward the Broomes and Demou. We now affirm.

Analysis

Under the facts of this case, Biondi cannot obtain indemnification for the punitive damages imposed for his acts of bad faith against Beekman. In the context of insurance indemnification, "the rule to be applied with respect to a punitive damage award made in a Civil Rights Act action is that coverage is proscribed as a matter of public policy."

So too, Beekman should not bear the burden of indemnifying its director for punitive damages imposed for acts of bad faith. Biondi's racial discrimination against the Broomes and retaliation against Demou is precisely the type of conduct for which public policy should preclude indemnification. The jury in the Federal action found that Biondi willfully violated the Broomes' and Demou's civil rights, and it imposed personal liability on Biondi. Indeed, the punitive damages assessed against Biondi were greater than those against any other director, confirming that Biondi was singled out for punishment. To allow Biondi now to shift that penalty to Beekman would eviscerate the deterrent effect of punitive damages, and "violate the 'fundamental principle that no one shall be permitted to take advantage of his own wrong.'"

Although Biondi acknowledges that public policy prohibits insurer indemnification for punitive damages, he argues that the prohibition does not apply to this case because, unlike New York's Insurance Law, the Business Corporation Law evinces a clear legislative policy of indemnifying corporate directors who act in good faith. While we recognize that "our determination of public policy * * * is limited by [existing] statutes," we conclude that neither the Business Corporation Law nor Beekman's by-laws entitle Biondi to indemnification, where the underlying judgment establishes that he acted in bad faith.

Business Corporation Law secs. 722(a) and 722(c) allow corporations to indemnify directors against third-party actions and derivative suits, respectively. Section 722(a) permits indemnification against judgments, fines, settlement payments and reasonable litigation expenses, while Section 722(c) limits indemnification to settlement payments and litigation expenses. In both cases, the standard of conduct is the same: a corporation may indemnify a director who acts "in good faith, for a purpose which he reasonably believed to be in * * * the best interests of the corporation * * * " (Business Corporation Law secs. 722[a] and [c] [emphasis added]). Termination of an action by a judgment or settlement does not, by itself, "create a presumption" that the standard of conduct has not been satisfied (Business Corporation Law sec. 722[b]).

While section 721's nonexclusivity language broadens the scope of indemnification, its "bad faith" standard manifests a public policy limitation on indemnification. That limitation is reflected in the statutory indemnification provisions, as well as Beekman's by-laws, both of which restrict indemnification to acts of "good faith" that are "reasonably believed to be in * * * the best interests of the corporation" (Business Corporation Law secs. 722[a], [c]).

With this background, we consider whether the adverse Federal judgment establishing Biondi's bad faith toward the Broomes and Demou precludes indemnification under Business Corporation Law sec. 721. Relying on section 722, Biondi argues that the Federal jury's finding of bad faith is not dispositive of his actions toward Beekman, and that he is entitled to prove that he acted in Beekman's interest. Beekman counters that a finding of bad faith toward a third party is, by itself, sufficient to bar indemnification under Business Corporation Law sec. 721.

Reading sections 721 and 722 together and applying them harmoniously and consistently as we are required to do (McKinney's Cons Laws of NY, Book 1, Statutes sec. 221), we hold that the key to indemnification is a director's good faith toward the corporation and that a judgment against the director, standing alone, may not be dispositive of whether the director acted in good faith. However, we conclude, as a matter of law, that in this case it is dispositive.

Based on the entire record before us, nothing in Biondi's conduct can be construed as being undertaken in good faith, for a purpose "reasonably believed" to be in the best interests of Beekman. By intentionally denying the Broomes' sublease application on the basis of race, Biondi knowingly exposed Beekman to liability under the civil rights laws. Indeed, a Beekman board member warned Biondi that if he felt "uneasy because Mr. Broome is black, we will be sued." Biondi's willful racial discrimination cannot be considered an act in the corporation's best interest.

Nor was it in Beekman's best interest for Biondi to breach his fiduciary duty to Demou, Beekman's shareholder. The Federal District Court in the underlying action instructed the jury that if it found that "the Board members made determinations in bad faith and with a purpose that was not in the best interest of all the people they represent, then you must find that the board breached its fiduciary duty" to Demou. The jury found that Biondi, acting in bad faith, breached his fiduciary duty to Demou. That finding was later upheld by the District Court, which denied Biondi's motion for a new trial on the ground that "the jury could reasonably find that the Beekman Board members acted in bad faith and with a purpose that was not in the best interests of the cooperative" (Broome v Biondi, supra, 17 F. Supp. 2d at 220 [emphasis added]). Because the underlying Federal judgment establishes that Biondi's acts were committed in bad faith, Biondi is not entitled to indemnification and cannot relitigate the good faith versus bad faith issue here (Business Corporation Law sec. 721).

Accordingly, the order of the Appellate Division should be affirmed, with costs.

OFFICERS

The New York law regarding corporate officers appears in section 715 of the BCL. There are no specific qualifications mandated to be a corporate officer under the BCL, and generally the officers are selected by the Board of Directors. One person may hold several corporate offices. The certificate of incorporation may reserve to the shareholders the right to approve the appointment of the officers.

The officers are the servants of the corporation, acting on its behalf under authority granted to them by the Board of Directors(the corporate agent). In this regard, all of the law of agency discussed in Chapter 1 applies. The BCL states that a corporation may have a president, one or more vice presidents, a treasurer, and a secretary, plus such other officers as may be established by the Board of Directors or provided for in the by-laws. Officers appointed by the Board of Directors may be removed by the Board with or without cause. Officers elected by the shareholders may only be removed by the shareholders with or without cause, or by judicial action for cause if suit is brought by the Attorney General or a holder of 10 percent of the outstanding shares. However, the Board of Directors may suspend an officer pending shareholder action for removal for cause.

Since officers are servants, or employees, of the corporation, most of their rights and obligations appear in the contracts they have entered into with the corporation, and all questions regarding their rights and obligations must be answered by specific reference to these agreements. These rights and obligations are governed by general contract and employment law.

SHAREHOLDERS

The shareholders are the owners of the corporation whose rights have been discussed in previous chapters. This chapter focuses on the BCL requirements regarding the shareholders' exercise of their rights and obligations.

The shareholders, as such, have no direct say in the operations of the corporation; they exercise their ownership rights by electing the Board of Directors. To exercise this right, the BCL mandates that there be an annual meeting of the shareholders on a day fixed by the by-laws and authorizes special meetings when such meetings are necessary, typically for emergency matters. A special meeting must be called if an insufficient number of directors have been elected to conduct the business of the corporation.

Shareholder meetings may be held in or outside of New York, and the shareholders must be given written notice of the meeting between ten and sixty days before the meeting takes place. The notice must state the date, place, and hour of the meeting, and, if it is a special meeting, the purpose for which the meeting is called. The written notice must be delivered personally or by mail, but the shareholders may waive such notice either by a signed waiver or by attending the meeting. If proper notice is not given, any action taken at such meeting is considered void.

Unlike the directors, for whom voting on corporate policy is an obligation, for the shareholders voting is a right that may or may not be exercised. The method whereby a shareholder may alienate his or her vote is delineated in Chapter 10.

The BCL provides for three types of quorum requirements for shareholders' meetings:

Normal quorum — majority.

Lesser quorum — fewer than a majority.

Greater quorum — more than a majority.

1. **Normal quorum**, which is a majority of the shares entitled to vote.
2. **Lesser quorum**, which is a number less than majority but in no event less than one-third of the shares entitled to vote; such requirement must appear in the certificate of incorporation.
3. **Greater quorum,** which is more than a majority; such provision must appear either in the certificate of incorporation or the by-laws.

Shareholder approval requires a simple majority vote, or a plurality for election of directors. For corporations formed prior to February 22, 1998, action effecting structural changes requires approval of two-thirds of the shareholders. For corporations formed on or after

February 22, 1998, such supermajority is only required for class voting or if so specified in the certificate of incorporation.

Shareholder action may be authorized without a meeting if 100 percent of the shareholders sign a written consent to such action and such written consent is delivered to the corporation within sixty days of such action. (The certificate of incorporation may provide for such written approval by fewer than 100 percent.)

As a general principle, shareholders are not fiduciaries and therefore owe no obligations to the corporation or the other shareholders; however, shareholders who acquire control of the corporation because of their percentage ownership of the company are required to exercise good faith with respect to the minority shareholders. This good faith requirement may come into play when the controlling shareholder sells his or her shares or votes to merge the corporation with another entity owned by the shareholder. When selling the shares, the controlling shareholder must not exercise bad faith with respect to the minority shareholders but otherwise is free to sell the shares to the highest bidder. For mergers, if the effect of the merger is a **freeze out,** in which minority shareholders are bought out, the court will set aside the merger if:

Freeze out — sale of stock intended to force out minority shareholders.

a. The transaction was the result of fraud, illegality, or self-dealing.

b. The minority shareholder was not dealt with fairly.

c. There was no legitimate corporate reason for the action.

Shareholder derivative suits — lawsuits brought by a shareholder for injury to the corporation.

As owners, shareholders have the right to maintain suits against any individual whose actions have injured the corporation if the corporation does not pursue such action on its own. These actions are called **shareholder derivative suits** and may be brought by any shareholder who was the legal or beneficial owner of the share at the time the action complained of took place and is still the shareholder at the time suit is brought. These actions are brought on behalf of the corporation for injury to the corporation, and any resulting award belongs to the corporation. Once it has been instituted, the action may only be dismissed by court authority. The shareholder bringing the action may be required to furnish surety unless the shareholder owns 5 percent of the outstanding shares or has shares with a value exceeding $50,000. Prior to instituting the suit, the shareholder must make a request to the Board of Directors to institute the action unless such request would be deemed futile. If successful, the shareholder may be entitled to attorneys' fees.

Since shareholders are the actual owners of the company, all corporate assets, after all obligations have been discharged, belong to the shareholders according to each shareholder's percentage of ownership in the corporation.

Robbins v. Panitz
61 N.Y.2d 967 (1984)

Plaintiff, as a former employee, shareholder and the president of the defendant corporation, brought the instant action seeking an accounting and other damages for his discharge and the alleged subsequent "freeze-out" of his interest in the corporation on or about August 1, 1979. Plaintiff alleged that it was the oral understanding of all the parties that he was to be the manager of the corporate restaurant-discotheque for as long as it operated. The restaurant operated from November, 1978 to August, 1980, but had ceased operation as of the date of trial. For the alleged breach of the oral employment agreement, plaintiff sought to hold the two individual defendants, who were officers of the corporation, liable for 52 weeks of his salary; for the ouster and alleged "freeze-out," plaintiff sought the value of his shares in the corporation as of August 1, 1979.

Memorandum.

The order of the Appellate Division insofar as appealed from should be reversed and the complaint dismissed, with costs.

The Trial Judge awarded plaintiff judgment against the individual defendants and two corporations for $39,000 as the value of plaintiff's one-third interest in the corporations and $31,200 as salary to which plaintiff would have been entitled during the 52 weeks following his discharge, and otherwise dismissed the complaint. The individual defendants appeal pursuant to our leave.

The salary award against the individuals cannot stand because the proof establishes no more than an employment by the corporation. Nor, although there was a motion to conform the pleadings to the proof at the end of the trial, can the salary award be sustained on the theory of interference with contractual relations. A corporate officer is not personally liable for causing the corporation to terminate an employment contract "unless his activity involves individual separate tortious acts" (A. S. Rampell, Inc. v Hyster Co., 3 NY2d 369, 378; accord Murtha v Yonkers Child Care Assn., 45 NY2d 913). The Trial Judge held these defendants liable notwithstanding his conclusion that whether plaintiff was discharged for cause was irrelevant.

Equally infirm is the award for the value of plaintiff's interest in the corporation. The predicate for the award was that defendants had offered to buy out plaintiff but no agreement as to the value of his interest had been reached. There thus having been no agreement reached, there was no contract basis for the award made. Nor did sections 1104-a and 1118 of the Business Corporation Law authorize determination of value by the Trial Judge. Those sections authorize a determination of value only in an action for dissolution of the corporation. No such cause of action was involved in the present action.

Order insofar as appealed from reversed, with costs, and complaint dismissed as against defendants-appellants in a memorandum.

CHAPTER REVIEW

As an artificial entity, a corporation may operate only by means of natural persons who act on its behalf. There are three categories of such persons who operate the corporate entity.

The Board of Directors is the manager of the corporation; the directors are fiduciaries who are mandated to create corporate policy. Directors must exercise a fiduciary standard of care and loyalty to the corporation and the shareholders, and must act personally with respect to all corporate decisions.

The officers of the corporation are the employees, or servants, and as such must fulfill all of the employment obligations as specified in their contracts.

As owners of the corporation, the shareholders are legally precluded from participating in the management of the corporation; they relinquish control of the business in order to achieve limited liability. As a general rule, shareholders owe no fiduciary duties to the corporation or the shareholders, unless they are controlling shareholders and consequently only have rights with respect to the company.

KEY TERMS

Bank resolution

Corporate books

Corporate opportunity doctrine

Freeze out

Greater quorum

Initial Board of Directors

Insider trading

Lesser quorum

Minutes

Normal quorum

Organizational meeting

Quorum

Regular meetings

Shareholder derivative suits

Special meetings

EXERCISES

1. Obtain a copy of corporate by-laws from the library or the Internet and analyze the provisions.

2. Discuss why controlling shareholders are held to a fiduciary obligation to the minority share-holders. Do you believe this is just if the majority shareholder only treats the shares as an investment and has nothing to do with the day-to-day operations? Discuss.

3. Why are shareholders given the ability to institute shareholder derivative suits? Explain.

4. When, if ever, may a shareholder formulate corporate policy? Discuss. Does this engender personal liability?

5. Discuss the reasons why a corporation may wish to vary the majority voting requirements of the BCL. Under what circumstances would this be beneficial or detrimental?

FACTUAL PROBLEM

A corporate majority shareholder has elected herself to the Board of Directors and has made herself the CEO. One of the perks of the office is the use of the corporate jet and the apartments the company maintains in Los Angeles and Houston, where it has major offices. When the company's profits decline, the minority shareholders want to have the CEO reimburse the company for her use of the jet and apartments because using commercial flights and staying in hotels would be less expensive. Argue for both sides.

Chapter

Chapter
9

Dividends
and Distributions

INTRODUCTION

Dividend — shareholder's yield on his or her investment.

A **dividend** is a distribution made by the corporation to its shareholders representing the profits the corporation has generated from its operations. A dividend represents the yield on the shareholder's investment in the same way that interest payments represent the yield on the creditor's loan. Most investors look for a return on their investment in two forms: capital growth, meaning the overall appreciation in the market value of the stock, and dividend distribution for income purposes.

The Board of Directors is entrusted with the exclusive authority and discretion to declare dividends for distribution. As discussed in Chapter 5, one of the common stock rights is the right to receive dividends *if* dividends are declared by the Board. Preferred shareholders, although they may be contractually entitled to receive a dividend, are also subject to the Board's decision with respect to the declaration of a dividend (Chapter 7). However, even though the Board has the discretion to declare dividends, that discretion is not absolute, and the declaration may only be made if certain financial tests are first met. Failure to meet these financial requirements may result in the personal liability of the directors for a breach of a fiduciary duty.

This chapter discusses the requirements for declaring a dividend, the method and type of permissible dividends, and the effect of a dividend declaration on the balance sheet of the corporation.

SOURCE OF FUNDS

The rules regarding the distribution of corporate dividends appear in Article 5 of the BCL. Section 510 of the BCL mandates that dividends and distributions may only be paid from surplus funds, except for certain corporations engaged in exploiting natural resources or

Surplus — excess.

wasting assets. "Exploiting natural resources" refers to extracting oil, gas, minerals, and so forth. "Wasting assets" refers to using nonreplaceable assets, such as patents and copyrights. This means that the corporation may only use funds from its **surplus** account for dividend distributions; the surplus account represents the profit the corporation has made, after taxes, from the operation of its business. The Board of Directors is precluded from using capital assets as the source of funds for dividends, except for the types of corporations that exploit natural resources or waste assets.

> *Example: A corporation has made a gross profit of $100,000 in the current quarter, and its taxes and other obligations equal $49,000. Therefore, the corporation has $51,000 available as surplus funds to be used for dividend distribution.*

The reason why this restriction to surplus funds does not apply to corporations that exploit natural resources or waste assets is because these entities never really make a profit; they are selling off their nonreplaceable **capital** assets. A manufacturing or service company can always reproduce its product, but a corporation that is engaged in oil drilling cannot simply manufacture additional petroleum. The oil that is extracted and sold cannot be replaced, and when the well runs dry, the assets are totally depleted. Therefore, in theory, such companies never make a "profit" because they are selling off their nonreplaceable assets.

Capital — property.

Basic accounting equation — Assets = Liabilities + Equity.

Balance sheet — document representing the basic accounting equation.

Assets — property of value owned by a company.

Liabilities — obligations.

Payables — name given to all liability accounts.

Equity — ownership interest in a business.

Retained earnings — profit or loss resulting from the operation of a business.

Income statement — document that indicates the sales, expenses, taxes, and profit or loss for a business.

Gross profit or loss — all profit or loss before taxes.

Net profit — gross profit less taxes.

Earned surplus — profit from the operation of a business.

Capital surplus — surplus other than earned surplus.

In order to understand what is meant by corporate surplus, it is necessary to discuss basic accounting. The **basic accounting equation,** which composes the **balance sheet,** is: Assets = Liabilities + Equity. **Assets** represent anything of value that the corporation owns or has a right to use. Typical assets include cash, property, plant and equipment, inventory, prepaid services, accounts receivable, and securities the corporation holds as an investor. **Liabilities** reflect all debts of the corporation, such as wages, rent, utilities, taxes, and so forth. Accounts that appear under liabilities are entitled **payables. Equity** represents the owners' (investors') interest in the corporation. The equity account is divided into two broad categories: stated capital and retained earnings. Stated capital, as discussed in Chapter 7, represents the consideration the investor has given in order to acquire a share of stock. The consideration may take the form of cash, property, or services. The other category of the equity account is called **retained earnings,** and this account represents the net profit the corporation has made from its operations. The amount of the profit or loss acquired during a given period is determined by reference to a second document known as the **income statement.** This document records all sales made by the company from which it deducts all expenses to be paid to determine the company's **gross profit or loss.** This amount determines the company's income tax liability, and the amount remaining after the taxes have been paid is the company's **net profit** for the period. This net profit is what appears on the balance sheet as retained earnings.

The equity account contains two different types of surplus balances. The amount appearing in the retained earnings account represents the company's **earned surplus** because it is derived from the business operations of the entity. All other surplus in the equity account is considered to be **capital surplus.** An example of capital surplus is the amount above par that a shareholder paid for his or her share of stock (Chapter 7).

The BCL mandates that the Board of Directors may only declare a dividend with the funds from the earned surplus account. Further, the BCL provides that the funds must be

Unrestricted, unreserved earned surplus — source of funds for a corporate dividend.

unrestricted, unreserved earned surplus in order to protect the corporation's creditors. Not all net profit earned by a corporation may be available for dividends. If the corporation has allocated a portion of its profit to some other legitimate corporate purpose, such as to acquire a new facility or to take advantage of a corporate opportunity, such funds are deemed to be restricted and/or reserved and are not available for dividend distribution.

> *Example: In the current quarter, a corporation has made a net profit of $600,000, which represents its earned surplus. The Board of Directors had previously decided to allocate 10 percent of its profit to a building fund to acquire a new plant. Further, the company has acquired another corporation and by contract is to pay off the debts assumed by the company to acquire the corporation with 25 percent of its net profits. Because of these previous restrictions and reservations, the company only has $390,000 available as unrestricted and unreserved earned surplus for a dividend declaration ($600,000 − $60,000 (10%) − $150,000 (25%) = $390,000).*

Once the Board of Directors declares a dividend, it becomes an enforceable right of the shareholders, but not until the dividend declaration had been made. At this point, the dividend becomes a debt, and it will appear on the books of the company as a liability until it is discharged by the actual distribution to the shareholders.

If the Board of Directors declares a dividend from an inappropriate source of funds or distributes a dividend only to selected shareholders, such dividend is deemed to be illegal. The shareholders may either sue the directors who participated in the distribution personally to have them reimburse the corporation for the funds so distributed or sue the shareholder who received such dividend to have the dividend returned to the company.

Deering Milliken, Inc. v. Clark Estates, Inc.
43 N.Y.2d 545 (1978)

On March 31 and April 5, 1967 Deering Milliken, Inc., executed agreements for the purchase from defendants, executors under a will and the Clark Estates, Inc., of some 480,000 shares of stock of Albany Felt Company. Under the first agreement, with the executors, a minimal payment was to be made at the time the contract was signed, a partial payment on May 1, 1967 and the substantial balance on August 1, 1967. Under the April agreement, with Clark Estates, payment was to be on such date between May 1 and August 1, 1967 as might be specified by the seller. Under each contract delivery of the stock certificates was to take place when the total purchase price was paid. Absent from both contracts was any provision as to which party would be entitled to dividends declared between the dates of the agreements and the dates of transfer of the shares. On May 24, 1967 the corporation declared a dividend payable July 1 to stockholders of record on June 16. Payment of the purchase price and delivery of the stock certificates held by Clark Estates took place on June 19, 1967, while final payment and delivery of the stock certificates held by the executors was made on August 1. The sellers rejected the buyer's demand under both contracts for delivery of the dividends distributed July 1. Special Term found this to be improper but the Appellate Division reversed, holding that the distribution belonged to the sellers, who were the beneficial owners of the shares when the dividend was declared.

On appeal, the Court of Appeals affirmed. In an opinion by Judge Jones, it was held that the agreements were contracts for future sales of stock rather than for a present change of beneficial ownership and that, accordingly, it was proper to grant defendants' cross motion for summary judgment dismissing plaintiff's claim for dividends declared after the date of the contracts and before the transfer of beneficial interest in the stock. When a contract is made for the future transfer of beneficial interest in stock and no provision is made therein by the buyer and seller as to which shall be entitled to receive regular dividends declared before the purchase price is paid and delivery of the stock certificates made, such dividends remain the property of the seller.

As in most contract questions, the intention of the parties, if manifested, would have controlled. In the March and April agreements between the parties, however, there were no express provisions with respect to entitlement to interim dividends, and no extrinsic evidentiary proof of the intention of the parties as to that subject has been tendered. That being so, the resolution of the resulting ambiguity by construction of the instruments is for determination by the court on the present cross motions for summary judgment.

Critical to the determination whether buyer or sellers were entitled to the May dividend is the question whether present sales—current transfers of substantial beneficial interest—or only agreements to make future sales were manifested by the execution of the contracts of March 1 and April 5, 1967. A purchaser of stock acquires "by a contract of present sale a right to the benefits which may accrue on the stock bought, and that right is, for convenience, called the 'beneficial ownership' of the stock." A different result attends the execution of a contract to make a sale in the future. "In the absence of an agreement to the contrary, the buyer under an executory contract to sell stock is not entitled to dividends until the legal title to the stock has passed to him, which is not until delivery is made to him or is due to him and is offered to be made, unless there is something in the contract specifying or implying a contrary intention. * * * Where there is a sale of stock in praesenti, but the date of delivery and payment is postponed, the vendee is entitled to all dividends declared between the date of the agreement and the date of closing to the purchaser."

Looking to the terminology used by these parties in their agreements, in addition to provisions for future dates for payments of the purchase price and deliveries of the stock certificates, we find: "Seller will sell to Buyer"; "Buyer * * * will purchase such shares from Seller"; the seller "agrees to cause to be sold to" the purchaser; the purchaser "agrees to buy such shares"; reference to "shares to be sold"—all terminology looking to future occurrences and inconsistent with a present transfer of beneficial ownership of the stock. Of similar import are the express conditions which precluded the subjection of the buyer to any obligation to pay until it had satisfied itself as to the existence of sufficient warrant in the financial condition of Albany Felt for the transactions described in the contracts. In view of that condition, it might have come about that the buyer would never be bound to pay. We conclude that, while at the time of execution of the March and April agreements Deering Milliken acquired certain enforceable rights with respect to a sale of the Albany Felt stock, there was then no present sale and no transfer of such beneficial interest as to carry with it the right to the regular quarterly dividend declared May 24, 1967. Defendants, as the actual and beneficial owners of the shares when the dividend was declared, were entitled to the distribution.

The extrinsic evidence bearing on the intention of the parties with respect to the timing of the completion of the sale by the executors (to be distinguished from extrinsic evidence with respect to the right to dividends—of which there is none) is consistent with the construction we have reached. Included among the papers offered by the buyer on its motion for summary judgment is an affidavit and an examination before trial of its president by whom it was represented in the stock transaction. This evidence discloses that the executors desired to defer the sale of stock for a tax advantage to them. The desire of the executors in this regard was communicated to the buyer's president and with that knowledge the parties executed the agreements, drafted on behalf of the sellers. Also included in the buyer's moving papers is a letter from the sellers' counsel, who had been involved in the discussions concerning the text of the instruments, referring to the executors' rejection of a proposal by the buyer's attorney that "the agreement be cast in terms of a present sale and purchase."

The cases of Currie v White (45 NY 822) and Johnson v Underhill (52 NY 203), relied on by Deering Milliken as support for its claim to the disputed dividend, are inapplicable. In each of those cases it was found that a present sale and transfer of beneficial interest had taken place; in the Johnson case the issue was only what consequence attended the failure to have effected a change in record ownership on the books of the corporation. So too, the trilogy of Broderick cases arising in the context of the collapse of the Bank of United States in 1930 (Broderick v Aaron, 264 NY 368; Broderick v Alexander [Kahn], 268 NY 306, supra; Broderick v Adamson [Greif], 270 NY 260), is not supportive of Deering Milliken's position. Those cases also dealt with the rights and liabilities attendant on present purchases and sales of stock, made in those instances through brokers on the open market, and with the degree of specification and identification necessary to effect a transfer of beneficial interest for the purpose of fixing the statutory liability of stockholders of a bank in liquidation.

Cases cited involving extraordinary or irregular dividends declared at or near the time of the striking of the agreement, which served to siphon off corporate assets and thereby unexpectedly to impair the bargain, are not in point; here it is undisputed that the dividend declared May 24, 1967 was a predictable regular, quarterly dividend of Albany Felt Company.

In reaching our decision we have not considered Rules of the New York Stock Exchange which have not been claimed or shown to be applicable to this transaction concluded directly between the prospective buyer and sellers.

Finally, because the Appellate Division took note of the fact that no provision for interest payments on the purchase price of the stock had been included in either agreement, we observe that we attach no significance to this omission. Although the inclusion of an obligation for payment of interest by the buyer from the date of the contract's execution would have supported a claim of a present sale (Currie v White, 45 NY 822, supra), its absence does not necessarily lead to a contrary result. An acceptable—perhaps, to a tax-conscious seller, even desirable—substitute might be a greater purchase price.

Inasmuch as the agreements executed March 31 and April 5, 1967 were contracts for future sales of Albany Felt stock, rather than for a present change of beneficial ownership, it was proper to grant defendants' cross motion for summary judgment dismissing plaintiff's claim for dividends declared after the date of the contracts and before the transfer of beneficial interest in the stock.

Accordingly, the order of the Appellate Division should be affirmed, with costs.

Cottrell v. Albany Card and Paper Manufacturing Company
142 A.D. 148 (1911)

This is an action brought by a trustee in bankruptcy against the sole stockholder of the bankrupt company to recover certain dividends amounting to $17,600 paid by it between December 27, 1902, and January 8, 1907, both inclusive, upon the ground that such dividends were paid in violation of the statute as being paid out of the capital and not out of the profits of the company. It is alleged in the complaint that defendant at such times owned all the capital stock of said bankrupt company; that during such times said company had three directors, two of whom were officers of defendant company and that both they and defendant company well knew that said dividends were paid from the capital of the bankrupt company and not from its profits; that the Schuylerville Paper Company, a domestic corporation, was adjudicated a bankrupt on or about July 28, 1908, and that the assets of said bankrupt are insufficient by more than $25,000 to pay its creditors. The answer sets up denials and the Statute of Limitations. The complaint was dismissed upon the opening of counsel upon the ground that it did not appear that the payment of the dividends in question rendered said bankrupt company insolvent at the time, and also that it did not appear but that any recovery had in this action would inure to the benefit of the stockholder of said company. Inasmuch as the complaint was dismissed upon the opening of counsel and that opening does not appear in the appeal book it must be assumed that his opening followed the lines of the complaint. The statement of defendant's counsel as to plaintiff's claim which appears in the record in no way binds the plaintiff, except as specifically assented to by plaintiff's counsel. The question thereupon arises as to whether said complaint contains allegations sufficient to constitute a cause of action in connection with the admitted fact that the payment of the dividends did not at that time cause the insolvency of the company.

It seems clear that the capital stock of a corporation is intended as a fund for the ultimate security and payment of all its creditors, both present and future. Thus section 28 of the present Stock Corporation Law (Consol. Laws, chap. 59; Laws of 1909, chap. 61) prohibits directors from declaring dividends "except from the surplus profits arising from the business of such corporation," and sections 62, 63 and 64 provide in detail for the reduction of the capital stock of a corporation, the provisions of all of these sections having long been the law of this State. In Williams v. Western Union Tel. Co. (93 N. Y. 162, 187, 188) Judge Earl says: "These provisions were intended to prevent the division, distribution, withdrawal and reduction of the property of a corporation below the sum limited in its charter or articles of association for its capital, but not to prevent its increase above that sum. The purpose was to prevent the depletion of the property of the corporation thereby endangering its solvency. * * * All these provisions show that it was the purpose of the Legislature, by means of them, to create a property capital for the corporation, and then to keep that intact so as to secure the solvency of the corporation and its responsibility to its creditors." The same holding appears in Hutchinson v. Stadler (85 App. Div. 424, 432, 436): "Among the obligations resting upon directors, one is to keep the corporate property intact, in order that it may remain solvent for the purpose of being answerable to the creditors of the corporation, and also that it may be kept intact as a going concern to enable it to carry out the purposes of its creation for the benefit of its shareholders, as was designed when the interests were united, and for which the incorporators and shareholders contributed their funds. It has long been settled that the directors are not authorized to declare dividends out of the capital stock of the corporation as between it and its creditors. Such distribution depletes the fund upon which the creditors have the right to rely for the payment of their obligations, and upon the faith of which the debts were contracted. (Williams v. Western Union Tel. Co., 93 N. Y. 162.)"

The complaint of the appellant here was dismissed upon the opening principally upon the ground that appellant disclaimed that the dividends in question, although paid out of capital, rendered the corporation actually insolvent at such times. But if the capital of a corporation be regarded as a fund for the ultimate payment of creditors, and so to be kept intact unless diminished in the manner prescribed by statute, the mere fact that the assets still remain equal to the liabilities cannot justify dividends such as these. The statute does not allow capital to be depleted by means of dividends up to the very point of insolvency; on the contrary, the capital is to be kept intact and unimpaired and creditors have a right to rely upon this policy of the law in their dealings with corporations. The argument of respondent, if admitted, would manifestly put a premium upon fraud, as then the entire net assets of a corporation, including capital paid in, over and above its actual debts and liabilities at any one time, could be secretly withdrawn by its stockholders in the form of dividends, thus forcing its creditors to bear all the risk of insolvency arising from any slight business loss or shrinkage of assets.

The unauthorized dividends are in effect property of the corporation unlawfully diverted and as such property recoverable by creditors, or by the trustee in bankruptcy as representing them. In Cook on Corporations (6th ed. p. 1496) it is said: "Hence the rule has been firmly established that, where dividends are paid in whole or in part out of the capital stock, corporate creditors, being such when the dividend was declared or becoming such at any subsequent time, may, to the extent of their claims, if such claims are not otherwise paid, compel the stockholders to whom the dividend has been paid to refund whatever portion of the dividend was taken out of the capital stock." The courts have sometimes refused to apply this rule when either the directors or stockholders, or both, have made and received the dividend in good faith, that is, not knowing or supposing it to have been paid out of profits, but such is not this case. It is alleged in the complaint that at the time of these dividends two of the officers of the stockholding company composed a majority of the directors of the bankrupt company, which fact would of itself be sufficient to charge the stockholding company with any knowledge possessed by its officers in their capacity of directors of the bankrupt company. It is further alleged both that such officers and the stockholding company knew that said dividends were not paid from profits. These allegations, if proved, would seem conclusive as to the actual fraud of the defendant as against the creditors of the bankrupt. When corporate stock deliberately and with full knowledge is withdrawn and diverted in violation of the statute bad faith must necessarily be present, and such bad faith raises immediately upon the receipt of the unlawful dividends an implied obligation to repay such dividends to the corporation or to its creditors. The diversion of assets being in bad faith no demand before suit is necessary, and accordingly after bankruptcy the trustee, without more, may sue at once for the recovery of the assets so diverted.

The judgment should be reversed and a new trial granted, with costs to abide the event.

Types of Dividends

Pursuant to New York law, a New York corporation may make a distribution to its shareholders in either cash, property, or shares of stock, provided that all such distributions are made on a pro rata basis to all shareholders of the same class of stock. The purpose of this requirement is to ensure that all shareholders of the same class of stock are treated equally. If there is a disproportionate distribution within a class, the shareholders may seek judicial relief.

The decision as to the nature of the distribution lies within the discretion of the Board of Directors, unless a given stock preference has mandated a specific type of distribution. The nature of the distribution has a direct impact on the company's finances.

Cash. Cash is everyone's favorite dividend. If the Board declares a dividend in cash (ten cents per share), the funds come directly from the retained earnings account, and the corporation no longer has those funds in its coffers.

Shares of stock. If the Board decides to declare a share dividend, the result provides the company with additional working capital. What happens is that the directors use the funds in retained earnings to "buy" the additional shares that will be distributed to the shareholders. As with all purchases of stock, the consideration the corporation receives becomes a corporate asset as cash, and is thereby available for use by the corporation. By declaring a share dividend, the directors convert earned surplus into working capital. For corporations formed on or after February 22, 1998, the corporation may distribute shares of one class of stock to the shareholders of a different class of stock. For corporations formed prior to that date, share dividends can only be made in shares of the same class as held by the recipient shareholder.

Property. A property distribution only occurs with small closely held corporations. The corporation does not go out to buy property to give to the shareholders; rather, it distributes to the shareholders the property it already owns, such as unwanted inventory or outdated equipment. Similar to a share dividend, the directors "buy" the property with the funds from the earned surplus account and thereby have the funds available for corporate business (and, as a by-product, unload assets of minimal value).

Decisions about the nature and type of dividends rest with the Board of Directors. If the shareholders are unhappy with the type of dividend they receive, their only recourse is to vote the directors out of office at the next shareholders' meeting.

Liebman v. Auto Strop Company
212 A.D. 306 (1925)

The primary relief sought is an injunction restraining the issue of a corporate stock dividend of the shares of a subsidiary company by the defendant Auto Strop Company. The Auto Strop Company owns 2,502 shares, a majority of the capital stock of the Auto Strop Safety Razor Company. Defendants Gaisman, Maas and Coleman own 1,002 shares of the Auto Strop Company. Liebman and Klein, two of the plaintiffs and the instigators of the suit, own with some relatives 998 shares of the Auto Strop Company.

By reason of certain amendments to the charters of the companies in December, 1913, and February, 1914, the control of the Safety Razor Corporation was considerably curtailed through requiring unanimous consent to certain activities of the companies, and this partial control by the minority was assured by a provision for cumulative voting of the stock of the minority shareholders, so that they were always enabled to elect two directors in each corporation.

The provision of the amendment of December, 1913, which gave this control in both companies is in this language:

> "[1] At all elections of directors of this corporation, each stockholder shall be entitled to as many votes as shall equal the number of his shares of stock multiplied by the number of directors to be elected, and he may cast all of such votes for a single director, or he may distribute them among the number to be voted for, or any two or more of them as he may see fit.

[2] Stock in any other corporation which may at any time be held by this corporation shall be voted at all elections of directors of such other corporation for the persons nominated for directors of such other corporation by the stockholders of this corporation at a regular or special meeting of stockholders held before any such election of directors of such other corporation, in like manner of cumulative voting, that is to say, each stockholder shall be entitled to as many votes as shall equal the number of his shares of stock multiplied by the number of directors of such other corporation to be elected, and he may cast all of such votes for a single nominee or may distribute them among the number to be voted for or any two or more of them as he may see fit."

The matters which required unanimous consent provided for in the amendments of February 9, 1914, to the charters both of the Auto Strop Company and of the Safety Razor Company were:

(1) Contracts of employment in excess of $3,000 per year;

(2) Agreements "relating to patents or trade marks or to rights or licenses in relation thereto";

(3) Agreements for borrowing money or incurring indebtedness;

(4) Engaging in any manufacturing business (in the case of the Safety Razor Company other than the manufacture and sale of auto strop razors and accessories).

The part of the amendment to the charter of the Auto Strop Company which is unusual gave the stockholders of that company the right to vote cumulatively for the nominees for directors of any other company of which the Auto Strop Company held stock, that is, the Safety Razor Company; and thus the stock of the Safety Razor Company held by the Auto Strop Company was automatically voted for the same directors of the Safety Razor Company as had been cumulatively elected in the Auto Strop Company.

After this arrangement had subsisted for many years and the minority directors had exercised the right of veto, due to the unanimous vote requirement, on certain occasions in May, 1923, the directors of the Auto Strop Company, with Liebman and Klein opposing, voted to distribute all the Safety Razor Company stock held by it, to wit, 2,502 shares, as a dividend to stockholders. It is this action which is sought to be restrained, and plaintiffs claim it is a waste of the Auto Strop Company's assets and is done in bad faith and will be injurious to their interests.

When the stock of the Safety Razor Company held by the Auto Strop Company (the 2,502 shares) is thus distributed pursuant to the resolution, the Auto Strop Company will no longer be a stockholder of the Safety Razor Company. The Gaisman interests will own a majority of the stock of the Safety Razor Company, and thus (as majority owners) will be in a position to elect, if they see fit, the entire board of directors of the Safety Razor Company.

The plaintiffs assert that so to distribute the valuable property in shareholdings of the parent company constitutes a "waste of the assets" of the Auto Strop Company, which they seek to prevent.

At trial the referee found that the provision of the charter allowing election of directors of the Safety Razor Company by nomination of stockholders of the Auto Strop Company ran counter to the General Corporation Law; that it was subversive of the policy of the corporation laws; and that, hence, it was invalid and a nullity. We will not determine whether such a provision is necessarily invalid under section 34 of the General

Corporation Law, because we have concluded that bad faith cannot be predicated of the action proposed here in any event.

We reach this result not only because the power of the Auto Strop Company to declare dividends of the Safety Razor Company's stock cannot be denied, but also because a reasonable exercise of the power was contemplated in view of the status of the business and the previous conduct of the plaintiff directors. In 1906 1,000 shares of the Safety Razor Company's stock out of 3,502 shares then held were distributed, and hence its character as surplus was not disputable. It is the directors' function to declare when and to what extent dividends may be paid. Their discretion controls, and when there is a surplus, whether of stock or otherwise, it is distributable upon their resolution among stockholders as a dividend. The power of directors to affect the rights of the minority must be exercised in good faith; and their action, even though lawful, may be restrained if a corporate purpose is not served and some selfish interest is promoted. A fraudulent destruction of the rights of non-assenting stockholders will not be permitted, and an act solely in the interest of the majority, greatly detrimental to the interests of the corporation and the minority, will be halted by equity, even though it is within lawful power. But the soundness or wisdom of the directors' judgment will not be judicially reviewed where there is neither bad faith nor fraud. An intent to injure the minority by some action which depreciates the worth of its holding may indicate bad faith in the exercise of legal power, or the sale of the property of the corporation to interests in which the majority bringing about the sale may have an interest would present the element of bad faith. An injury to the minority, however, in respect of control cannot of itself support the assertion that the scheme is grounded in fraud. If there were no possibility of the act of the directors being regarded as an honest conclusion, and no beneficial result accrued to the company or the minority, the court might interpose.

The claim here is that the deprivation of Liebman and Klein of their power to name two of the seven directors of the Safety Razor Company is evidence that the act indicated in the distribution of this surplus stock held by the Auto Strop Company is in bad faith, and that, therefore, distribution of the stock to accomplish this purpose constitutes a waste of the corporate assets. There is no doubt that the distribution of the stock by the Auto Strop Company does take away this right of the minority stockholders, and the provisions requiring unanimous consent with respect to the various mentioned activities of the company would fail. This incident of the act of the directors, however, does not make for its mala fides without any indication of proof of loss to the corporate body affected or to the minority.

The corporation is the owner of the property, and its directors are trustees clothed with the power of controlling the property and with its management. The act of the defendants in distributing the stock of the Safety Razor Company to the stockholders of the Auto Strop Company, all of whom are stockholders in that same company, and who thereby become proportionately increased in ownership, cannot be said to be affected with bad faith, unless we can find some legal detriment to plaintiffs under which they are entitled to prevent the accomplishment of the project, of which this transaction appears barren. Nothing of a waste of assets as such is shown, because the surplus to be distributed has been held as such through many years and is a part of a total of shares some of which have been distributed. There is ground for holding, too, that the unanimous consent provision of the Safety Razor Company's charter concerning action by directors in the matters of loans, salaries and agreements relating to patents and engaging in any business other than the manufacture and sale of auto strop razors, ought to be changed so as not to embarass the business now conducted on a much larger scale than when these provisions were adopted. The non-assent of a minority who have a veto by exercise of a refusal of unanimous consent in these details may seriously hamper the proper conduct of a large business. The Auto Strop Company is the only licensor of the auto strop patents operated by the Safety Razor Company, and is interested in the royalties secured by the manufacture and sale under these patents. All of the business operations of the Safety Razor Company are, therefore, of necessity such as ought not to be obstructed by such opposition as the evidence discloses as heretofore occurring, and a desire for co-operation with new directors is not an indication necessarily of judgment of the majority brought about solely through selfish reasoning.

We think the judgment should be affirmed, with costs.

TAXATION OF THE DIVIDEND

For the Shareholder

Dividends are considered ordinary income to the shareholder in the tax year in which the shareholder has actual or constructive receipt of the dividend. The value of the dividend is taxed by the Internal Revenue Service, but the actual tax consequences vary depending on the nature of the dividend.

Cash As with all receipts of cash, the value is the amount of the cash received, and it is taxed accordingly, just like wages or interest received on a bank savings account.

Shares of stock Because the distribution is made on a pro rata basis, a shareholder does not have to pay any taxes on the value of the share received as a dividend in the year of distribution. This is true because the share dividend does not provide any direct benefit or income to a shareholder. If a shareholder owns 1,000 shares of stock that represent a 1 percent ownership interest in the corporation, when he or she receives three additional shares as a dividend, he or she still owns 1 percent of the corporation which is now represented by 1,003 shares. The only practical benefit the shareholder receives is when these shares are sold. When the share is distributed, the value of that share at that moment constitutes the shareholder's **basis** in the stock (consideration given for the stock—the cost). If and when the shareholder sells those shares, the difference between the basis and the amount received from the sale represents the **capital gain or loss** to the shareholder.

> *Example: A shareholder receives five shares of stock as a dividend. At the date of distribution, each share is valued at $5. Several years later, the shareholder sells these five shares for $6 per share. In the year of the sale, the shareholder must report a gain of $5, the difference between the basis and the selling price.*

Since shares of stock are considered **capital assets** to the shareholder, property of value owned by the shareholder, the tax consequences of the sale will be treated as either short-term or long-term capital gain or loss depending on the length of time the shareholder held the stock before selling it.

If the shareholder held the stock for less than six months prior to selling it, the gain or loss is taxed as a **short-term capital gain or loss.** Short-term gains are taxed as ordinary income; short-term losses may be used to offset other capital gains and ordinary income. If the loss is greater than $3,000 after offsetting capital gains, the taxpayer may carry the loss

Basis — all consideration given for acquiring an asset.

Capital gain or loss — amount realized on the sale or distribution of a capital asset; the difference between the basis and the selling price.

Capital assets — property held for investment and appreciation.

Short-term capital gain or loss — amount realized from the sale of a capital asset held for no more than six months.

forward to succeeding tax years, deducting $,3000 per year of the carried-forward loss until accounting for the entire loss.

If the shareholder holds the stock for more than six months, the resulting sale is considered a **long term capital gain or loss.** A long-term capital gain is taxed at a special rate for capital gains; long-term capital losses may be used to offset long-term capital gains and carried forward to succeeding years.

Long-term capital gain or loss — amount realized on the sale of a capital asset held for more than six months.

Property If a shareholder receives a property distribution, he or she must report the property as ordinary income at its fair market value. Property dividends are not favored by shareholders. If a shareholder receives inventory that the corporation could not sell as a dividend, the fair market value is meaningless because it is an item that could not sell. Regardless, the shareholder must report and pay taxes on the fair market value of this property even though it has no practical value to the shareholder.

For the Corporation

Excess business holdings tax — additional tax imposed on corporations that retain more than a minimum amount as unrestricted, unreserved earned surplus.

Although the Board of Directors is granted the discretion to declare a dividend, there may be some negative tax consequences if the Board fails to do so. The IRS imposes an **excess business holdings tax** on all unrestricted earned surplus over a specified amount that is not distributed to shareholders as a dividend. The tax rationale behind this is that if the funds are distributed to the shareholder, the IRS can tax the value of the dividend, but if the corporation retains the funds, the IRS loses tax dollars. Therefore, the IRS imposes a penalty for corporations that do not make these distributions. Also, because the IRS will impose this additional tax, it may be a breach of the directors' fiduciary obligation if the Board fails to declare a dividend and thereby subjects the corporation to an additional tax burden.

Depreciate — loss in value due to time and/or use.

Accelerated depreciation —depreciation taken at a rate faster than straight-line depreciation.

Even if the corporation does make the distribution, there still may be some negative tax consequences. Corporations are permitted to **depreciate** property used for their business; depreciation represents the decrease in value of an asset due to use and time. Corporations are also permitted to take **accelerated depreciation,** a deduction at a faster rate than the property is actually wearing out. If the corporation distributes property for which it had taken accelerated depreciation but "pays" itself the fair market value of the property (the value on which the shareholder will have to report), the corporation may have to file amended tax returns and pay extra taxes and perhaps pay a penalty for the tax benefit it received from taking the depreciation as an operating expense.

CHAPTER REVIEW

One of the major factors that influence a potential investor's decision with respect to acquiring a specific stock is the dividend history of the corporation. Most investors are interested in receiving a healthy yield on their investments of funds, and if a corporation's dividend history represents too low a yield, the potential investor will take his or her funds elsewhere.

Once the decision to invest in a given corporation has been made, the shareholder has no automatic right to a dividend (except for certain preferred issues). The authority and discretion to declare a dividend rests with the Board of Directors, and only if such dividend declaration is made by the Board does the shareholder have an actual right to a dividend.

The BCL permits a corporation to distribute cash, property, or shares of stock as a dividend, but may only do so if funds are available for such distribution from unrestricted, unreserved earned surplus. If the Board of Directors declares a dividend from an inappropriate source of funds, the directors who voted for such a dividend may be personally liable to the corporation, as will be the shareholder who actually received such dividend.

There are differing tax consequences for the shareholders depending on the nature of the dividend. Cash dividends are taxed as ordinary income in the tax year of actual or constructive receipt. A share dividend is only taxed when it is sold by the shareholder; the date of the actual or constructive receipt only determines the shareholder's basis in the shares. Property distributions are taxed as ordinary income to the shareholder at the property's fair market value.

If a corporation retains more than a statutorily determined amount as unrestricted, unreserved earned surplus, the corporation may be subject to an excess business holdings tax, and the directors may be liable for a breach of fiduciary obligations in causing the corporation to be subjected to this additional tax.

KEY TERMS

Accelerated depreciation
Assets
Balance sheet
Basic accounting equation
Basis
Capital
Capital assets
Capital gain or loss
Capital surplus
Depreciate
Dividend
Earned surplus

Equity
Excess business holdings tax
Gross profit or loss
Income statement
Liabilities
Long-term capital gain or loss
Net profit
Payables
Retained earnings
Short-term capital gain or loss
Surplus
Unrestricted, unreserved earned surplus

EXERCISES

1. Discuss the benefits and detriments of different types of dividend distributions.

2. Briefly list some legitimate restrictions and reservations that may be placed on an earned surplus account.

3. Why do you believe the BCL gives the Board of Directors the discretion to declare dividends? Explain. How would this affect a potential investor's decision with respect to purchasing shares?

4. Obtain and analyze the federal tax schedule for capital gains and losses.

5. Discuss the circumstances under which an investor would prefer greater dividends as opposed to greater capital growth. What could a shareholder do to change the corporate dividend policy to reflect the shareholder's financial needs.

FACTUAL PROBLEM

A shareholder of a close corporation has been audited by the IRS for failing to report as income the value of the electric typewriter she received as a distribution from the corporation. The shareholder maintains the typewriter represents a return of capital, but the IRS says it is income. Argue for both sides.

Chapter **10**

Shareholder Agreements

INTRODUCTION

As a general principle, shareholders, as owners of the corporation, are free to alienate their interests and rights without restriction. However, despite this general rule, under certain circumstances the shareholders of a corporation, either publicly or privately held, may enter into agreements that in some way limit this right of alienation. This chapter focuses on four such agreements.

The first of these agreements is a shareholder restrictive agreement, which is only encountered in closely held corporations. These agreements limit a shareholder's ability to sell or otherwise dispose of his or her shares. The second arrangement detailed is a proxy, a vehicle by which a shareholder transfers his or her right to vote to another individual for a limited period of time. The third agreement viewed is a voting trust, a legal relationship by which a shareholder relinquishes his or her right to vote by giving that ability to a trustee for a period of time not to exceed ten years. The final agreement detailed is a shareholder pooling agreement, whereby a group of shareholders contract to vote their shares as a block for a particular corporate vote. These four agreements, perfectly valid under the BCL, have the effect of limiting a shareholder's freedom with respect to share ownership.

SHAREHOLDER RESTRICTIVE AGREEMENT

Shareholder restrictive agreement — agreement limiting the ability of a shareholder to alienate his or her shares.

A **shareholder restrictive agreement** is a contract, encountered in closely held corporations, in which the shareholders agree to limit their freedom of alienation in order to maintain ownership of the corporation in a select group of individuals. New York law prohibits any unreasonable restriction on a shareholder's ability to alienate his or her shares but does permit some restrictions on the transferability of stock. The only prohibition is that no such

179

agreement may completely and irrevocably prohibit the sale or transfer of the stock. Any such restriction on transferability must appear in either the certificate of incorporation, the by-laws, or a separate shareholders' agreement.

Example: A group of lawyers decide to form a law office and incorporate as a professional corporation. Under New York law (Chapter 5), professional corporations, by statute, must limit share ownership to professionals licensed to perform the professional services for which the corporation was formed. This restriction appears not only in the statute, but also in the certificate of incorporation, and limits the shareholders' ability to transfer their shares.

When dealing with a restrictive agreement, two specific problems must be addressed: under what circumstances the shares may be transferred and the price that is to be paid for such shares. Generally, these agreements provide for the transferability of the shares by limiting the alienation to one of several possibilities: first option, mandatory buyout, or consent of the other shareholders.

First option — requirement that a shareholder offer his or her shares to the other shareholders before he or she may sell them to outsiders.

An agreement that provides for **first option** states that if a shareholder wishes to sell his or her shares, the shareholder must first offer the shares to the other shareholders or the corporation. If the other shareholders or the corporation do not exercise the option to purchase, the shareholder is free to sell the shares to outsiders.

Example: A shareholder of a closely held corporation is dissatisfied with the manner in which the company is managed and wishes to sell her shares to make a different investment. The shareholder is a party to a restrictive shareholder agreement in which she had agreed to give the other shareholders the first option to purchase the shares. The shareholder offers the shares to the other shareholders, according to the provisions of the agreement. If the other shareholders do not exercise the option to purchase, the dissatisfied shareholder may sell the shares to an outsider.

Mandatory buyout — provision in a shareholder's restrictive agreement in which the corporation must repurchase the shares if a shareholder wishes to sell.

A **mandatory buyout** provision requires the remaining shareholders or the corporation to repurchase the shares of a shareholder who wishes to divest himself or herself of the stock. If the agreement includes a mandatory buyout provision, it usually also indicates the conditions that will trigger such obligation on the part of the remaining shareholders or the corporation. The most typical of these triggering provisions are:

1. *The death of the shareholder.* When a shareholder dies, automatically all of the shareholder's property passes to someone else, either by will or by intestate succession. Because the purpose of the restrictive agreement is to limit the persons who may own the shares, this event will trigger the buyout provision.

2. *The retirement of the shareholder.* In the case of a professional corporation or a corporation that requires shares to be owned by persons actively engaged in the business of the company, the shareholder's retirement will trigger the buyout provision.

3. *The disability of the shareholder.* If the shareholder becomes disabled and funds are needed for the shareholder's care, the provisions of the agreement will become operative.

4. *The bankruptcy of the shareholder.* If a shareholder is declared bankrupt, the corporation or remaining shareholders must purchase the shares so that the bankrupt shareholder's creditors can have assets to attach. Because the shares cannot be freely transferred, the creditors cannot attach the shares outright.

5. *The loss of the shareholder's occupational license.* This affects professional corporations as indicated in the preceding example.

6. *The written notice by the shareholder of the intent to sell the shares.* Because New York law prohibits the complete prohibition on the alienation of shares, if the shareholder wishes to divest himself or herself of the stock, the agreement cannot prohibit such divestment.

Because mandatory buyouts are only encountered with close corporations, the second problem that is encountered is the price that will be paid for these shares because there is no open market value for the stock. Well-drafted shareholder restrictive agreements, therefore, usually include a pricing provision used to determine the price the remaining shareholders or the corporation will pay for the shares. The most typical pricing provisions used are:

1. *Firm price.* A specific dollar amount per share is written into the agreement.

2. *Adjusted stated value.* This is an accounting method whereby the value of the corporation's assets less liabilities, plus its anticipated earnings, are quantified and then divided by the number of outstanding shares.

3. *Earnings multiple formula.* This is another accounting method whereby the earnings of the company for a given period are multiplied by a standard indexed number determined for every industry by financial analysts. The resulting number is then divided by the number of outstanding shares to arrive at a price per share.

4. *Book value.* Under this method, only the assets of the company are considered at the number that appears in the corporate accounting book. This number is then divided by the number of outstanding shares to arrive at a price per share.

5. *Matching a bona fide offer.* If the dissatisfied shareholder had been given a bona fide offer, the agreement may provide that the corporation or remaining shareholders must match that price.

6. *Appraisal.* Some agreements provide that the price of the shares will be determined by an independent appraiser who is mutually agreed on by the parties.

7. *Arbitration.* Because of the cost-effectiveness of the arbitration process, many agreements provide that disputes over the price of the shares will be determined by submission of the problem to an arbitrator.

If the corporation or the remaining shareholders are unable to make the purchase, the dissatisfied shareholder is then free to sell the shares to outsiders. As previously noted, New York law prohibits the shareholders from any unreasonable restriction on the sale of the shares.

Amodio v. Amodio
70 N.Y.2d 5 (1987)

The only issue before the court in this divorce action is the value, for equitable distribution purposes, of defendant's 15% stock interest in Capitol Electrical Supply Co., Inc., a closely held corporation. Defendant acquired the stock in 1980 for $87,500 pursuant to the terms of a shareholder's agreement which provides that if defendant seeks to sell his stock within 20 years, the other shareholders may exercise a right of first refusal and purchase his shares for the price paid. The agreement also provides that if defendant dies within its 20-year term, the surviving stockholders can acquire his interest for $87,500. After a trial the court concluded that the stock was worth $87,500 and the Appellate Division affirmed.

There is no uniform rule for valuing stock in closely held corporations. "One tailored to the particular case must be found, and that can be done only after a discriminating consideration of all information bearing upon an enlightened prediction of the future" (Snyder's Estate v United States, 285 F2d 857, 861). The Internal Revenue Service has declared that appropriate factors to be considered in valuing such stock for tax purposes include: (1) the nature and history of the business, (2) its particular economic outlook and that of its industry generally, (3) the book value of the stock and the financial condition of the business, (4) the company's earning capacity, (5) its dividend paying capacity, (6) its goodwill and other intangible assets, (7) other sales of the corporation's stock, and (8) the market price of stock of comparable corporations (Rev Rul 59-60, IRS Cum Bull 1959-1, at 237).

The Internal Revenue Service's formulation is not the only method of valuing stock in a closely held corporation, but it has been recognized by authors and applied by appellate courts and was one of the two methods used by plaintiff's expert witness in this case.

Whatever method is used, however, must take into consideration inhibitions on the transfer of the corporate interest resulting from a limited market or contractual provisions (see, 3 Foster, Law and the Family, op. cit., at 645; 11C Zett, NY Civ Prac, op. cit., at 69-25, 69-46 - 69-48; cf., Matter of Blake v Blake Agency, supra, at 149). If transfer of the stock of a closely held corporation is restricted by a bona fide buy-sell agreement which predates the marital discord, the price fixed by the agreement, although not conclusive, Is a factor which should be considered .

The decisions below, however, could be read as indicating that the courts found the price fixed in the agreement controlling because under the agreement the stock was not currently transferable. That the stock could not immediately be sold is not dispositive; marital property may have a value to the holder notwithstanding that it has no present market value. The court must consider all the circumstances reflecting on the present worth of the property to the titleholder. It need not rely solely on the price set forth in a buy-sell agreement if other evidence exists.

In this case plaintiff's expert witness, using two different methods of appraisal, testified that the value of defendant's stock was between $172,000 and $253,000. His first method computed the value of the stock by dividing the corporation's estimated shareholder equity by defendant's 15% interest in the corporation. The other valued the corporation, and defendant's stock interest in it, by applying the guidelines for valuing close corporations set forth in Revenue Ruling 59-60. However, the witness did not consider the stock transfer restrictions contained in the shareholders' agreement in either method. That being so, the courts properly determined defendant's stock was worth $87,500, the price contained in the shareholders' agreement, because that was the only evidence in the record of its actual value.

Accordingly, the order of the Appellate Division should be affirmed, with costs.

Gallagher v. Lambert
74 N.Y.2d 562 (1989)

Plaintiff Gallagher purchased stock in the defendant close corporation with which he was employed. The purchase of his 8.5% interest was subject to a mandatory buy-back provision: if the employment ended for any reason before January 31, 1985, the stock would return to the corporation for book value. The corporation fired plaintiff prior to the fulcrum date, after which the buy-back price would have been higher.

We must decide whether plaintiff's dismissed causes of action, seeking the higher repurchase price based on an alleged breach of a fiduciary duty, should be reinstated. We think not and affirm, concluding that the Appellate Division did not err in dismissing these causes of action by summary judgment because there was no cognizable breach of any fiduciary duty owed to plaintiff under the plain terms of the parties' repurchase agreement.

Gallagher was employed by defendant Eastdil Realty as a mortgage broker from 1968 to 1973. Three years later, in 1976, he returned to the company as a broker, officer and director, serving additionally as president and chief executive officer of defendant's wholly owned subsidiary, Eastdil Advisors, Inc. Gallagher was at all times an employee at will. Still later, in 1981, Eastdil offered all its executive employees an opportunity to purchase stock subject to a mandatory buy-back provision, which provided that upon "voluntary resignation or other termination" prior to January 31, 1985, an employee would be required to return the stock for book value. After that date, the formula for the buy-back price was keyed to the company's earnings. Plaintiff accepted the offer and its terms.

On January 10, 1985, Gallagher was fired by Eastdil Realty. He did not and does not now contest the firing. But he demanded payment for his shares calculated on the post-January 31, 1985 buy-back formula. Eastdil refused and Gallagher sued, asserting eight causes of action. Only three claims, based on an alleged breach of fiduciary duty of good faith and fair dealing, are before us. The trial court denied defendants' motion for summary judgment on these claims, stating that factual issues were raised relating to defendants' motive in firing plaintiff. The Appellate Division, by divided vote, reversed, dismissed those claims and ordered payment for the shares at book value. That court then granted leave and certified the following question to us: "Was the order of this Court, which modified the order of the Supreme Court, properly made?"

The parties negotiated a written contract containing a common and plain buy-back provision. Plaintiff got what he bargained for—book value for his minority shares if his employment in the corporation ended before January 31, 1985. There being no basis presented for the courts to interfere with the operation and consequences of this agreement between the parties, the order of the Appellate Division granting summary judgment to defendants, dismissing the first three causes of action, should be affirmed and the certified question answered in the affirmative.

Earlier this year, in Ingle v Glamore Motor Sales (73 NY2d 183), we expressly refrained from deciding the precise issue presented by this case. There, the challenge was directed to the at-will discharge from employment and was predicated on a claimed fiduciary obligation flowing from the shareholder relationship. Relying principally on Sabetay v Sterling Drug (69 NY2d 329, 335-336) and Murphy v American Home Prods. Corp. (58 NY2d 293, 300), we held that "[a] minority shareholder in a close corporation, by that status alone, who contractually agrees to the repurchase of his shares upon termination of his employment for any reason, acquires no right from the corporation or majority shareholders against at-will discharge." (Ingle v Glamore Motor Sales, 73 NY2d, supra, at 188 [emphasis added].) However, we cautioned that "[it] is necessary * * * to appreciate and keep distinct the duty a corporation owes to a minority shareholder as a shareholder from any duty it might owe him as an employee." (Id., at 188.)

The causes before us on this appeal are based on an alleged departure from a fiduciary duty of fair dealing existing independently of the employment and arising from the plaintiff's simultaneous relationship as a minority shareholder in the corporation. Plaintiff claims entitlement to the higher price based on a breach flowing from Eastdil's premature "bad faith" termination of his at-will employment because, he asserts, the sole purpose of the firing at that time was to acquire the stock at a contractually and temporally measured lower buy-back price formula.

The claim seeking a higher price for the shares cannot be neatly divorced, as the dissent urges, from the employment because the buy-back provision links them together as to timing and consequences. Plaintiff not only agreed to the particular buy-back formula, he helped write it and he reviewed it with his attorney during the negotiation process, before signing the agreement and purchasing the minority interest. These provisions, which require an employee shareholder to sell back stock upon severance from corporate employment, are designed to ensure that ownership of all of the stock, especially of a close corporation, stays within the control of the remaining corporate owners-employees; that is, those who will continue to contribute to its successes or failures (see, Kessler, Share Repurchases Under Modern Corporation Laws, 28 Fordham L Rev 637, 648 [1959–1960]). These agreements define the scope of the relevant fiduciary duty and supply certainty of obligation to each side. They should not be undone simply upon an allegation of unfairness. This would destroy their very purpose, which is to provide a certain formula by which to value stock in the future (Allen v Biltmore Tissue Corp., 2 NY2d 534, 542-543). Indeed, the dissenters in Ingle itself acknowledged that employee shareholders would be precluded from complaining about the terms of an otherwise enforceable buy-back provision (Ingle v Glamore Motor Sales, 73 NY2d, supra, at 192, n 1).

Gallagher accepted the offer to become a minority stockholder, but only for the period during which he remained an employee. The buy-back price formula was designed for the benefit of both parties precisely so that they could know their respective rights on certain dates and avoid costly and lengthy litigation on the "fair value" issue (see, Coleman v Taub, 638 F2d 628, 637). Permitting these causes to survive would open the door to litigation on both the value of the stock and the date of termination, and hinder the employer from fulfilling its contractual rights under the agreement. This would frustrate the agreement and would be disruptive of the settled principles governing like agreements where parties contract between themselves in advance so that there may be reliance, predictability and definitiveness between themselves on such matters. There being no dispute that the employer had the unfettered discretion to fire plaintiff at any time, we should not redefine the precise measuring device and scope of the agreement. Defendant agreed to abide by these terms and thus fulfilled its fiduciary duty in that respect.

Accordingly, the order of the Appellate Division should be affirmed, with costs, and the certified question answered in the affirmative.

Example: A shareholder agreement provides that a shareholder may sell his shares provided that he first offers the shares to the other shareholders. A shareholder wants to sell his shares and has been offered a good price for his holdings by the corporation's major competitor. The other shareholders will not buy the shares and refuse to give their consent to the sale because of the possibility of a takeover by the competitor. In this instance, the court may deem this withholding of consent "unreasonable."

Any restriction on the transferability of shares must appear on the face of the share certificate itself in order to protect potential purchasers of the stock. Any restriction on transferability is not enforceable against any person who had no actual notice of such restriction.

Example: A shareholder whose shares are subject to an agreement restricting transferability sells his shares to a bona fide purchaser who has no notice of the restriction. (The restriction does not appear on the share certificate and the purchaser was not told of the restriction.) The other shareholders attempt to have the sale rescinded. The court will not enforce the restriction against the bona fide purchaser who has no notice.

PROXIES

Proxy — authorization by a shareholder to have someone else vote the shares.

A **proxy** is a written authorization by a shareholder directing the proxy holder to vote the shares on the shareholder's behalf. Proxies are permitted pursuant to the provisions of section 609 of the BCL, but the BCL does not indicate any specifics for the form of the proxy itself. (See Exhibit 10–1 for a sample proxy.)

Under section 609(b), a proxy is valid for a period of eleven months from the date it is given unless the proxy specifies a different period. Generally, proxies are agencies created by the shareholder, and the death or incompetence of the shareholder automatically revokes the proxy provided that written notice has been received by the officer of the corporation who validates the list of current shareholders before the authority of the proxy holder has been exercised.

Under certain circumstances, outlined in section 609(f) of the BCL, a proxy may be irrevocable. The requirements are that the proxy must state that it is irrevocable, and the proxy holder must be either:

a. a pledgee (security holder)

b. a person who has agreed to purchase the shares

c. a creditor of the shareholder if the proxy was given in consideration of the debt

d. an officer whose employment contract calls for the proxy

e. a person designated by a shareholder pooling agreement (see following)

Proxy solicitation — request to a shareholder to give his or her proxy to the person making the request.

Solicitation — formal request, or any part of a continuing plan leading the way to a formal request, for a proxy.

Whereas a shareholder may freely give his or her proxy to anyone, if someone requests the proxy from the shareholder, this is known as a **proxy solicitation.** Such solicitation is regulated by the Securities and Exchange Commission for securities traded on a national exchange or for securities issued by a corporation whose assets and number of shareholders meet statutorily specified minimum numbers. **Solicitation** is defined as a formal request or any part of a continuing plan preparing the way to a formal request for a proxy. Any such solicitation requires the solicitor to make full disclosure to the shareholder of the following information:

1. the identity of all proxy participants
2. the compensation the corporate officers and directors receive if they are the ones making the solicitation
3. any conflict of interest between the solicitor and the corporation
4. all material factors that would influence the shareholder's decision

Persons solicit proxies in order to gain control of a corporation. Although ownership of a corporation vests in the shareholders, the ability to control the corporation lies in the right to vote. Consequently, the person with the ability to exercise the shareholder's right to vote may control the corporation by electing the directors who manage the business.

If the current directors solicit the proxies, which they always do in the notice of the shareholder's annual meeting, a shareholder of a New York corporation may have a shareholder proposal included in the proxy solicitation, provided that the proposal does not exceed 300 words and is reasonable and related to proper corporate matters.

If two or more persons seek the proxies of a shareholder, the solicitation is referred to as a **proxy contest.** The current management of the corporation may be reimbursed for its expenses in a proxy contest, provided that the matter in dispute is one of policy rather than the directors' desire to remain in office. The insurgents (noncurrent management) in a proxy contest have no right to reimbursement, but the corporation may voluntarily reimburse them (and usually does so if the insurgents win).

> *Example: A corporation has excellent assets but has not been able to utilize them to their full extent. A corporate raider wishes to take over the company in order to sell its assets and eventually dissolve the corporation. Current management wishes to keep the corporation operating. In this situation, the proxy contest is one of policy, and the management's expenses may be reimbursed by the corporation.*

Proxy contest — two or more persons seeking a shareholder's proxy.

VOTING TRUSTS

Voting trusts are permitted under section 621 of the BCL. A **voting trust** is a written agreement among shareholders to transfer their shares to a trust that is managed by a trustee. The trustee has legal title to the shares, meaning that the trustee votes the shares, and the shareholders retain the beneficial title to the shares entitling them to receive any dividends that are declared.

New York law limits voting trusts to a period of ten years, but the trust may be extended if the shareholders so agree in writing within six months of the trust's termination. If a trust is created, the shareholders and the trust agreement are sent to the corporation, which then reissues the shares in the name of the trust. The trustee is a fiduciary to the shareholders and must maintain accounts, books, and records. Voting trusts are irrevocable for the period of the trust.

Voting trust — trust created for not more than ten years in which the trustee has the authority to vote the shares and the beneficiaries receive the dividends.

> *Example: A father wishes to transfer some shares to his children but wants to retain some control over the corporation. He places the shares in a voting trust, naming himself as the trustee and the children as the beneficiaries. In this fashion, the father gets to vote*

the shares, and the children receive the dividends for the period of the trust. When the trust terminates, the shares will be reissued to the children outright.

Ronnen v. Ajax Electric Motor Corp.
88 N.Y.2d 582 (1996)

The opposing parties to this litigation are brother and sister who, with their children, collectively hold a bare majority of the issued and outstanding shares of the capital stock of Ajax Electric Motor Corp., a closely held corporation based in Rochester. Respondent Neil Norry has been the chief executive officer of Ajax. The immediate matter in dispute is the validity of the election of the board of directors of the corporation at its annual shareholders' meeting held March 13, 1995.

Central to that dispute is a March 5, 1982 shareholders' agreement between Norry (and his two sons) and his sister, appellant Deborah Ronnen, on behalf of herself and as custodian for her children. The shareholders' agreement granted Norry certain rights to vote Ronnen's stock and that of her children.

The March 13, 1995 shareholders' meeting began in acrimony between Ronnen and Norry, who initially chaired the meeting. Immediately prior to the meeting, Ronnen served Norry with a temporary restraining order prohibiting him from voting the Ronnen shares regarding proposed amendments to the Ajax bylaws and certificate of incorporation, which were on the agenda for the meeting. When the meeting convened, Ronnen's attorney had the proceedings videotaped, without prior notice to Norry. In response to these actions, Norry announced that the meeting was being adjourned. Over Ronnen's protest, he voted the Ronnen shares with the Norry shares for a combined majority vote to adjourn and left the meeting. In his absence, Ronnen and the remaining shareholders of Ajax, including appellants Bruce Lipsky and Joseph Livingston, elected a slate of directors.

Norry then brought a proceeding, pursuant to Business Corporation Law sec. 619, to invalidate the election of directors in his absence and for an order directing a new election. Ronnen, Lipsky and Livingston petitioned under section 619 to confirm the election. Supreme Court interpreted the shareholders' agreement as giving Norry the right to vote the Ronnen shares in any election of a board of directors. This factor, together with the hostile atmosphere permeating the March 13, 1995, meeting, led Supreme Court to conclude that a new election should be held. The Appellate Division affirmed the order for a new election of directors, with two Justices dissenting on the ground that the shareholders' agreement did not transfer Ronnen's voting rights to Norry for board of directors elections and that the election was in other respects properly conducted. Ronnen, Lipsky and Livingston appeal as of right on the basis of the double dissent (see, CPLR 5601 [a]).

We now affirm. The parties are not in dispute over the circumstances leading up to the March 5, 1982 agreement between the Norry shareholders and Ronnen. Ajax had been a highly prosperous distributor of electric motors nationwide, founded by Irving Norry (the father of Neil Norry and Deborah Ronnen), Sydney Gilbert and David Lipsky. Irving Norry and his wife had, by 1980, transferred by gift or sale all of their shareholdings in Ajax to their two children and their families. Friction developed between Norry and Ronnen regarding, among other things: Norry's acquisition for his children of his mother's Ajax shares, upsetting the equality of the Norry siblings' interests in the corporation; Ronnen's displeasure over an irrevocable option her brother had been granted in 1967 to acquire her Ajax shares under what she considered an inadequate price formula; the level Norry had fixed for his compensation and other alleged financial self-dealing in Ajax and in Norry Electric Co., a separate family business; and Ronnen's objection to not being kept informed of financial decisions Norry made in connection with the management of both corporations. Ronnen wished to ensure that her interest in Ajax could be passed on to her children free of interference by Norry. Norry expressed willingness to accommodate Ronnen, provided he was guaranteed continued managerial control of Ajax and was given the opportunity to acquire the Ronnen shares in Ajax before they could be sold to an outsider. He also wished to buy out his sister's interest in Norry Electric Co. These various objectives of the parties were implemented in the shareholders' agreement and other contemporaneous transactions.

The shareholders' agreement recited as one of its purposes "to provide for the vote of [the Norry and Ronnen families'] Shares in order to provide for continuity in the control and management of Ajax." The primary voting control provision was set forth in paragraph 8 of the agreement. Subparagraph 8 (a) provided that the Ronnen shareholders "agree that Neil Norry shall exercise voting rights over the Shares owned by them . . . with respect to any and all matters relating to Ajax's day-to-day operations and corporate management" (emphasis supplied). Norry was also given the right to vote the Ronnen shares regarding any sale of substantially all of Ajax's assets or stock to an outside party, provided that the transaction treated the Norry and Ronnen interests equivalently. The agreement, however, reserved to Ronnen the right to vote the Ronnen shares "[i]n connection with other major corporate policy decisions," and listed as examples of such major decisions, "other types of corporate reorganizations" and other similar actions. Subparagraph 8 (b) gave Norry an irrevocable proxy to vote the Ronnen shares as provided in the preceding subparagraph.

The unambiguous words of paragraph 8 and the recital purpose clause of the agreement present an issue of pure contract interpretation for the court (see, Bethlehem Steel Co. v Turner Constr. Co., 2 N.Y.2d 456, 460, 161 N.Y.S.2d 90, 141 N.E.2d 590; Brainard v New York Cent. R. R. Co., 242 N.Y. 125, 133, 151 N.E. 152), and admit of no construction other than the conferral to Norry of the right to vote the Ronnen shares in any election of a board of directors of Ajax. The undisputed background facts support this interpretation as well (see, Brainard v New York Cent. R. R. Co., supra). The parties have not cited to any provision of the Ajax certificate of incorporation transferring corporate management decisions from the board of directors to the shareholders (see, Business Corporation Law sec. 620 [b]). Therefore, management of the business of Ajax was, by statute, exclusively "under the direction of its board of directors" (Business Corporation Law sec. 701; see, McQuade v Stoneham, 263 N.Y. 323, 329, 189 N.E. 234, rearg. denied 264 N.Y. 460).

We have held that "the law in force at the time [an] agreement is entered into becomes as much a part of the agreement as though it were expressed or referred to therein, for it is presumed that the parties had such law in contemplation when the contract was made and the contract will be construed in the light of such law" (Dolman v United States Trust Co., 2 N.Y.2d 110, 116, 157 N.Y.S.2d 537, 138 N.E.2d 784). Thus, without the right to vote the Ronnen shares to elect the directors of the corporation, the transfer of voting rights regarding "corporate management" under subparagraph 8 (a) of the agreement would be essentially meaningless since management control was vested in the directors and not the shareholders. We have long and consistently ruled against any construction which would render a contractual provision meaningless or without force or effect.

The reservation to Ronnen of the right to vote the Ronnen shares "[i]n connection with . . . major corporate policy decisions" is consistent with the parties' intent to confer on Norry the right to vote the Ronnen shares in the election of board of directors, since major corporate decisions, such as corporate mergers, connote extraordinary change while director elections are the ordinary subject matter of a shareholder meeting. It, therefore, follows that by agreeing to transfer to Norry the right to vote the Ronnen shares "with respect to any and all matters relating to Ajax's . . . corporate management," the parties must have intended, on the facts of this case, to give Norry the right to vote the shares to elect a board of directors.

By the same token, in the absence of having an irrevocable proxy to vote their cumulative majority interests for the election of directors, the shareholders' agreement's recited purpose to ensure "continuity in the control and management of Ajax" could not be achieved. We should not adopt a construction of subparagraph 8 (a) which would frustrate one of the explicit central purposes of the agreement.

Ronnen, however, points to the language of paragraphs 10, 12 and 14 of the shareholders' agreement as negating any inference that Norry was given the right to vote the Ronnen shares in elections of the board of directors. Paragraph 10 of the agreement recites that "[t]he parties agree that . . . they shall vote the Shares" to ensure a seat on the board of directors for Deborah Ronnen. Paragraph 12 provides that "[t]he parties agree that . . . they shall vote the Shares in the election of Directors" to ensure Ronnen's access to all reports concerning the management of Ajax, and paragraph 14 similarly requires the "parties" to "vote the Shares in the election of Directors" so as to generally cap Norry's total executive compensation at $125,000 a year.

Ronnen, thus, argues that the literal language of paragraphs 10, 12 and 14 militates against an interpretation of the agreement ceding the right of Ronnen, "a party" to the agreement, to vote the Ronnen shares for the election of directors, and that such an interpretation would deprive those provisions of any force or effect. Ronnen further argues that the use of the plural, "parties," in those paragraphs was ignored by the courts below, who rewrote the clauses in question as an agreement that, singularly, "Neil Norry shall vote the Shares" in accordance with the substantive requirements of paragraphs 10, 12 and 14. We disagree.

As we have already discussed, subparagraph 8 (a) of the shareholders' agreement unequivocally guarantees the right of Norry to vote a majority block of shares on all matters "relating to . . corporate management" of Ajax, which in this case necessarily entails majority voting rights to elect a board of directors favorable to the continuation of his corporate policies. Construing paragraphs 10, 12 and 14 literally, to permit Ronnen to vote the Ronnen shares in board of directors elections to form a majority with shareholders possibly unfavorable to Norry's management role would, thus, take away from Norry the bargained for management rights and privileges promised in paragraph 8. We have previously applied the principle that a contract which confers certain rights or benefits in one clause will not be construed in other provisions completely to undermine those rights or benefits (see, Two Guys from Harrison-N.Y. v S.F.R. Realty Assocs., supra, 63 N.Y.2d at 405 ["generally, a contract which expressly permits an activity will not be construed to prohibit other conduct necessary to carrying out that activity"]; Premium Point Park Assn. v Polar Bar, 306 N.Y. 507, 511, 119 N.E.2d 360 ["(w)e may not construe the covenant as prohibiting in one subdivision that which it expressly sanctions in another"]).

Contrary to Ronnen's contention, a transfer of Ronnen's voting rights to Norry on election of a board of directors will not render paragraphs 10, 12 and 14 meaningless. These three provisions were manifestly intended to suit the purposes of Ronnen, guaranteeing her a seat on the board of directors and requiring the three Norry shareholders (Neil Norry and his sons) to vote the majority block of shares for directors who will be favorable to her position on access to corporate information and on imposing a ceiling on Norry's compensation. Thus, the pluralized language in paragraphs 10, 12 and 14 that "[t]he parties agree that . . . they shall vote the Shares" in board of directors elections can readily be construed to refer to the three Ronnens who were parties to the agreement, all of whose shares would be necessary to form a majority voting block with the Ronnen shares. That interpretation should be favored, as it would reconcile paragraphs 10, 12 and 14 with paragraph 8 of the agreement and effectuate all of the parties' objectives in entering into the agreement.

For all the foregoing reasons, we hold that the courts below properly construed the shareholders' agreement as giving Neil Norry the right to vote the Ronnen shares in board of directors elections. The position on appeal of appellants Lipsky and Livingston that, as thus construed, the shareholders' agreement is void as against public policy is unpreserved and, hence, has not been considered.

Finally, in view of the irrevocable proxy Ronnen gave Norry to vote the Ronnen shares in any election of directors, together with the other circumstances surrounding the March 13, 1995 shareholders' meeting alluded to by Supreme Court, the ordering of a new board of directors election in this case was within that court's discretionary equity powers under Business Corporation Law sec. 619 to "confirm the election, order a new election, or take such other action as justice may require" (emphasis supplied).

Accordingly, the order of the Appellate Division should be affirmed, with costs.

SHAREHOLDER POOLING AGREEMENTS

Shareholder pooling agreement — contract among shareholders to vote their shares as a block.

A **shareholder pooling agreement,** permitted under section 620 of the BCL, is a written agreement among shareholders to vote their shares as a block. Pursuant to the agreement, the shareholders specify that the shares will be voted:

a. as specified in the agreement

b. as they may agree by vote

c. as determined by a procedure delineated in the agreement

These agreements may be supported by a mutual exchange of proxies. If a shareholder breaches the agreement, the other signatories may seek specific performance under the court's equitable jurisdiction.

Example: In order to be able to have some say in corporate management, a group of minority shareholders enter into a shareholder pooling agreement to vote their shares as a block to have a particular person elected as a director. This is an example of a valid shareholder pooling agreement.

McQuade v. Stoneham
263 N.Y. 323 (1934)

A contract is illegal and void so far as it precludes a board of directors, at the risk of incurring legal liability, from changing officers, salaries or policies or from retaining individuals in office, except by consent of the contracting parties.

In an action to compel specific performance of a contract, entered into at the time of the purchase of stock in a corporation by plaintiff and one of the defendants from the other, a majority stockholder, whereby the three agreed to use their best endeavors to continue each other as a director and an officer of the corporation at stated salaries so long as they or the representative of any of them own stock as set forth in the agreement, where it appears that defendants did not keep their agreement to use their best endeavors to keep plaintiff in office as treasurer of the corporation but permitted him to be dropped, both as officer and director, though they controlled sufficient votes to elect him, a judgment in favor of plaintiff for damages for wrongful discharge is erroneous. Stockholders may unite to elect directors, but may not, by agreement among themselves control the directors in the exercise of the judgment vested in them by virtue of their office to elect officers and fix salaries, and bad faith or improper motives on the part of stockholders entering into such an agreement does not change the rule.

Contentions that an agreement among directors to continue a man as an officer of a corporation is enforceable so long as the officer remains loyal to the corporation and that in the determination of the action heed should be given to the morals involved, cannot be sustained. Directors may not by agreements entered into as stockholders abrogate their independent judgment and courts do not enforce mere moral obligations.

In any event plaintiff cannot recover for the reason that at the time the contract was made and until after its repudiation he was a magistrate of the city of New York and section 102 of the Inferior Criminal Courts Act (L. 1910, ch. 659; amd., L. 1915, ch. 531) provided that "no city magistrate shall engage in any other business * * * but * * * shall devote his whole time and capacity, so far as the public interest demands, to the duties of his office." The by-laws of the corporation impose upon the treasurer regular duties and provide that he shall perform such other duties as may be assigned to him. The performance of regular duties in the management of a business corporation for a substantial remuneration constitutes engaging in business within the meaning of the statute and the defendants cannot be held in damages for refusal to continue plaintiff's illegal occupancy of a corporate office.

In the Matter of the Arbitration between Glekel and Gluck
30 N.Y.2d 93 (1972)

Petitioner, the purchaser, and respondent in this proceeding, the seller, entered into an agreement for the sale of 90,000 shares of stock. The agreement provided that, while respondent held not less than 40,000 shares, both parties would vote their shares together for a majority of the directors nominated by petitioner and for a minority nominated by respondent. It was further agreed that if the directors designated by petitioner were elected and, if so requested by respondent, petitioner should use his best efforts to cause the company to register under appropriate laws for the sale or distribution of stock owned by respondent. An arbitration provision was addressed particularly to this provision. Respondent requested petitioner to cause the corporation to register 295,412 shares then owned by him for sale or distribution, but the president and board of directors felt that the best interest of the corporation was not to agree to respondent's registration request. The Appellate Division granted a stay of arbitration of the question whether petitioner had used his best efforts on the ground that, since petitioner had become a director of the corporation after the agreement was executed, the agreement precluded petitioner from exercising his judgment and discretion in the discharge of his duties and hence was void as against public policy. The clause in dispute does not require petitioner to interfere with the directors, to elect officers or to do any act of interference with corporate management. His agreement that, if the directors designated by him are elected, he "shall use his best efforts" to cause the company to register the stock is a proper arrangement between two stockholders.

Even if the purported illegality were more clearly manifest, and it were fairly arguable whether this was in fact an interference with the lawful directors and officers, the issue of illegality would be for the arbitrators.

The agreement could not be deemed illegal because petitioner later became a director and thereupon came to regard his contract as an interference with his independent duty. His acceptance of a directorship which frustrated the undertaking by him could itself be deemed a breach. The order denying a motion to stay arbitration is reinstated.

The leading New York case on the subject (Manson v. Curtis, 223 N. Y. 313 [1918]), relied on by both sides, holds that an agreement between stockholders and officers to control and circumvent the normal powers of officers and directors is illegal and in violation of section 34 of the General Corporation Law (now Business Corporation Law, @ 701), providing that the business of a corporation shall be managed by its board of directors (223 N. Y., p. 322).

But the court carefully preserved the general freedom of stockholders to agree to control corporate policies. The opinion stated: "It is not illegal or against public policy for two or more stockholders owning the majority of the shares of stock to unite upon a course of corporate policy or action, or upon the officers whom they will elect. An ordinary agreement, among a minority in number, but a majority in shares, for the purpose of obtaining control of the corporation by the election of particular persons as directors is not illegal. Shareholders have the right to combine their interests and voting powers to secure such control of the corporation and the adoption of and adhesion by it to a specific policy and course of business" (223 N. Y., pp. 319–320).

The general principle on which illegality is based was reiterated in McQuade v. Stoneham (263 N. Y. 323) where the agreement between stockholders to control directors in the election of officers was found illegal, although it was noted by Judge Pound, on the basis of Justice Holmes' opinion in Brightman v. Bates (175 Mass. 105, 111), that stockholders may "combine to elect directors" (263 N. Y., p. 329).

The clause here in dispute, however, does not require Glekel to interfere with the directors, to elect officers or to do any act of interference with corporate management. He agrees, if the directors designated by him are elected, that he "shall use his best efforts" to cause the company to register the stock. This seems to be a perfectly proper arrangement between two stockholders.

Indeed, it was on Glekel's own interpretation of his obligation that he had actually tried to do this and failed because the president and board of directors felt the best interest of the corporation was not to agree to appellant's registration request, i.e., "I requested the President of the company to take up the question of registration of your shares." If the arbitrators found this was using "his best efforts" they would find in his favor. This is very different from agreements to intermeddle with corporate management in violation of statute.

Even if the purported illegality were more clearly manifest, and it were fairly arguable whether this was in fact an interference with the lawful directors and officers, the issue of illegality would be for the arbitrators.

The agreement could not possibly be deemed illegal because Glekel later became a director and thereupon came to regard his contract as an interference with his independent duty. If he is right in this theory, then his acceptance of a directorship which frustrated the undertaking by him could itself be deemed a breach. Appellant seems right in concluding: "What the respondent is arguing is that by his own act of designating himself as a director he made illegal an agreement otherwise fully legal."

The order should be reversed, with costs, and the order at Special Term reinstated.

CHAPTER REVIEW

Two of the most important rights associated with being a shareholder of a corporation are the ability to transfer one's shares and the right to vote. Although in principle these rights are unfettered, under New York law the shareholder may enter into agreements that specifically limit these rights.

The shareholder may enter into a shareholder agreement restricting the transferability of shares. These agreements are found in closely held or professional corporations and are utilized to limit the persons who may own shares of the company. These agreements restricting the transferability of shares are valid and enforceable provided that they do not completely and irrevocably prohibit the transfer of shares. To meet this requirement, such an agreement must indicate the manner in which a shareholder may divest himself or herself of his or her shares. Such restrictions are unenforceable against a bona fide purchaser of shares who has no notice of the restriction on transferability.

With respect to limiting the shareholder's right to vote, three methods of alienation are permitted: proxies, by which a shareholder authorizes another person to vote the shares; voting trusts, in which the shares are reissued to the trust and the trustee votes the shares; and shareholder pooling agreements, in which a group of shareholders contract to vote their shares as a block.

KEY TERMS

First option	Shareholder pooling agreement
Mandatory buyout	Shareholder restrictive agreement
Proxy	Solicitation
Proxy contest	Voting trust
Proxy solicitation	

EXERCISES

1. Briefly discuss the benefits and detriments of the different pricing provisions for shareholder restrictive agreements. Which would you recommend for a client, and what factors would influence your recommendation?

2. Draft a shareholder restrictive agreement.

3. Draft a shareholder pooling agreement.

4. Indicate some benefits and detriments of having a voting trust. Draft a voting trust.

5. Discuss some of the reasons why a shareholder might enter into an agreement to limit his or her right to vote.

FACTUAL PROBLEM

A wealthy and elderly man still supports his middle-aged children. Unfortunately, he does not receive a sufficient tax benefit for taking the children as dependents to offset this tax liability for the income his stock generates. He would like to hand over sufficient shares to the children so that they are liable for their own taxes, thereby reducing his tax liability, but he wants to retain voting control of his shares, especially for several close corporations. Discuss the alternative methods he might employ.

Z 241—Proxy. 6-91

Blumbergs Law Products

JULIUS BLUMBERG, INC., PUBLISHER, NYC 10013

Know Everyone by these Presents,

That I ....

....

do hereby constitute and appoint ....

Attorney and Agent for me and in my name, place and stead, to vote as my proxy at any election of

....

according to the number of votes I should be entitled to cast if then personally present.

In Witness Whereof, I have signed this Proxy on .... 19...........

Witness

....

Exhibit 10–1

Proxy *(Forms may be purchased from BlumbergExcelsior, Inc. or any of its delers. Reproduction prohibited.)*

Chapter *11*

Structural Changes

INTRODUCTION

Structural change — any transaction affecting a corporation's certificate of incorporation.

Generally speaking, a **structural change** for a corporation is any transaction that has an effect on its certificate of incorporation because a certificate of incorporation is the document that establishes the corporate entity. One of the common stock rights is the right to vote for any extraordinary corporate matters, and structural changes come within this concept. Therefore, these transactions have a direct impact on both the corporate operations and the rights of the shareholders.

This chapter focuses on the four most important corporate structural changes: amendments to the certificate of incorporation; the bulk transfer of all or substantially all of the corporate assets; transactions that involve the corporation with other corporate entities such as mergers, exchanges, and consolidations; and the ultimate dissolution of the corporation.

AMENDMENTS AND CHANGES

Amendment — document used to change a certificate of incorporation.

An **amendment** is any change that is made to the certificate of incorporation, excluding any change that acts to dissolve the corporate entity. The right to amend a certificate of incorporation is granted to the corporation pursuant to section 801 of the BCL. The procedures for effectuating an amendment start with a Board of Directors' resolution specifying the proposed amendment which then must be submitted to the shareholders for their approval. However, under section 803(a) of the BCL, there are three types of amendments that may be authorized by Board of Directors' action alone:

1. an amendment to specify or change the location of the corporate office
2. an amendment to change the post office address to which the Secretary of State is to send service of process
3. an amendment to make, revoke, or change the designation of a registered agent or to specify a change of address for the registered agent

Certificate of change — document filed to effectuate an amendment to a certificate of incorporation that does not require shareholder approval.

If these changes are proposed before there are any shareholders of record, subscribers for shares, or directors, these amendments may be made by the incorporators under authority of section 803(d) of the BCL. For these three amendments, the Board can file a document called a **certificate of change** with the Secretary of State which acts to amend the certificate of incorporation.

Example: In its certificate of incorporation, the promoters designated a registered agent who no longer works for the company. The directors, by Board action alone, decide to appoint a new registered agent, and the change is effectuated by the filing of a certificate of change with Secretary of State.

All other amendments to the certificate of incorporation require shareholder approval. Proposed amendments require the approval of holders of a majority of all the outstanding shares entitled to vote. If any amendment affects only one class or series of shares and does not affect any other class or series, holders of a majority of the shares affected must approve the amendment. See BCL § 804(a).

Example: The Board of Directors propose to increase the authorized number of common stock shares from 1,000 to 5,000. To accomplish this change, a majority of the outstanding shareholders must approve.

Certificate of amendment — document filed to effectuate an amendment to a certificate of incorporation.

Once the proposed amendment has been approved by the shareholders, the Board of Directors must file a **certificate of amendment** with the Secretary of State. The information required to appear in a certificate of amendment appears in section 805 of the BCL, and includes:

a. name of the corporation
b. date of incorporation
c. text and effect of the proposed amendment
d. manner in which the amendment was authorized

The amendment takes effect once the certificate is filed with the Secretary of State. New York law does not require the publication of amendments or changes.

Restated certificate of incorporation — superceding document that incorporates a certificate of incorporation and all of its amendments.

If a corporation has made numerous amendments to its certificate of incorporation, section 806 of the BCL permits the corporation to file a **restated certificate of incorporation,** which acts as a superceding document incorporating the original certificate and all of the amendments into one document. The restated certificate of incorporation must include:

a. name of the corporation
b. date of incorporation
c. a statement that the certificate of incorporation is being restated, if no amendment or change is being made at the same time
d. a statement that the certificate of incorporation is being amended or changed, specifying each such amendment or change if the restatement is being used to make such changes

    e. effect on the shares if the amendment changes the issuance of shares

    f. effect on stated capital if the amendment changes stated capital (changes par value)

    g. manner in which the restated certificate was authorized

Amendments to the by-laws, even if such amendment requires shareholder approval, are not deemed to be structural changes because they do not affect the certificate of incorporation. The most typical amendments to a certificate of incorporation are:

    a. change of name or purpose for which the corporation was formed

    b. change in the number of authorized shares

    c. changes that affect the rights or designation of shares

    d. creation of a new class of stock

    e. creation or denial of preemptive rights

    f. changes to stated capital, such as changing par value

If the proposed amendment is to change a requirement for a supermajority vote or quorum for shareholders, such amendment requires approval by two-thirds vote of the authorized shares. Amendments changing the Board of Directors' powers with respect to management must be approved by all of the shareholders (or all of the incorporators if there are no shareholders) for corporations formed prior to February 22, 1998. For corporations formed after that date, a majority vote is all that is required.

Any shareholder who has voted against the amendment and whose rights as a shareholder have been adversely affected by the amendment is entitled to receive fair market value for his or her shares of stock. The types of amendment that would trigger these **appraisal rights** are:

Appraisal rights — right of a dissenting shareholder of a close corporation to have his or her shares bought by the corporation.

    a. an amendment that alters or abolishes an existing right, such as an amendment to change a preferred class to common

    b. changes to redemption rights, such as reducing the amount maintained in the sinking fund

    c. changes in preemptive rights

    d. changes to voting rights, such as the abolishment of cumulative voting

In order to obtain the appraisal rights, the dissenting shareholder must give a written objection to the proposed amendment prior to the vote and must give written notice of his or her intention to assert appraisal rights.

Example: A corporation wishes to abolish preemptive rights that were granted to its shareholders in the certificate of incorporation. Notice of a special shareholders' meeting is sent out, and a shareholder writes to the corporation noting his objection to the amendment. The amendment is approved, after which the shareholder sends the corporation written notice of his intention to assert his appraisal rights. The corporation must now buy his shares at their fair market value. (Such appraisal rights only exist for close corporations.)

In the Matter of Sutton
84 N.Y.2d 37 (1994)

In this CPLR article 78 proceeding, petitioners seek (1) a declaration that an amendment to the certificate of incorporation of Bag Bazaar, Ltd. is valid and (2) to compel respondent David S. Sutton, as a director of the corporation, to sign and deliver a certificate of amendment to petitioners for filing. Respondent has refused to execute the certificate, contending it is not valid because the amendment had the support of only 70% of the shareholders when the certificate of incorporation required unanimous approval. The appeal requires an interpretation of section 616 (b) of the Business Corporation Law which states that supermajority provisions in a certificate of incorporation may be amended by a two-thirds vote unless the certificate "specifically" provides otherwise.

In 1963, the certificate of incorporation of Bag Bazaar, Ltd. was amended to provide that "[t]he unanimous vote or consent of the holders of all the issued and outstanding shares of Common Stock of the corporation shall be necessary for the transaction of any business . . . of the corporation, including amendment to the certificate of incorporation." At that time the business was run by Abraham Sutton and none of the parties to this litigation was a shareholder. In 1971 Abraham's brother, respondent David S. Sutton, purchased 30 shares. Two years later Abraham's son, petitioner Solomon A. Sutton, joined the business and subsequently acquired 30 shares. On Abraham's death, in 1987, his widow, petitioner Yvette Sutton, inherited Abraham's remaining 40 shares. Thus, petitioners now own 70% of the outstanding shares of the corporation and respondent and his wife own 30 shares. Petitioner Solomon A. Sutton serves as one of the two directors of the company and respondent David S. Sutton as the other.

The corporation was run without incident for nearly 30 years under Abraham's leadership. After he relinquished control of the company, however, disputes arose between Solomon and David Sutton concerning the management of the corporation. These disputes culminated in an April 1992 shareholders' meeting, where petitioners voted their 70% of the shares in favor of a resolution to strike the unanimity provision, while respondent's 30% of the shares voted against the resolution.

Respondent, as a director of the corporation, refused to sign a certificate of amendment reflecting the deletion of the unanimity provision, thereby preventing the amendment from taking effect. Accordingly, petitioners commenced this proceeding and moved for judgment declaring the resolution valid and enforceable and compelling respondent to sign the certificate of amendment. Respondent cross-moved to dismiss the petition, for reformation of the certificate of incorporation and to compel arbitration of the dispute. Supreme Court granted the petition and denied the cross motion. The Appellate Division reversed and denied the petition.

To support their position on this appeal, petitioners contend that the Legislature added the word "specifically" to section 616 (b) because it recognized that a unanimity provision gives minority shareholders the ability to deadlock any and all corporate action. The amendment was intended to minimize deadlocks by permitting a two-thirds majority of the shareholders to alter or delete the unanimity requirement unless the certificate of incorporation explicitly stated otherwise. Respondent maintains that "specifically" was added to the statute to clarify that if more than a two-thirds vote was required to amend a unanimity provision, the certificate should state exactly what greater percentage is needed. They maintain that this certificate satisfied that requirement by declaring that a unanimous vote was required for any amendment.

In 1961, the Business Corporation Law was adopted to replace the Stock Corporation Law, and section 9 was substantially reenacted as Business Corporation Law sec. 616

(b) and sec. 709 (b). However, in 1962, prior to the 1963 effective date of the Business Corporation Law, a series of changes were made, including the addition of the word "specifically" in section 616 (b). As finally enacted, section 616 (b) provides that "[a]n amendment of the certificate of incorporation which changes or strikes out a [super-majority] provision . . . shall be authorized at a meeting of shareholders by vote of the holders of two-thirds of all outstanding shares entitled to vote thereon, or of such greater proportion of shares . . . as may be provided specifically in the certificate of incorporation" (emphasis added). According to the Legislative Study Committee the word "specifically" was one of a number of "technical" amendments added to the chapter to clarify existing language and avoid minor inconsistencies. It was not intended to effect a substantive change in the law (Mem of Joint Legis Comm To Study Revision of Corp Laws, Bill Jacket, L 1962, ch 834, at 86).

Thus, nothing in the legislative history or the statute itself suggests the necessity for a discrete paragraph addressed solely to the supermajority provision and explicitly declaring the vote required for its amendment. The history reveals that Stock Corporation Law sec. 9 stated that a provision in the certificate of incorporation requiring unanimous consent could only be amended by unanimous consent and this provision was substantially reenacted in the Business Corporation Law. Inasmuch as the Legislature did not intend the "technical" revisions added before the effective date of the Business Corporation Law to change the existing law substantively, the present statute should be construed as section 9 of the Stock Corporation Law was. Unanimity was required under the prior law to amend a unanimity provision, such as this one, and the addition of the word "specifically" merely provides that a two-thirds majority may now amend a unanimity provision unless the certificate requires a greater percentage.

The provision in Bag Bazaar's certificate is unambiguous: it requires unanimous shareholder consent for the transaction of "any business . . . including amendment to the certificate of incorporation." To read section 616 (b) as requiring more to address amendment of the supermajority provision would be unnecessarily restrictive in light of the legislative history. The certificate need only clearly state what vote, if greater than two thirds, is required to amend a unanimity provision. The certificate of Bag Bazaar, Ltd. does so.

The commentaries relied on by petitioners do not support petitioners' position (see, Hoffman, New Horizons for the Close Corporation in New York Under its New Business Corporation Law, 28 Brooklyn L Rev 1, 5 [New Horizons]; Israels, Corporate Practice sec. 4.20, at 91-92 [Hoffman 4th ed]; Kessler, A Close Corporation Checklist for Drafting the Certificate of Incorporation under the New York Business Corporation Law, 31 Fordham L Rev 323, 336 [Close Corporation]). They suggest only the obvious: that under prior law unanimity was required to amend a unanimity provision and that under the Business Corporation Law, unanimity is required only when "specifically" called for by the certificate of incorporation (see generally, Hoffman, New Horizons, op. cit., at 5; Kessler, Close Corporation, op. cit., at 336). They do not address the question before us, i.e., what language will fulfill the specificity requirement.

Finally, petitioners note that unless section 616 (b) is read as requiring an explicit certificate provision governing the amendment of unanimity provisions, majority shareholders will be unable to conduct the business of a corporation in the face of opposition from the minority. But as respondent notes, there is nothing inherently unfair or improper about a voluntary organization's consensual decision to assure protection for minority shareholders, and shareholders are not without remedies where deadlocks do arise (see generally, Business Corporation Law sec. 1104).

Accordingly, the order of the Appellate Division should be affirmed, with costs.

BULK TRANSFERS

Bulk transfer — sale of all or substantially all of a corporation's assets otherwise than in the ordinary course of business.

A **bulk transfer** occurs whenever a corporation disposes of all, or substantially all, of its assets otherwise than in the regular course of business. These types of transactions are covered in Article 9 of the BCL as well as in the New York adaptation of the Uniform Commercial Code. Although technically not a structural change, since the certificate of incorporation remains unaffected, the transaction is deemed to be so substantial to the interests of the shareholders, because the entity no longer possesses its original assets, that it qualifies as a structural change.

For corporations formed on or after February 22, 1998, a bulk transfer requires the approval of a majority of all outstanding shares entitled to vote. For corporations in existence prior to that date, bulk transfers require the approval of two-thirds of the outstanding shares entitled to vote. In either instance, notice must be sent of the proposed transfer to all shareholders.

If the transfer is approved, the seller corporation must prepare an affidavit indicating the names and business addresses of all its creditors and specifying the amounts owed to them at the date of the transfer. The seller corporation must also prepare a schedule of all the property being transferred. The list of creditors and schedule of property must be retained by the purchaser and made available for inspection by any business creditor for a period of six months following the transfer. Written notice of the transfer must be sent to all creditors of the seller at least ten days prior to the purchaser taking possession of the property or paying for it, whichever comes first.

Any shareholder who dissents from the transfer is entitled to appraisal rights—having his or her shares bought at their fair market value—unless the transfer was for cash and was effectuated as a preliminary step toward the corporation's dissolution which is planned to take effect within one year of the transfer.

See Exhibit 11–1 for a bulk transfer form and Exhibit 11–2 for a security agreement.

Cross Properties, Inc. v. Brook Realty Co., Inc.
31 N.Y.2d 938 (1972)

Appeal, by permission of the Appellate Division of the Supreme Court in the Second Judicial Department, from an order of said court, entered July 6, 1971, which unanimously affirmed (1) an interlocutory judgment of the Supreme Court, entered in Westchester County upon a decision of the court at a Trial Term (Hugh S. Coyle, J.), (a) dismissing the amended complaint in an action to enjoin a proposed sale of properties to defendant Brook Realty Co., under a contract of sale dated September 13, 1968, to have that contract declared invalid, and for damages, (b) adjudging that the contract of September 13, 1968 was valid and binding upon all of the parties, and (c) granting leave to all of the parties to apply for a hearing to determine whether and upon what terms, if any, specific performance should be decreed and in what amount money damages, if any, should be awarded, and (2) a subsequent order of the Supreme Court at Special Term (John J. Dillon, J.), entered in Westchester County, denying a motion to modify said interlocutory judgment so as to dismiss a cross claim by defendant Brook Realty Co. for specific performance, or, in the alternative, for summary judgment dismissing that cross claim. The Appellate Division affirmed the findings of fact made by the Supreme Court and also made new findings. Plaintiffs were shareholders of defendant Dollar Land Holdings Limited (Dollar England), an English corporation which owned approximately 90% of the outstanding stock of defendant Dollar Land Corporation Limited (Dollar Canada). Dollar Canada wholly owned the stock of defendant County Dollar Corporation (County Dollar), a New York corporation, which, in turn, wholly owned the stock of defendant Dollar Land Corporation Limited (U. S.) (Dollar U. S.), also a New York corporation. County Dollar owned the Cross County Shopping Center in Yonkers, New York, and Dollar U. S. owned a shopping center in Texas and a bank building in Florida. After a decision was made by the then management of Dollar England to liquidate corporate assets, County Dollar and Dollar U. S. entered into the contract of September 13, 1968, to sell their properties to defendant Brook Realty Co. They obtained authorization for execution of the contract at meetings of their boards of directors which were held earlier that day, and on September 24, 1968 Dollar Canada's board of directors authorized execution and delivery of its consent to the sale by County Dollar. In October, 1968 plaintiffs gained management control of Dollar England. Reconstituted boards of directors of Dollar England, Dollar Canada, County Dollar and Dollar U. S. thereafter adopted resolutions to rescind all prior authorization for the sale. In the present action plaintiffs alleged, inter alia, that section 909 of the Business Corporation Law, requiring shareholder approval of a sale of all or substantially all of the assets of a corporation, required the approval of such a sale by the shareholders of an ultimate parent corporation, or ultimate beneficial owners, even though title to the assets was in the name of subsidiary corporations; that, in any event, under the circumstances of this case, said section 909 required disregard of the corporate entities of the subsidiary corporations in order to protect the rights of the shareholders of the parent corporation; that the consent purportedly given by Dollar Canada to the sale by County Dollar was invalid; that the rescission of the consents given by Dollar Canada and County Dollar effectively invalidated the contract of sale; that the former directors had acted in breach of fiduciary obligations; that defendant Brook Realty Co. was not a bona fide purchaser for value without notice, and that English law, under which the proposed sale was ultra vires the powers of Dollar England, was applicable to the case. The following question was certified by the Appellate Division: "Was the order of this court, dated July 6, 1971, properly made?"

Affirmed.

MERGERS, CONSOLIDATIONS, AND EXCHANGES

Merger — one corporation absorbs another corporation.

Survivor corporation — corporation that continues in existence after a merger.

Target corporation — corporation taken over in a merger.

Consolidation — two or more corporations join to form a new corporation, combining all their assets and liabilities and transferring them to the new entity.

Exchange — swap of stock between two corporations.

Mergers and consolidations are statutory devices used to convert two or more corporations into a single legal entity. A **merger** occurs when one or more constituent corporations merge into and become part of another constituent corporation. The **survivor corporation** assumes all of the assets and liabilities of the **target corporation.** In a **consolidation**, two or more constituent corporations join to form a new corporate entity, pooling all of their assets and liabilities and transferring them to a new consolidated entity. In between these two configurations exists the **exchange**, a procedure in which two or more corporations swap stock or assets. An exchange is a more conservative method of combining separate corporate entities.

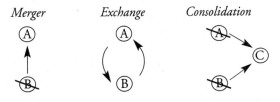

Diagrammatically, the three combinations are as follows:

The procedures for effectuating a merger or consolidation are the same. The Board of Directors must adopt a plan of merger or consolidation, detailing all the material terms of the transaction. This plan must be accepted by the shareholders in order for the merger or consolidation to take place. For corporations in existence prior to February 22, 1998, the approval must be by a vote of two-thirds of the shares entitled to vote; for corporations formed on or after February 22, 1998, the plan must be approved by a majority vote. If the plan concerns the merging of classes or series of stock, the plan must be approved by a majority of each affected class or series. See BCL § 903(a). A copy of the proposed plan of merger or consolidation must be attached to the notice of the shareholders' meeting at which the plan will be voted on.

If the plan is approved by the shareholders, the Board of Directors files a **certificate of merger or consolidation,** which must be signed and verified. The merger or consolidation becomes effective on the date of the filing of the certificate with the Secretary of State or on a later date not to exceed ninety days of the filing, if such date is specified in the certificate. See BCL § 906(a) and 907(a).

New York law provides for a procedure known as **short-form merger** if one corporation owns 90 percent of the outstanding shares of each class of stock of another corporation. The shareholding corporation is referred to as the **parent corporation** because it controls, by its voting rights, the other corporation, known as a **subsidiary corporation.** In this situation, a merger may be effectuated without shareholder approval provided the following procedures are followed:

a. The Board of Directors of the parent corporation adopts a plan of merger.

b. A copy of the plan is given to the other shareholders of the subsidiary.

c. A certificate of merger is filed no less than thirty days after notice is given.

Shareholders of a merged or consolidated corporation who do not assent to the transaction are entitled to appraisal rights, except for shareholders of the surviving corporation or if the shares are traded on a national exchange.

Certificate of merger or consolidation — document filed to effectuate a merger or consolidation of two or more corporations.

Short-form merger — merger resulting when one corporation owns 90 percent of the voting stock of another corporation.

Parent corporation — corporation that owns a controlling block of stock of another corporation.

Subsidiary corporation — corporation controlled by another corporation.

Friedman v. Beway Realty Corp.
87 N.Y.2d 161 (1995)

Petitioners are minority stockholders in nine family owned close corporations, each of which had as its sole asset a parcel of income-producing office, commercial or residential real estate in New York City. In 1986, the board of directors and the requisite majority of stockholders of each corporation voted to transfer all of its property to a newly formed partnership. Petitioners voted their shares against the transfers and, pursuant to Business Corporation Law sec. 623, timely elected to exercise their appraisal rights and receive the "fair value" of their shares in each corporation. When the corporations failed to offer to purchase their shares, petitioners commenced this proceeding to have a judicial determination of the fair value of the shares (see, Business Corporation Law sec. 623 [h]).

I

The corporations' primary argument for reversal is that Supreme Court erred as a matter of law in refusing to take into account in its fair value determination the financial reality that minority shares in a close corporation are worth less because they represent only a minority, rather than a controlling interest. Although the corporations' argument may have validity when corporate stock is valued for other purposes, it overlooks the statutory objective here of achieving a fair appraisal remedy for dissenting minority shareholders. Mandating the imposition of a "minority discount" in fixing the fair value of the stockholdings of dissenting minority shareholders in a close corporation is inconsistent with the equitable principles developed in New York decisional law on dissenting stockholder statutory appraisal rights (a position shared by the courts in most other jurisdictions), and the policies underlying the statutory reforms giving minority stockholders the right to withdraw from a corporation and be compensated for the value of their interests when the corporate majority takes significant action deemed inimical to the position of the minority.

Several principles have emerged from our cases involving appraisal rights of dissenting shareholders under Business Corporation Law sec. 623 or its predecessor statute. (1) The fair value of a dissenter's shares is to be determined on their worth in a going concern, not in liquidation, and fair value is not necessarily tied to market value as reflected in actual stock trading (Matter of Fulton, 257 N.Y. 487, 492). "The purpose of the statute being to save the dissenting stockholder from loss by reason of the change in the nature of the business, he [or she] is entitled to receive the value of his [or her] stock for sale or its value for investment" (id., at 494 [emphasis supplied]). (2) The three major elements of fair value are net asset value, investment value and market value. The particular facts and circumstances will dictate which element predominates, and not all three elements must influence the result (Matter of Endicott Johnson Corp. v Bade, 37 N.Y.2d 585, 587–588, 376 N.Y.S.2d 103, 338 N.E.2d 614). (3) Fair value requires that the dissenting stockholder be paid for his or her proportionate interest in a going concern, that is, the intrinsic value of the shareholder's economic interest in the corporate enterprise (Matter of Cawley v SCM Corp., 72 N.Y.2d 465, 474, 534 N.Y.S.2d 344, 530 N.E.2d 1264). (4) By virtue of the 1982 amendment to Business Corporation Law sec. 623 (h) (4) (L 1982, ch 202, sec. 9), fair value determinations should take into account the subsequent economic impact on value of the very transaction giving rise to appraisal rights, as supplemental to the three basic value factors (net asset, investment and market values). (5) Determinations of the fair value of a dissenter's shares are governed by the statutory provisions of the Business Corporation Law that require equal treatment of all shares of the same class of stock.

Further, contrary to the corporations' contention here, there is no difference in analysis between stock fair value determinations under Business Corporation Law sec. 623, and fair value determinations under Business Corporation Law sec. 1118. The latter provision governs the rights of minority stockholders when the corporation has elected to purchase their interests, also at "fair value," following their petition for corporate dissolution under Business Corporation Law sec. 1104-a for oppressive majority conduct. The corporations' opposing argument is that considerations of the oppressive conduct of the majority stockholders enter into fair value considerations conducted under Business Corporation Law sec. 1118; therefore, the cases decided under that section are distinguishable and not authoritative for fair value considerations under Business Corporation Law sec. 623. The corporations' position in this regard is untenable because their basic underlying assumption—that oppressive majority conduct enters into the court's fair value equation under section 1118—is in error. As we stated in Matter of Pace Photographers (Rosen) (71 N.Y.2d 737), once the corporation has elected to buy the petitioning stockholders' shares at fair value, "the issue of [majority] wrongdoing [is] superfluous . . . [f]ixing blame is material under [Business Corporation Law] sec. 1104-a, but not under [Business Corporation

Lawsec.] 1118" (id., at 746; see also, Matter of Seagroatt Floral Co., 78 N.Y.2d at 445, supra).

Thus, we apply to stock fair value determinations under section 623 the principle we enunciated for such determinations under section 1118 that, in fixing fair value, courts should determine the minority shareholder's proportionate interest in the going concern value of the corporation as a whole, that is, "'what a willing purchaser, in an arm's length transaction, would offer for the corporation as an operating business.'"

Consistent with that approach, we have approved a methodology for fixing the fair value of minority shares in a close corporation under which the investment value of the entire enterprise was ascertained through a capitalization of earnings (taking into account the unmarketability of the corporate stock) and then fair value was calculated on the basis of the petitioners' proportionate share of all outstanding corporate stock.

Imposing a discount for the minority status of the dissenting shares here, as argued by the corporations, would in our view conflict with two central equitable principles of corporate governance we have developed for fair value adjudications of minority shareholder interests under Business Corporation Law sec. 623 and 1118. A minority discount would necessarily deprive minority shareholders of their proportionate interest in a going concern, as guaranteed by our decisions previously discussed. Likewise, imposing a minority discount on the compensation payable to dissenting stockholders for their shares in a proceeding under Business Corporation Law sec. 623 or 1118 would result in minority shares being valued below that of majority shares, thus violating our mandate of equal treatment of all shares of the same class in minority stockholder buyouts.

A minority discount on the value of dissenters' shares would also significantly undermine one of the major policies behind the appraisal legislation embodied now in Business Corporation Law sec. 623, the remedial goal of the statute to "protect[ ] minority shareholders 'from being forced to sell at unfair values imposed by those dominating the corporation while allowing the majority to proceed with its desired [corporate action].'" This protective purpose of the statute prevents the shifting of proportionate economic value of the corporation as a going concern from minority to majority stockholders. As stated by the Delaware Supreme Court, "to fail to accord to a minority shareholder the full proportionate value of his [or her] shares imposes a penalty for lack of control, and unfairly enriches the majority stockholders who may reap a windfall from the appraisal process by cashing out a dissenting shareholder."

Furthermore, a mandatory reduction in the fair value of minority shares to reflect their owners' lack of power in the administration of the corporation will inevitably encourage oppressive majority conduct, thereby further driving down the compensation necessary to pay for the value of minority shares. "Thus, the greater the misconduct by the majority, the less they need to pay for the minority's shares."

We also note that a minority discount has been rejected in a substantial majority of other jurisdictions. "Thus, statistically, minority discounts are almost uniformly viewed with disfavor by State courts" (id., at 48l). The imposition of a minority discount in derogation of minority stockholder appraisal remedies has been rejected as well by the American Law Institute in its Principles of Corporate Governance.

We likewise find no basis to disturb the trial court's discretion in failing to assign any additional diminution in value of petitioners' shares here because they were subject to contractual restrictions on voluntary transfer. As we noted in Matter of Pace Photographers (Rosen) (supra), a statutory acquisition of minority shares by a corporation pursuant to the Business Corporation Law is not a voluntary sale of corporate shares as contemplated by a restrictive stockholder agreement and, therefore, "the express covenant is literally inapplicable" (71 N.Y.2d at 749). Nor is there any reason to disturb Supreme Court's award of prejudgment interest.

. . .

III

While we have concluded that Supreme Court correctly applied the legal doctrines respecting fair value determinations of dissenting minority stockholders' shares in the instant case, we find error in the court's calculation of the unmarketability discount which must be applied here. As previously explained, Supreme Court generally adopted the net asset valuation approach of McGraw, the corporations' expert, and his two-step evaluation process. However, the court added back the 9.8% discount McGraw took in the first step of that process because the court concluded that it actually represented a minority discount. Then, when it reached the second step of the evaluation process, the court removed what it regarded as the same minority discount from the 30.4% unmarketability discount McGraw applied at that stage. Thus, Supreme Court added back McGraw's minority discount twice, once in each of the stages of the process. Apparently, this was based upon the court's erroneous finding that McGraw arrived at the 30.4% discount by analyzing privately transacted sales of stock "with restrictive sale provisions and [McGraw] found that they exhibited a median discount of 30.4 percent relative to net asset value" (emphasis supplied). Supreme Court further reasoned that, because the sales McGraw analyzed were of minority shares, his unmarketability discount also must have contained an element of reduced value because of their minority status. The evidence in the record does not support the foregoing conclusions. In actuality, McGraw did not arrive at the 30.4% discount by comparing shares with "restrictive sale provisions" to their net asset values. He calculated the unmarketability factor by comparing the purchase prices of registered, publicly traded minority shares in comparative corporations, to the purchase prices of the same class of minority shares in the same corporations that were unregistered and, therefore, not publicly traded but purchased under trading restrictions in private placements. Because McGraw in his calculations always compared the prices of a marketable set of minority shares to the prices of a set of minority shares when the same stock was unmarketable, the difference in prices of the shares did not contain any additional minority discount element, and the discount was solely attributable to the difference in the marketability of the shares in the same stock.

Thus, Supreme Court erred in removing a nonexistent minority discount element from the reduction in value of petitioners' shares McGraw attributed to their lack of marketability. It is unclear, however, as to whether Supreme Court would have accepted in full McGraw's 30.4% discount as a proper reflection of diminution in value due to unmarketability had the court been aware that it did not also reflect a reduction in value due to the shares' minority status. Because of this uncertainty, the matter must be remitted to Supreme Court for a new determination of the appropriate discount for unmarketability of petitioners' shares and a recalculation of fair value when that discount is applied to the proportionate net asset value of petitioners' stockholdings in the nine corporations.

Accordingly, the order should be reversed, without costs, and the matter remitted to Supreme Court for further proceedings in accordance with this opinion.

Example: A shareholder of a target corporation does not approve of the merger and wants to be bought out pursuant to her appraisal rights. If the corporation's stock is traded on a national exchange, she is not entitled to be bought out. However, if the corporation is closely held, appraisal rights do attach.

Albert v. Salzman
41 A.D.2d 501 (1973)

Taking, as we must for the purposes of this motion, the allegations of the complaint to be true, the following facts appear.

Odell, Inc. was a Delaware corporation engaged in marketing certain brand products. Papercraft Corporation is a corporation engaged in the manufacture of various paper products. Both are publicly owned companies. Following negotiations in the fall of 1969 the boards of directors of both companies informally approved an agreement of merger whereby the stockholders of Odell would receive .59375 of a share of Papercraft for each share of Odell. This proposed arrangement accorded roughly with the respective market prices of the stocks of the two companies, namely, Odell $16.50 per share and Papercraft $31 per share. However, on October 21, 1969, the Odell board of directors rejected this offer.

Following the rejection a series of private negotiations between Papercraft and various officers, directors and stockholders of Odell ensued. As a result of those negotiations the following transactions resulted. On November 25, 1969, defendant Salzman, a director of Odell, sold his shares (45,406 common and 1,270 preferred) to Papercraft for $30 a share, an excess of $11.50 per share over the market price. For this Salzman agreed to and did resign as an officer and director of Odell, although his salary was to continue until December, 1970. He further agreed to use his best efforts to have Odell reduce the number of its directors from 12 to 9, to provide for an easier method of amending the by-laws, to bring about the resignation of 7 of the 12 directors, and to cause the election of nominees of Papercraft in their stead. Two days previously Papercraft had made an agreement with Laurence, a director of Odell who owned individually and with his wife 28% of the outstanding Odell stock (237,000 shares) to buy 85,000 shares. Laurence agreed to vote his remaining shares for a board of directors mutually agreeable to Papercraft and himself. In addition Laurence had the right, for six months, to "put" to Papercraft 70,000 shares of Odell, or, if it had been merged with Papercraft, the equivalent number of shares of Papercraft at $22.44 per share.

The substitution of directors did not, however, go smoothly, despite the co-operation of Salzman and Laurence. Thereupon Papercraft had further negotiations with the remaining directors. Papercraft agreed to buy the stock of director Wessenger (8,500 shares) for $30 a share, the sale to become effective when the new board was seated. The market price of Odell at that time was between $20.25 and $21.75 per share. Wessenger was also guaranteed against any loss of his pay on an employment agreement. He agreed to vote for Papercraft's nominees for the board. At the time Wessenger's Odell stock was transferred to Papercraft, its market price was about $4.50 per share. Arrangements were made with director Marcus to lift restrictions on the 10,000 Odell shares he owned, which required him to offer the stock to Odell at 12 1/2 cents a share. Marcus was also promised the presidency of Odell. Director Schur was given a two-year extension of his employment contract and a substantial salary increase. Directors Eisenberg and Wishingrad received beneficial, but less favorable, contract changes.

Thereupon a new board took office and immediately approved a merger offer by which Odell stockholders would receive one share of Papercraft for each four shares of Odell.

The above are the allegations of the first cause of action. The second is not under separate attack.

The third cause of action alleges that between the date of the election of the new board and the effective date of the merger the board adopted new and improper accounting practices which made it appear that Odell's financial position was greatly inferior to what it had been. This practice, together with the added expense of the employment contracts referred to above, is alleged to have depressed the price of Odell stock, with the result that the merger offer was made to appear beneficial to Odell stockholders.

The fourth cause of action alleges that Salzman, Laurence and Wessenger were aware of the fact that Odell was in serious financial difficulties due to several facts set out and that they concealed this knowledge, enabling them to make the sales of their stock referred to.

Upon this motion by Salzman, two of the new directors and Papercraft to dismiss the complaint, it appears that the plaintiff Albert, a former stockholder of Odell, sold his stock after this suit was initiated. It is conceded that he can no longer maintain the action. However, another stockholder of Odell, Fine, has sought to intervene in the action, and it is his application that provides the meat of the appeal. Special Term denied the application, and with the disqualification of Albert dismissal was inevitable.

Three grounds for denying the intervenor's motion are urged. The first, considering the experience of counsel urging it, must be regarded as a tongue-in-cheek makeweight designed to trap the unwary. It is that the original action having been dismissed, there is no viable action in which to make the application. An equally simplistic answer would be that if the court considered the intervenor's application to intervene before it took up the defendant's application to dismiss, both being presented simultaneously, there would be a pending action in which intervention was permissible. But, adopting an adult approach, it will be seen that in no reported decision has a valid derivative or representative action been doomed to fail for this reason, and the decisions are unanimous that intervention for the purpose of survival, if seasonably sought, is invariably granted (Matter of Eberlin, 18 A D 2d 1068; Mann v. Compania Petrolera Trans-Cuba, 17 A D 2d 193; Matter of Petroleum Research Fund, 3 A D 2d 1). In the very situation presented here, namely, disqualification of the original plaintiff by disposal of his stock, intervention was allowed (Pikor v. Cinerama Prods. Corp., 25 F. R. D. 92; Winkelman v. General Motors Corp., 44 F. Supp. 960). Even if the original plaintiff was never qualified to bring the action, intervention has been allowed (cf. Pikor, supra).

The second, and really serious, ground is that the first, third and fourth causes of action do not state a cause of action. The gravamen of this contention is that the causes of action belong to Odell, a stockholder of Odell having derivative rights only, and Odell being now merged into Papercraft prosecution of the action would amount to Papercraft suing itself. In other words, by so classifying the actions, the individual defendants, despite the alleged blatant betrayal of their trust, would walk away secure in the retention of their illegal profits, and equity should regard the transactions with philosophical equanimity. If the Chancellor's stomach is sufficiently strong he need not concern himself with his conscience. We fail to see it that way.

A merged corporation does not by merger lose a cause of action which it had prior to the merger (Business Corporation Law, sec. 906, subd. [b], par. [3]). Consequently a derivative action on its behalf survives merger (Marco v. Sachs, 201 Misc. 934, affd. 279 App. Div. 1085, affd. 304 N. Y. 912). So far as the individual defendants are concerned, whether the action be regarded as derivative or representative there is no difficulty. Concededly if the action is representative no obstacle to suit is presented.

As regards Papercraft, the situation is different. The relief demanded against this defendant is the setting aside of the merger and an accounting for any gain Papercraft received. The gain referred to is the acquisition of the Odell stock, other than that acquired from the individual defendants at less than its fair price. The latter relief is not available, as its equivalent has been provided for by the right of refusal and having the stock appraised (Greene & Co. v. Schenley Ind., 281 A. 2d 30 [Del., 1971]). As regards setting aside the merger, that would clearly be a right belonging to Odell and not its stockholders or any of them. The right to sue despite the merger does not extend to the corporation into which the other is merged (Basch v. Talley Ind., 53 F. R. D. 9).

The third cause of action is plainly derivative and cannot survive.

All of the relief sought in the fourth cause of action is obtainable in the first. Moreover, it is difficult to see how Odell or its stockholders were damaged by the deception practiced on Papercraft by the defendants charged. At most this cause of action seeks to have the remaining stockholders of Odell participate in the benefits of the fraud practiced on Papercraft. While profits gained from the use of special information belong either to the corporation or the other stockholders, it does not appear that this is such a situation. The facts alleged would base a cause of action in favor of Papercraft only.

The third reason urged for denying intervention is that the proposed intervenor had assented to the merger by exchanging his Odell stock for Papercraft stock. At most this would constitute a defense dependent for its validity on principles applicable to all waivers, namely, intention as affected by the surrounding circumstances. In any event, it would not preclude recovery against the individuals on the first cause of action for the reasons already stated.

The decision of Special Term should be modified, on the law, to allow intervention of the intervenor Fine and to allow the action to continue against the individual defendants on the first cause of action, and the order should otherwise be affirmed, without costs.

Corporate reorganization — a merger, consolidation, or exchange.

"A" reorganization — IRS designation for a corporate merger or consolidation.

"B" reorganization — IRS designation for a corporate exchange of stock.

"C" reorganization — IRS designation for a corporate exchange of stock of one corporation for substantially all of the assets of another corporation.

Dissolution — termination of a corporation.

Voluntary dissolution — corporate termination brought about by the wishes of the owners.

An exchange follows a similar but much more simplified procedure. With a corporate exchange, the Boards of the corporations adopt a plan of exchange which must be approved by the shareholders according to the approval procedures described earlier. If approved, each corporation signs and verifies the plan which is then filed with the Secretary of State. Appraisal rights attach to exchanges as well as to mergers and consolidations.

In addition to filing with the New York Secretary of State, the corporations also must be aware of the tax consequences of these transactions. In order to keep the shareholders from being taxed on any gain in the value of their shares resulting from such combinations, the corporation must get the Internal Revenue Service to have the transaction determined to be a **corporate reorganization,** which avoids immediate tax liability. Mergers and consolidations are called **"A" reorganizations,** share exchanges are **"B" reorganizations,** and exchanges that swap stock for substantially all of the assets of another corporation are called **"C" reorganizations.** By acquiring IRS approval, the shareholders are only tax liable when the shares are eventually sold. Additionally, participants should be aware that these types of combinations may give rise to the spectre of antitrust violations.

DISSOLUTION

If the corporation has indicated a perpetual existence, or even a specified period of time for its life, and it wishes to terminate its existence at a prior date, certain procedures must be followed pursuant to New York law.

The BCL provides for two types of corporate **dissolution** (the termination of the corporate existence): voluntary and involuntary. **Voluntary dissolution** procedures are detailed in Article 10 of the BCL. Voluntary dissolution occurs when the shareholders of the corporation wish to terminate the corporate existence. The proposal to dissolve may come from either a Board of Directors resolution or by means of a shareholder proposal. In each situation, the proposed dissolution must be approved by the shareholders. For corporations in existence prior to February 22, 1998, the vote to dissolve requires approval by two-thirds of the shares entitled to vote; for corporations formed after that date, a simple majority will suffice.

Certificate of dissolution — document filed to terminate a corporation.

If the dissolution is approved, the Board of Directors must cause a **certificate of dissolution** to be filed with the Secretary of State (see Exhibit 11–3). Section 1003 of the BCL specifies the information that must appear in the certificate:

1. name of the corporation
2. date of incorporation
3. names and addresses of the officers and directors of the corporation
4. statement that the corporation has elected to dissolve
5. statement indicating the manner in which such dissolution was authorized

The certificate of dissolution must have the approval of the New York State Tax Commission attached as evidence that the corporation is not dissolving in an attempt to avoid tax liability, and the corporation must print a notice of dissolution in the newspaper to alert creditors. If the corporation so wishes, the dissolution may be supervised by the New York Supreme Court.

Involuntary dissolution — corporate termination brought about by court order for a legal violation.

The procedures for involuntary dissolution appear in Article 11 of the BCL. An action for **involuntary dissolution** may be brought by:

1. the Attorney General for any corporate violation, including:
   (a) failure to file an annual report
   (b) fraud
   (c) ultra vires action
   (d) failure to appoint a registered agent
2. the directors of the corporation if the corporation has insufficient assets to continue operations and the dissolution will benefit the shareholders
3. a majority of the shareholders for the same reasons the directors can petition for dissolution
4. holders of 20 percent of the voting shares of a corporation whose shares are not publicly traded if:
   (a) the directors or controlling shareholders have been guilty of fraudulent, illegal, or oppressive conduct against the complaining shareholders, or
   (b) the corporate assets are being wasted or looted

Liquidation — process of terminating a business.

After dissolution, the corporation must not accept any new business but must simply wind up its affairs. This process is known as **liquidation,** whereby the corporation discharges its obligations, marshals its assets, and terminates the business.

CHAPTER REVIEW

Few corporations retain their initial form or operations throughout their entire existences. At some point, many corporations decide to reorganize in order to create a more financially profitable business. If any of the changes affects the structure of the corporation, the certificate of incorporation, New York law requires shareholder approval of the action.

The most typical situation involves simple amendments to the certificate, usually involving changes to the number or type of authorized shares. Mergers, exchanges, and consolidations are more drastic actions, combining two or more corporations into a single entity. In these situations, two or more corporations lose their individual identities and become absorbed into a larger corporate being.

Whenever a corporation divests itself of all, or substantially all, of its assets, although the structure of the corporation may remain, this divestment is considered extreme enough to be deemed a structural change that also requires shareholder approval.

At some point, many corporations terminate their existences by a procedure known as dissolution. In New York, dissolution may be either voluntary, being brought about by the owners of the corporation themselves, or involuntary, in which the corporation is terminated because of some violation of law. Voluntary termination requires shareholder approval, whereas involuntary termination comes about by order of the court.

In all situations in which a shareholder approval is required, the BCL mandates appraisal rights for dissenting shareholders. For corporations in existence prior to February 22, 1998, a two-thirds vote of the shares entitled to vote is required to approve corporate action; for corporations formed after that date, a simple majority vote is sufficient.

KEY TERMS

"A" reorganization

Amendment

Appraisal rights

"B" reorganization

Bulk transfer

"C" reorganization

Certificate of amendment

Certificate of change

Certificate of dissolution

Certificate of merger or consolidation

Consolidation

Corporate reorganization

Dissolution

Exchange

Involuntary dissolution

Liquidation

Merger

Parent corporation

Restated certificate of incorporation

Short-form merger

Structural change

Subsidiary corporation

Survivor corporation

Target corporation

Voluntary dissolution

EXERCISES

1. Indicate several reasons why two corporations would wish to enter into a corporate exchange.

2. Briefly discuss the importance of appraisal rights for a shareholder. How would a shareholder find a qualified appraiser?

᠎

3. Indicate several situations in which a shareholder might wish to cause the dissolution of a corporation. How could the shareholder be stopped from dissolving the corporation?

4. Why would the tax consequences of a corporate reorganization be important to a shareholder? Discuss.

5. Indicate the various items that should be specified in a plan of merger or consolidation. Using the library or the Internet, find a sample plan of merger and consolidation and analyze its provisions.

FACTUAL PROBLEM

Two corporations plan to consolidate. However, the Boards of Directors cannot decide on the value of the new shares that would be given to the current shareholders of the corporations. Further, one of the corporations has a preferred issue, and no such issue is planned for the consolidated entity. How can the Boards determine the proper apportionment of the new stock? Could the preferred shareholders demand appraisal rights and/or stop the consolidation? Explain.

W 82—Contract for Sale of Business, Ind. or Corp.
(Uniform Commercial Code—Bulk Transfers) 12-89

Blumbergs Law Products

© 1964 BY JULIUS BLUMBERG, INC.,
PUBLISHER, NYC 10013

AGREEMENT, made the   day of   in the State of

between

whose address is

hereinafter called the Transferor, and

whose address is

hereinafter called the Transferee.

SUBJECT MATTER OF SALE

1. The Transferor agrees to sell to the Transferee and the Transferee agrees to buy the following described business:

located at

including the stock in trade, fixtures, equipment, accounts receivable, contract rights, lease, good will, licenses, rights under any contract for telephone service or other rental, maintenance or use of equipment, machinery and fixtures at the said premises, more particularly described in Schedule A hereto attached, free and clear of any debts, mortgages, security interests or other liens or encumbrances except as herein stated. Title shall be closed on the   day of

closing date at   M. at the office of

PURCHASE PRICE

2. The purchase price to be paid by the Transferee is $

TERMS OF PAYMENT

3. The terms of payment are as follows:

Upon execution of this agreement
By cash or certified check, receipt of which is hereby acknowledged $

Upon execution and delivery of Bill of Sale
By cash or certified check $

By execution and delivery of   promissory note   of the following tenor, to be secured by a security interest in the goods and chattels and all other personal property mentioned in Schedule A hereof and all other personal property, goods and chattels thereafter acquired used in connection with the aforesaid business; together with all proceeds thereof and all increases, substitutions, replacements, additions and accessions thereto. $

Transferee agrees to perfect such security interest by executing and delivering to Transferor a Security Agreement and a Financing Statement, in accordance with the provisions of the Uniform Commercial Code, and all other instruments or documents as may be required by the Transferor. The filing fees thereof shall be paid by the Transferee.

By taking title subject to and assuming payment of the sum of $
secured by a
now a lien affecting the business and assets or a portion thereof and paying same according to the terms thereof.

ADJUSTMENTS

4. At the closing the following adjustments shall be made: rents, insurance premiums, taxes, electricity, gas, fuel, water, interest on mortgages or other liens.

GUARANTY AS TO RECEIPTS

5. Transferor represents that the gross weekly receipts (for a week of   business days) of the business, for the past   weeks averaged the sum of $ per week, and hereby guarantees that the gross receipts for the period from   M., to   M.   will aggregate at least the sum of $.

TRIAL PERIOD

6. The aforesaid period shall be deemed the trial period during which full opportunity shall be afforded the Transferee or representatives to keep tally of said gross receipts, and in the event the total of such gross receipts for said period is less than the guaranteed sum, the Transferee shall be repaid in full any deposit or payment on account hereunder, on demand. The Transferee shall not be deemed to have taken possession during this trial period.

Exhibit 11–1

Bulk Transfer Form *(Forms may be purchased from BlumbergExcelsior, Inc. or any of its dealers. Reproduction prohibited.)*

CREDITORS LIST

7. Transferor shall furnish Transferee with a list of Transferor's existing creditors, containing the names and business addresses of all creditors of the Transferor, with the amounts owed to each and also the names of all persons who are known to the Transferor to assert claims against the Transferor even though such claims are disputed. Such list shall be signed and sworn to or affirmed by the Transferor or his agent and, unless such list is appended hereto, it shall be delivered to Transferee at least 15 days before the closing date; provided that if Transferee takes possession of the goods or pays for them before that date such list shall be furnished at least 15 days before the happening of either event.

PRESERVATION OF LIST AND SCHEDULE

8. Transferee shall preserve the list of creditors aforementioned as well as the schedule of property (Schedule A hereof) for a period of 6 months next following the date of transfer of title and shall permit inspection of either or both and copying therefrom at all reasonable hours by any creditor of the Transferor; in lieu thereof, Transferee may file such list and schedule in the Office of the Secretary (Department) of State.

NOTICE TO CREDITORS

9. Transferee shall give notice to creditors of the transfer at least 10 days before taking possession of the goods or paying for them, whichever happens first. Notice shall be given in the form and manner as provided in the Uniform Commercial Code.

RESTRICTIVE COVENANT

10. The bill of sale shall contain a covenant by the Transferor and all other persons heretofore active in the said business or in any way interested therein with the Transferor, not to reestablish, re-open, be engaged in, nor in any manner whatsoever become interested, directly or indirectly, either as employee, as owner, as partner, as agent, or as stockholder, director or officer of a corporation, or otherwise, in any business, trade or occupation similar to the one hereby agreed to be sold, within the area bounded:

northerly by...

southerly by...

easterly by...

and westerly by...

for a term of...years from the closing date.

LEASE

11. Transferor further agrees, at the time of closing, to assign and transfer as part of this sale the existing lease or to execute and deliver, or to procure the execution and delivery, to the Transferee of a new lease or an extension of the term of the existing lease, covering the premises used in connection with said business and providing for a continuous term which shall expire on the   day

term

of

rent

The rent during such term shall not exceed $ per month.

assumption

Transferee shall assume full performance of the existing lease, if assigned. Security in the sum of

security

$ now held by the landlord under the existing lease, is hereby added to the amount of the purchase price and is to be paid to the Transferor by the Transferee at the closing, less any valid set-off or counterclaim asserted by the landlord. Transferor shall also assign and transfer to the Transferee all of the Transferor's right, title and interest in said security. Any default on the part of the Transferor with respect to the provisions of this paragraph shall forthwith entitle the Transferee to repayment in full, on demand, of any deposit or payment on account hereunder.

LIQUIDATED DAMAGES

12. Any willful, capricious or other inexcusable default hereunder on the part of either party shall entitle the aggrieved party to the sum of $ as liquidated damages for breach of this contract in addition to repayment in full of any sum paid hereunder as aforesaid, said amount being hereby agreed upon by reason of the difficulty in reducing the exact damages actually sustained to a mathematical certainty.

BROKER

13. The parties agree that
of No.

is the only broker who brought about this sale. The Transferor shall pay to the Broker when and if

commissions

title closes a commission at the rate of   per cent of the purchase price.

WARRANTIES SURVIVE

14. The warranties and covenants contained herein shall survive the Bill of Sale and become a part thereof and continue in full force as though set forth at length therein.

PRIOR NAMES AND ADDRESS

15. Transferor represents that Transferor has not used any other business names and/or addresses within the three years last past except as follows:

DEFINITION OF GOODS

16. The term "goods" as defined and used in the Uniform Commercial Code shall apply to this agreement.

CAPTIONS

17. The captions are inserted only as a matter of convenience and for reference and in no way define, limit or describe the scope of this agreement nor the intent of any provision thereof.

Exhibit 11–1

Continued *(Forms may be purchased from BlumbergExcelsior, Inc. or any of its dealers. Reproduction prohibited.)*

The terms, warranties and agreements herein contained shall bind and inure to the benefit of the respective parties hereto, and their respective legal representatives, successors and assigns.

The gender and number used in this agreement are used as a reference term only and shall apply with the same effect whether the parties are of the masculine or feminine gender, corporate or other form, and the singular shall likewise include the plural.

This agreement may not be changed orally.

IN WITNESS WHEREOF, the Parties have respectively signed and sealed these presents the day and year first above written.

....L.S.

....L.S.

....L.S.

....
Broker

STATE OF   COUNTY OF   ss.:

being duly sworn deposes and says that:

He is the   Transferor;

The following is a true and complete list of: the existing creditors of the Transferor, showing their business addresses and the amounts owed to each; the names and addresses of all persons known to the Transferor who have asserted claims which the Transferor disputes.

Creditor — indicate if a Claimant	Business Address	Amount — indicate if disputed

Sworn and subscribed to before me,

this   day of

....

....

Exhibit 11–1

Continued *(Forms may be purchased from BlumbergExcelsior, Inc. or any of its dealers. Reproduction prohibited.)*

T 84—Security Agreement in the nature of a Conditional Sales Contract.
Uniform Commercial Code; Ind. or Corp.

© 1964 BY JULIUS BLUMBERG, INC.,
PUBLISHER, NYC 10013

SECURITY AGREEMENT   (Conditional Sales Contract)

THIS AGREEMENT, made the   day of   19   under the laws of the state of

BETWEEN   Buyer, herein called the Debtor

whose business address is (if none, write "none")

and whose residence address is
and
whose address is   Seller, herein called the Secured Party

WITNESSETH:

The Secured Party hereby agrees to sell and hereby sells, and the Debtor hereby agrees to buy and hereby buys upon the terms stated below the property described in the schedule herein (hereinafter called the collateral), which collateral the Debtor represents will be used primarily

☐ for personal, family or household purposes   ☐ in farming operations   ☐ in business or other use

at the agreed price of $ which Debtor agrees to pay to the Secured Party as follows: $ on the date hereof, the receipt whereof is hereby acknowledged and the balance in   successive   installments as evidenced by a note or series of notes of even date herewith until the balance of $ together with interest shall have been paid in full.

As security for the said indebtedness and also to secure any other indebtedness or liability of the Debtor to the Secured Party direct or indirect, absolute or contingent, due or to become due, now existing or hereafter arising, (all hereinafter called the "obligations") Debtor hereby grants and conveys to the Secured Party a purchase money security interest in the collateral, all proceeds thereof, if any, and all additions and accessions thereto.

1. DEBTOR WARRANTS, COVENANTS AND AGREES AS FOLLOWS:

PAYMENT   1a To pay and perform all of the obligations secured by this agreement according to their terms.

EXECUTE DOCUMENTS   1b On demand of the secured party; execute any written agreement or do any other acts necessary to effectuate the purposes and provisions of this agreement, execute any instrument or statement required by law or otherwise in order to perfect, continue or terminate the security interest of the Secured Party in the collateral and pay all costs of filing in connection therewith.

POSSESSION   1c To retain possession of the collateral during the existence of this agreement and not to sell, exchange, assign, loan, deliver, lease, mortgage or otherwise dispose of same without the written consent of the Secured Party.

LOCATION   1d To keep the collateral at the location specified in the schedule and not to remove same (except in the usual course of business for temporary periods) without the prior written consent of the Secured Party.

LIENS   1e To keep the collateral free and clear of all liens, charges, encumbrances, taxes and assessments.

TAXES   1f To pay, when due, all taxes, assessments and license fees relating to the collateral.

INSURANCE   1g To keep the collateral insured against loss by fire (including extended coverage), theft and other hazards as the Secured Party may require and to obtain collision insurance if applicable. Policies shall be in such form and amounts and with such companies as the Secured Party may designate. Policies shall be obtained from responsible insurors authorized to do business in this state. Certificates of insurance or policies, payable to the respective parties as their interest may appear, shall be deposited with the Secured Party who is authorized, but under no duty, to obtain such insurance upon failure of the Debtor to do so. Debtor shall give immediate written notice to the Secured Party and to insurors of loss or damage to the collateral and shall promptly file proofs of loss with insurors. Debtor hereby appoints the Secured Party the attorney for the Debtor in obtaining, adjusting and cancelling any such insurance and endorsing settlement drafts and hereby assigns to the Secured Party all sums which may become payable under such insurance, including return premiums and dividends, as additional security for the indebtedness.

REPAIRS   1h To keep the collateral, at Debtor's own cost and expense, in good repair and condition and available for inspection by the Secured Party at all reasonable times.

RETENTION OF TITLE   1i Until full performance by the Debtor of the obligations hereunder, the Secured Party shall retain and the Debtor shall not obtain title to the collateral hereby sold.

CHANGE OF ADDRESS   1j To immediately notify the Secured Party in writing of any change in or discontinuance of Debtor's place or places of business and/or residence.

AFFIXED TO REALTY   1k That if the collateral is to be affixed to real estate, a description of the real estate and the name and address of the record owner is set forth in the schedule herein; if the said collateral is attached to real estate prior to the perfection of the security interest granted hereby, Debtor will on demand of the Secured Party furnish the latter with a disclaimer or disclaimers, signed by all persons having an interest in the real estate, of any interest in the collateral which is prior to Secured Party's interest.

2. THE PARTIES FURTHER AGREE

NOTES   2a Notes, if any, executed in connection with this agreement, are separate instruments and may be negotiated by Secured Party without releasing Debtor, the collateral, or any guarantor or co-maker. Debtor consents to any extension of time of payment. If there be more than one Debtor, guarantor or co-maker of this agreement or of notes secured hereby, the obligation of all shall be primary, joint and several.

NON-WAIVER   2b Waiver of or acquiescence in any default by the Debtor, or failure of the Secured Party to insist upon strict performance by the Debtor of any warranties or agreements in this security agreement, shall not constitute a waiver of any subsequent or other default or failure.

NOTICES   2c Notices to either party shall be in writing and shall be delivered personally or by mail addressed to the party at the address herein set forth or otherwise designated in writing.

LAW APPLICABLE   2d The Uniform Commercial Code shall govern the rights, duties and remedies of the parties and any provisions herein declared invalid under any law shall not invalidate any other provision of this agreement.

DEFAULT   2e The following shall constitute a default by Debtor:

non-payment   Failure to pay the principal or any installment of principal or of interest on the indebtedness or any notes when due. Failure
violation   by Debtor to comply with or perform any provision of this agreement. False or misleading representations or warranties made
misrepresentation   or given by Debtor in connection with this agreement. Subjection of the collateral to levy of execution or other judicial process.
levy - insolvency   Commencement of any insolvency proceedings by or against the Debtor. Death of the Debtor. Any reduction in the value of the
death   collateral or any act of the Debtor which imperils the prospect of full performance or satisfaction of the Debtor's obligations
impairment of security   herein.

REMEDIES ON DEFAULT   2f Upon any default by the Debtor and at the option of the Secured Party, the obligations secured by this agreement shall
acceleration   immediately become due and payable in full without notice or demand and the Secured Party shall have all the rights, remedies and privileges with respect to repossession, retention and sale of the collateral and disposition of the proceeds as are accorded by the applicable sections of the Uniform Commercial Code respecting "Default".

assembling collateral   Upon any default and upon demand, Debtor shall assemble the collateral and make it available to the Secured Party at the place and at the time designated in the demand.

attorneys' fees etc.   Upon any default, the Secured Party's reasonable attorneys' fees and the legal and other expenses for pursuing, searching for, receiving, taking, keeping, storing, advertising and selling the collateral chargeable to the Debtor.

deficiency   The Debtor shall remain liable for any deficiency resulting from a sale of the collateral and shall pay any such deficiency forthwith on demand.

monies advanced   If the Debtor shall default in the performance of any of the provisions of this agreement on the Debtor's part to be performed, Secured Party may perform same for the Debtor's account and any monies expended in so doing shall be chargeable with interest to the Debtor and added to the indebtedness secured hereby.

FINANCING STATEMENT   2g The Secured Party is hereby authorized to file a Financing Statement.

CAPTIONS   2h The Captions are inserted only as a matter of convenience and for reference and in no way define, limit or describe the scope of this agreement nor the intent of any provision thereof.

Exhibit 11–2

Security Agreement *(Forms may be purchased from BlumbergExcelsior, Inc. or any of its dealers. Reproduction prohibited.)*

The terms, warranties and agreements herein contained shall bind and inure to the benefit of the respective parties hereto and their respective legal representatives, successors and assigns.

The gender and number used in this agreement are used as a reference term only and shall apply with the same effect whether the parties are of the masculine or feminine gender, corporate or other form, and the singular shall likewise include the plural.

This agreement may not be changed orally.

IN WITNESS WHEREOF, the Parties have respectively signed and sealed these presents the day and year first above written.

....

....

....

SCHEDULE OF PROPERTY SOLD

Describe items of collateral and the address where each item will be located. If property is to be affixed to real estate describe the real estate and state the name and address of the owner of record thereof.

Items   *Location, etc.*

The chief place of business of the Debtor, if other than stated in this agreement, is:

GUARANTEE

The undersigned guarantees prompt and full performance and payment according to the tenor of the within agreement, to the holder hereof, and, in the event of default, authorizes any holder hereof to proceed against the undersigned, for the full amount due including reasonable attorneys' fees, and hereby waives presentment, demand, protest, notice of protest, notice of dishonor and any and all other notices or demand of whatever character to which the undersigned might otherwise be entitled. The undersigned further consents to any extension granted by any holder and waives notice thereof. If more than one guarantor, obligation of each shall be joint and several.

WITNESS the hand and seal of the undersigned this   day of   19

.... (L.S.)

Address..

Security Agreement
(CONDITIONAL SALES CONTRACT)

TO

DATED,

To perfect lien, file UCC 1 (see UCC §9-401)
N. Y. CONSUMER GOODS OR FARM CONNECTED COLLATERAL:
—resident debtor; with filing officer in county of debtor's residence.
—non-resident debtor; Dept. of state: if debtor has a place of business in only one county in N. Y., also with filing officer of such county.
—crops: Dept. of state and also with filing officer in county where land lies, on which crops are grown.
FIXTURES attached to realty; in county where land lies.
ALL OTHER CASES: Dept. of state: if debtor has a place of business in only one county in N. Y., also with filing officer in such county.
'filing officer' in N.Y.C. the City Register of the county; elsewhere in state, the county clerk.

N. J.: CONSUMER GOODS OR FARM CONNECTED COLLATERAL:
—with clerk of county of debtor's residence.
—if non-resident debtor, in county where goods are kept.
—crops: in county where land lies.
FIXTURES attached to realty; with register of county where land lies or with county clerk if no register.
ALL OTHER COLLATERAL; with secretary of state.

CONN.: FIXTURES attached to realty; with clerk of town or city where land lies.
ALL OTHER COLLATERAL; with secretary of state.

Exhibit 11–2

Continued *(Forms may be purchased from BlumbergExcelsior, Inc. or any of its dealers. Reproduction prohibited.)*

T 333—Certificate of Dissolution.
Business Corporation Law, 9-98

©1998 BY **Blumberg**Excelsior Inc.
NYC 10013

Certificate of Dissolution of

under Section 1003 of the Business Corporation Law

IT IS HEREBY CERTIFIED THAT:

(1)   *The name of the corporation is*

If the name of the corporation has been changed, the name under which it was formed is

(2)   *The certificate of incorporation was filed by the Department of State on*

(3)   *The name, title and address of each of its officers and directors are:*

Name	*Title*	*Street and Number*

(4)   *The corporation elects to dissolve.*

(5)   ✻ *The dissolution was authorized at a meeting of shareholders by vote of the holders of †*
of all the outstanding shares entitled to vote.
✻ *The dissolution was authorized by unanimous written consent of the holders of all the outstanding shares*
entitled to vote thereon.
✻ *The dissolution was authorized, pursuant to and in the manner required by the certificate of incorporation,*
on written consent signed by the holders of †
of all outstanding shares entitled to vote.
✻ *The dissolution was authorized pursuant to and in the manner required by the provisions of the certificate*
of incorporation authorizing dissolution, which provisions are as follows:

✻ Strike out if inapplicable
† Publisher's note: In most cases, if the corporation was formed before February 22, 1998, insert "two-thirds"; if the corporation was formed after February 22, 1998, insert "a majority". See BCL § 1001.

Exhibit 11–3
Certificate of Dissolution *(Forms may be purchased from BlumbergExcelsior, Inc. or any of its dealers. Reproduction prohibited.)*

Chapter 12

Limited Liability Companies

INTRODUCTION

The most recent addition to the pantheon of business entities permitted under New York law is the limited liability company. As of July 26, 1994, New York has permitted the formation of a **limited liability company (LLC)**, which is defined by the statute as an association of one or more persons who are operating a business that provides limited liability for its owners. It is specifically defined as not being a corporation.

New York law provides for several different types of limited liability companies:

1. The basic LLC, which is the format used to operate a general business.
2. The **professional limited liability company (PLLC)**, which is designed to operate professional occupations.
3. The **registered limited liability partnership (RLLP),** which is designed for professionals who would otherwise be operating as a partnership. (This form of LLC requires at least two owners.)

Under New York law, one person may form an LLC; this is not true in several other jurisdictions in which LLCs are permitted but in which the laws require LLCs to be formed by at least two persons. This may create problems for a New York LLC consisting of one owner who operates the business in a different state that mandates the business be owned by two or more persons to be considered an LLC. If the second state does not recognize the limitations on liability for the foreign New York LLC, the owner may be subject to unlimited personal liability in the second state. Almost every state permits LLCs. However, the LLC is not universal, and problems may be encountered for New York LLCs operating in a jurisdiction in which they are not permitted at all.

The LLC was designed to provide its owners with limited personal liability for the obligations of the business but without the formalities incident to creating a corporation.

Limited liability company (LLC) — business entity offering owners limited personal liability.

Professional limited liability company (PLLC) — a limited liability company for professionals.

Registered limited liability partnership (RLLP) — a limited liability company for partnerships.

Also, there may be some tax advantages for the owner who operates the business as an LLC.

Limited liability companies may be managed by either the owners themselves, who are called **members,** or by persons the owners hire as managers for the business. In either event, the members' or managers' personal liability is limited to their own malfeasance, not for the obligations of the LLC.

Members — owners of a limited liability company.

CREATION

Articles of Organization —document filed to create a limited liability company.

Certificate of Registration — document filed to create a registered limited liability partnership.

New York imposes several specific requirements on those who wish to form an LLC. The LLC and PLLC must have **Articles of Organization** (see Exhibit 12–1) that must be filed with the Secretary of State; the RLLP must, in addition to the Articles of Organization, file a **Certificate of Registration** (see Exhibit 12–2) with the Secretary of State. The Articles of Organization for the LLC and PLLC must include:

1. Title.
2. Name of the LLC, which must be unique to LLCs in the state of New York. (The name must include the words "Limited Liability Company" or "LLC" or "Professional Limited Liability Company" or "PLLC.")
3. Location of the business office.
4. Designation of the Secretary of State as the agent for service of process.
5. Name of a registered agent, either a natural person over the age of eighteen who lives or works in New York or a New York corporation.
6. A statement regarding the liability of its members.
7. A statement indicating that it is to be either member or manager operated.
8. The duration of the LLC.
9. Signature of the members.

For PLLCs, in addition to the foregoing, the Articles of Organization must include:

1. Profession to be practiced.
2. Names and addresses of its members.
3. History of the entity if it was originally a professional corporation.
4. Copies of the members' licensing certificates from the state, as well as a Certificate of Good Standing.

An RLLP must file, in addition to the Articles of Organization, a Certificate of Registration that includes:

1. Title.
2. Name (including the words "Registered Limited Liability Partnership" or "RLLP").

3. Profession to be practiced.
4. Location of the office.
5. Statement that the RLLP has no limited partners.
6. Statement that it intends to register as an RLLP.
7. Designation of the Secretary of State as agent for the service of process.
8. Name of the appointed registered agent.
9. Statement of the liability of its members.
10. Signature of the members.

Operating Agreement — contract between members of a limited liability company regarding the business's operation.

In addition to these filings, all LLCs are required to publish notices in two newspapers once per week for six weeks, similar to the publication requirement of limited partnerships (Chapter 3), and file an affidavit of publication with the Department of State within 120 days after filing its Articles of Organization or Certificate of Registration. Limited liability companies are also required to have an **Operating Agreement** similar to the limited partnership agreement discussed in Chapter 3.

Once the preceding documents have been filed, the LLC comes into existence and is deemed to be a legal entity separate and distinct from its owners.

OPERATION

Limited liability companies may be managed either by their members or by managers. This determination must be made in the company's Articles of Organization. The amount of a member's capital contribution determines the degree to which the member may participate in the management of the business. A new member may be added to an LLC on the vote or written consent of a majority in interest of its members, and a member may withdraw with the vote or written consent of at least two-thirds of the members. Unlike partnerships, withdrawal of a member does not automatically cause the dissolution of the LLC.

All of the general operational requirements that apply to the other forms of business organizations operating in New York also apply to LLCs. For tax purposes, the LLC is treated similarly to a general partnership (Chapter 3) or a Subchapter S corporation (Chapter 6).

For one-member LLCs, this can be a great advantage over operating the business as a sole proprietorship, which affords no limitation on personal liability, or as a Subchapter S corporation because, as a general rule, LLCs have fewer reporting requirements than do corporations.

An LLC dissolves when:

1. the time period specified in the Articles of Organization elapses
2. specific events specified in writing in the Operating Agreement come to pass
3. at least a majority of the members agree by vote or written consent

4. the bankruptcy, death, expulsion, incapacity, or withdrawal of any member occurs *unless* the Operating Agreement permits the LLC to continue under those circumstances

5. the court issues a judicial decree of dissolution

Articles of Dissolution — document filed to terminate a limited liability company.

Once the LLC is dissolved, it must file **Articles of Dissolution** with the Department of State and then distribute its assets in the following order:

1. creditors

2. members in satisfaction of liabilities

3. members for return of capital

4. members for membership interests

ADVANTAGES AND DISADVANTAGES OF OPERATING A BUSINESS AS AN LLC

There are several distinct advantages of operating a business as an LLC:

1. The members and managers are shielded from personal liability for the obligations of the business.

2. The membership interest is freely transferable and assignable, subject to any restriction in the Operating Agreement.

3. The LLC can continue to exist even after the death, incapacity, expulsion, and so forth of a member.

4. The business can obtain additional capital by selling additional membership certificates.

5. The owners are not prohibited from directly managing the business.

6. The LLC is taxed like a general partnership with profits and losses passing directly to the owners.

The disadvantages of operating a business as an LLC are:

1. There are certain formalities and regulatory requirements that must be met to form the LLC.

2. The members' ability to manage is determined by the degree of their capital contribution, not necessarily by their experience or expertise.

3. There may be problems transacting business in other states that either do not permit LLCs or define LLCs differently than does New York.

Because LLCs were not formed until recently, there are virtually no judicial decisions in New York demonstrating how the LLC will be viewed when the courts interpret the statute. It is believed that the courts will use as analogies previous decisions concerning limited partnerships and corporations that form the basis of the New York LLC law.

Office of the Attorney General of the State of New York
Informal Opinion No. 98-47
1998 N.Y. AG LEXIS 57

You have asked whether a sewage-works corporation organized under the New York Transportation Corporations Law may reorganize as a limited liability company. You note that the Tracy Sewer Works Corporation now provides sewage treatment to two commercial developments within the Town of Southeast. Tracy's counsel has asked the Town to approve its reorganization as a limited liability company. You have advised us that the owners of the two developments served by Tracy also are owners of the corporation and that Tracy does not serve any other customers.

Article 10 of the Transportation Corporations Law was enacted to authorize an alternate means of providing sewer services to areas of the State not served by a municipal sewer district. See, Governor's Approval Memorandum, Bill Jacket, L 1960, ch 1067; Op Atty Gen (Inf) No. 95-49. Sewage-works corporations are designed to be limited entities whose authority is prescribed by the Transportation Corporations Law and the scope of the franchise granted by the local governing body under that law. See, *1977 Op Atty Gen (Inf) 117.* There is no specific legislative authorization for entities other than sewage-works corporations or municipalities to perform these functions.

Article 10 includes a number of provisions ensuring local government oversight of sewage-works corporations. The relevant local government body must consent to the formation of the corporation and inspect any plans and actual construction it undertakes. Transportation Corporations Law §§ 116, 118. The local government must require the posting of a performance bond for the completion of construction of a sewage-works system and obtain a reasonable guarantee that the corporation will continue to operate the system for at least five years. Id., § 119(1), (2). In addition to making these assurances, the corporation must place its stock in escrow. Title to the stock will pass to the local governing body if the corporation fails to finish construction of the system, or if the corporation abandons or discontinues the operation and maintenance of the system. Id., § 119(3). In our view, these requirements demonstrate the Legislature's intent that only entities formed and operated in this manner may provide private sewage treatment. Also, these legislative controls indicate that once a sewage-works corporation is formed, only the municipality may succeed to ownership of the sewage system if the corporation fails to finish construction or abandons or discontinues operation and maintenance.

Section 201 of the Limited Liability Company Law provides that:

> A limited liability company may be formed under this chapter for any lawful business purpose or purposes except to do in this state any business for which another statute specifically requires some other business entity or natural person to be formed or used for such business.

We conclude that the Town may not approve the reorganization of the Tracy Sewer Works Corporation as a limited liability company. Article 10 of the Transportation Corporations Law specifically requires that sewage-works corporations be formed to supply sewer services to areas not served by a municipal sewer system. There is no specific authorization for other entities to perform this function. The detailed requirements of the statute indicate that the Legislature intended that only corporations formed and operated in the manner set forth in article 10 may provide private sewage treatment. The Limited Liability Company Law precludes formation of a limited liability company when a statute requires another form of business entity for a particular purpose.

The Attorney General renders formal opinions only to officers and departments of State government. This perforce is an informal and unofficial expression of the views of this office.

CHAPTER REVIEW

The limited liability company is the most recent form of business entity permitted under New York law. The LLC affords the owner the opportunity to have direct control in the business while still maintaining limited personal liability for the enterprise's obligations.

The LLC statute requires that the LLC file Articles of Organization, and a Certificate of Registration for RLLPs, with the Department of State in order to form; publish notices in two newspapers for a six-week period; and adopt an Operating Agreement to specify its internal operations. (See Exhibit 12–3 for an additional form used by limited liability companies, the Certificate of Assumed Name of Limited Liability Company.) Although many businesses have converted to LLCs, the statute is too recent to provide any judicial guidance as to the actual benefit or detriment of operating a business under this format.

KEY TERMS

Articles of Dissolution

Articles of Organization

Certificate of Registration

Limited liability company (LLC)

Members

Operating Agreement

Professional limited liability company (PLLC)

Registered limited liability partnership (RLLP)

EXERCISES

1. Under what circumstances would a business consider forming as an LLC?
2. Go to the library and compare New York's LLC laws to those of another state.
3. Explain why a professional corporation might organize as a PLLC.
4. Discuss the items that should appear in an Operating Agreement.
5. Briefly discuss the advantages and disadvantages of member management versus manager management.

FACTUAL PROBLEM

A sole proprietor wants to convert his sole proprietorship to an LLC as part of his estate plan to protect his family. The sole proprietor practices as a certified public accountant. Discuss some of the problems he may encounter in attempting to form the LLC.

Blumbergs Law Products **T 14—** Articles of Organization, §203, Limited Liability Company Law, 10-94. Prepared by the New York State Department of State. Reprinted with permission.

JULIUS BLUMBERG, INC., PUBLISHER, NYC 10013

Articles of Organization of

Under Section 203 of the Limited Liability Company Law

FIRST: The name of the limited liability company is:

SECOND: The county within this state in which the office of the limited liability company is to be located is: *

THIRD: (Optional) The latest date on which the limited liability company is to dissolve is:

FOURTH: The Secretary of State is designated as agent of the limited liability company upon whom process against it may be served. The post office address within or without this state to which the Secretary of State shall mail a copy of any process against the limited liability company served upon him or her is:

FIFTH: (Optional) The name and street address within this state of the registered agent of the limited liability company upon whom and at which process against the limited liability company can be served is:

SIXTH: The future effective date of the Articles of Organization, if not effective upon filing, is:

SEVENTH: The limited liability company is to be managed by (check appropriate box)
- ☐ One or more members
- ☐ A class or classes of members
- ☐ One or more managers
- ☐ A class or classes of managers

EIGHTH *If all or specified members are to be liable in their capacity as members for all or specified debts, obligations or liabilities of the limited liability company as authorized pursuant to Section 609 of the Limited Liability Company Law, a statement that all or specified members are so liable.*

IN WITNESS WHEREOF, this certificate has been subscribed on
by the undersigned who affirms that the statements made herein are true under the penalties of perjury.

....
Signature   Name and capacity of signer

Exhibit 12–1
Articles of Organization *(Forms may be purchased from BlumbergExcelsior, Inc. or any of its dealers. Reproduction prohibited.)*

*   If the limited liability company shall maintain more than one office in this state, set forth the county in which the principal office is to be located.

(1)   The future effective date may not exceed 60 days from the date of filing and must be a date certain.

The articles may include any other provisions not inconsistent with law.

𝕬𝖗𝖙𝖎𝖈𝖑𝖊𝖘 𝖔𝖋 𝕺𝖗𝖌𝖆𝖓𝖎𝖟𝖆𝖙𝖎𝖔𝖓

of

under Section 203 of the Limited Liability Company

Filed By:

Office and Post Office Address

Publisher's Note: This document is printed on 25% cotton paper. Unlike ordinary photocopy paper, this stock resists turning brittle and brown with age. Insist on genuine Blumberg forms to ensure the longevity of this important document.
    The publisher maintains property rights in the layout, graphic design and typestyle of this form as well as in the company's trademarked logo and name. Reproduction of blank copies of this form without the publisher's permission is prohibited. Such unauthorized use may constitute a violation of law or of professional ethics rules. However, once a form has been filled in, photocopying is permitted.

Exhibit 12–1

Continued *(Forms may be purchased from BlumbergExcelsior, Inc. or any of its dealers. Reproduction prohibited.)*

T 16— Certificate of registration of a domestic registered Limited Liability Partnership,§121-1500(a), Partnership Law, 10-94. Prepared by the New York State Department of State. Reprinted with permission.

JULIUS BLUMBERG, INC., PUBLISHER, NYC 10013

Certificate of Registration of

Under Section 121-1500(a) of the Partnership Law

FIRST: The name of the registered limited liability partnership is:

SECOND: The address of the principal office of the partnership without limited partners is:

THIRD: The profession(s) to be practiced by such partnership without limited partners is:

and such partnership without limited partners is eligible to register as a "registered limited liability partnership" pursuant to 121-1500(a) of the Partnership Law.

FOURTH: The Secretary of State* is designated as agent of the registered limited liability partnership upon whom process against it may be served. The post office address within or without this state to which the department of state shall mail a copy of any process served against it is:

FIFTH: (Optional) The name and street address within this state of the registered agent of the registered limited liability partnership upon whom and at which process against the registered limited liability partnership can be served against is:

SIXTH: The future effective date, if the registration is not to be effective upon filing, is:

SEVENTH: The partnership without limited partners is filing a registration for status as a registered limited liability partnership.

EIGHTH: *If all or specified partners are to be liable in their capacity as partners for all or specified debts, obligations, or liabilities of the registered limited liability partnership as authorized pursuant to Section 26(d) of the Partnership Law, a statement that all or specified partners are so liable.*

IN WITNESS WHEREOF, this certificate has been subscribed on by the undersigned who affirms that the statements made herein are true under the penalties of perjury.

....
Signature   Name and capacity of signer

Exhibit 12–2

Certificate of Registration *(Forms may be purchased from BlumbergExcelsior, Inc. or any of its dealers. Reproduction prohibited.)*

The registration shall be executed by one or more partners of the partnership without limited partners.

    *   Although the relevant provision of Section 121-1500(a) refers to the "department of state" as agent for service, the actual party for service within the department is the Secretary of State, and the form reflects this. It is expected that the statutory provision will be amended to reflect this.

    (1)   The future effective date may not exceed 60 days from the date of filing and must be a date certain.

    (2)   The registration may include any other matters the partnership without limited partners determines.

Certificate of Registration

of

under Section 402 of the 121-1500(a) Partnership Law

Filed By:

Office and Post Office Address

Exhibit 12–2

Continued *(Forms may be purchased from BlumbergExcelsior, Inc. or any of its dealers. Reproduction prohibited.)*

Certificate of Assumed Name of Limited Liability Company

The undersigned do hereby certify the following:

1. The undersigned are conducting or transacting business as members of a limited liability company under the name _____ (the Company)

2. The principal place of business of the Company is located at _____ , New York.

2. The offices of the Company are located in the County of _____ , State of New York.

4. The Company has filed with the Secretary of State its Articles of Organization under the name _____ , LLC.

5. The full names of all the persons conducting or transacting such limited liablity company business are as follows:

IN WITNESS WHEREOF, we have this _____ day of _____, 200__ made and signed this Certificate of Assumed Name.

STATE OF NEW YORK

COUNTY OF   ss.:

On the _____ day of _____ , 200__ , before me personally came _____ to me known to be the individual who executed the foregoing instrument, and who, being duly sworn by me, did depose and say that he is a member of _____ LLC, a New York limited liability company and that he has authority to sign the same, and acknowledged that he executed the same as the act and deed of said limited liability company.

Exhibit 12–3
Certificate of Assumed Name of Limited Liability Company

Glossary

A

"A" reorganization — IRS designation for a corporate merger or consolidation.

Absence of fraud test — test used by the courts to ascertain whether the directors have received adequate consideration for the sale of the corporate shares.

Accelerated depreciation — depreciation taken at a rate faster than straight-line depreciation.

Actual authority — agent's ability to act derived from principal's manifestations to the agent.

Agency by agreement — agency formed by mutual assent.

Agency by estoppel — agency relationship created by equitable concepts where it would be unjust to permit the principal to deny the agency.

Agency by ratification — agency created retroactively when principal affirms unauthorized acts.

Agent — person who has the legal ability to enter into contracts on another's behalf.

Alien corporation — corporation formed under the laws of a foreign nation.

Alter ego — a shareholder disregarding the corporate existence as a separate entity.

Amendment — document used to change a certificate of incorporation.

Apparent authority — ability to act created by principal's manifestations to a third party.

Application for Certificate of Authority — document filed by a foreign corporation that regularly conducts business in New York.

Appraisal rights — right of a dissenting shareholder of a close corporation to have his or her shares bought by the corporation.

Articles of Dissolution — document filed to terminate a limited liability company.

Articles of Organization — document filed to create a limited liability company.

Assets — property of value owned by a company.

Assignee — transferee of contract rights.

Assignment — transfer of contract rights.

Authority by estoppel — agent's ability to act created under equitable concepts when it would be unjust to permit the principal to escape liability.

Authorized shares — the number of shares specified in a corporation's certificate of incorporation.

B _____

"B" reorganization — IRS designation for a corporate exchange of stock.

Balance sheet — document representing the basic accounting equation.

Bank resolution — document used to establish a depository for corporate funds.

Basic accounting equation — Assets = Liabilities + Equity.

Basis — all consideration given for acquiring an asset.

Beneficiary — person with equitable title to a trust.

Best efforts underwriting — method of compensating underwriters by paying them a commission on each share sold.

Blue sky laws — state security laws.

Board of Directors — managers of a corporation.

Board of managers — persons who manage a joint stock company.

Bond — secured debt security.

Bondholders — owners of a secured debt.

Bulk transfer — sale of all or substantially all of a corporation's assets otherwise than in the ordinary course of business.

Business Certificate for Partners — document that must be filed before a partnership can operate.

Business Corporation Law (BCL) — New York's corporate statute.

Business judgment rule — fiduciary standard of care for corporate directors, using the skill of the reasonable prudent businessperson.

Business tax — franchise tax.

Business trust — trust used to create a business.

By-laws — document delineating the day-to-day operations of a corporation.

C _____

"C" reorganization — IRS designation for a corporate exchange of stock of one corporation for substantially all of the assets of another corporation.

Capital — property.

Capital assets — property held for investment and appreciation.

Capital gain or loss — amount realized on the sale or distribution of a capital asset; the difference between the basis and the selling price.

Capital surplus — surplus other than earned surplus.

Cartage — business's obligation to dispose of waste.

Certificate of amendment — document filed to effectuate an amendment to a certificate of incorporation.

Certificate of beneficial interest — document identifying beneficiary.

Certificate of change — document filed to effectuate an amendment to a certificate of incorporation that does not require shareholder approval.

Certificate of dissolution — document filed to terminate a corporation.

Certificate of incorporation — document filed with the Secretary of State to form a corporation.

Certificate of Limited Partnership — document that must be filed to create a limited partnership.

Certificate of merger or consolidation — document filed to effectuate a merger or consolidation of two or more corporations.

Certificate of Registration — document filed to create a registered limited liability partnership.

Classified Board of Directors — Board of Directors whose positions are allocated to different classes of stock.

Close or closely held corporation — corporation whose shares are not publicly traded and are held by a small number of shareholders.

Cognovit — contract provision confessing judgment.

Collateral — security for a debt.

Commission — fee paid to seller of a security.

Common stock rights — the right to vote, the right to receive dividends, and the right to the assets of the corporation on dissolution.

Condition precedent — act or event that gives rise to an absolute duty to perform.

Consolidation — two or more corporations join to form a new corporation, combining all their assets and liabilities and transferring them to the new entity.

Contribution — what a person gives to acquire an ownership interest.

Conversion rights — preference giving the security holder the ability to exchange one type of security for another at a set ratio.

Corporate books — where corporate minutes are kept.

Corporate minutes — record of what occurs at corporate meetings.

Corporate opportunity doctrine — requirement that directors offer all business opportunities to the corporation and not take advantage of them personally.

Corporate reorganization — a merger, consolidation, or exchange.

Corporation by estoppel — equitable doctrine precluding a challenge to a business's corporate status; not permitted in New York.

Corpus — trust property.

Coupon bond — bond that makes periodic distributions of interest.

Creator — person who created a trust.

Cumulative dividend rights — stock preference giving the holder the right to have undeclared dividends accumulated for him until a dividend is eventually declared.

D _____

DBA form — document used to register an assumed business name.

Debenture — unsecured debt security.

Debt-equity ratio — proportion of capitalization that is derived from loans as opposed to ownership.

Debt security — bonds and debentures.

De facto corporation — business that has acted in good faith as a corporation so that the courts will consider it to be a corporation.

De jure corporation — validly formed corporation.

Depreciate — loss in value due to time and/or use.

Discount — purchasing a debt security at less than face value to increase the actual rate of return.

Dissolution — termination of a corporation.

Dividend — shareholder's yield on his or her investment.

Domestic corporation — corporation formed under the laws of New York.

E _____

Earned surplus — profit from the operation of a business.

Equitable or beneficial title — title held by trust beneficiary.

Equity — ownership interest in a business.

Equity security — stock.

Estimated taxes — quarterly income tax obligation.

Excess business holdings tax — additional tax imposed on corporations that retain more than a minimum amount as unrestricted, unreserved earned surplus.

Exchange — swap of stock between two corporations.

Executive committees — groups of directors and officers who investigate matters for the full board.

Express authority — ability to act created by direct statements.

F _____

Face value — amount appearing on debt security representing amount debtor will pay on maturity.

Fellow servant exception — principal is not liable for servant's tortious act committed against another of the principal's servants.

Firm commitment underwriting — underwriting in which the underwriter purchases the securities outright at a discount.

First option — requirement that a shareholder offer his or her shares to the other shareholders before he or she may sell them to outsiders.

Foreign corporation — corporation formed under the laws of a state other than New York.

Four unities — time, title, interest, and possession.

Freeze out — sale of stock intended to force out minority shareholders.

Frolic of his own — exception to doctrine of respondeat superior.

G _____

General agent — nonspecial agent.

General partner — person who manages a limited partnership or who is a partner in a general partnership.

General partnership — business operated and owned by two or more persons with unlimited personal liability.

Greater quorum — more than a majority.

Gross profit or loss — all profit or loss before taxes.

H _____

Holder of record — shareholder who appears on the corporate books at the close of business on the record date.

I _____

Implied authority — ability to act arising from custom, usage, and past.

Income statement — document that indicates the sales, expenses, taxes, and profit or loss for a business.

Incorporator — natural person over eighteen years of age who files and signs the certificate of incorporation, calls the organizational meeting of the corporation, and appoints the initial Board of Directors.

Independent contractor — person hired exclusively for the results to be accomplished.

Initial Board of Directors — first Board of Directors appointed by the incorporators.

Insider trading — buying or selling stock based on nonpublic information that was acquired by reason of being a fiduciary of the corporation.

Interest rate — return on investment for a creditor.

Involuntary dissolution — corporate termination brought about by court order for a legal violation.

Issued shares — shares available for sale to the public.

J _____

Joint and several liability — partners' liability for tort actions.

Joint liability — partners' liability for contract actions.

Joint stock company — business format that operates like a corporation but without retaining unlimited liability for its owners.

Joint tenancy — multiple ownership of property with rights of survivorship.

Joint tenant — title holder of a joint tenancy.

Joint venture — partnership for a limited operation or purpose.

Junk bond — bond issued by a financially risky issuer.

L _____

Legal title — title held by a trustee.

Lesser quorum — fewer than a majority.

Liabilities — obligations.

Limited liability company (LLC) — business entity offering owners limited personal liability.

Limited partner — investor in a limited partnership.

Limited partnership agreement — contract used to form a partnership.

Limited partnership share — evidence of ownership interest.

Limited partnership — partnership with one or more general partners and one or more limited partners.

Liquidation — process of terminating a business.

Long-term capital gain or loss — amount realized on the sale of a capital asset held for more than six months.

M _____

Mandatory buyout — provision in a shareholder's restrictive agreement in which the corporation must repurchase the shares if a shareholder wishes to sell.

Mark — word, symbol, or group of words that designates a specific product or service.

Master-servant relationship — form of employment relationship.

Maturity date — day when debt security must be repaid.

Members — owners of a limited liability company.

Merger — one corporation absorbs another corporation.

N

Name reservation form — document used to reserve a company name.

Negligent hiring — master's personal liability when he hires an incompetent servant.

Net profit — gross profit less taxes.

Noncumulative dividend rights — undeclared dividend does not accumulate for the shareholder.

No par — no minimum value for corporate stock.

Normal quorum — majority.

Not-for-profit corporation — corporation organized for charitable purposes.

Novation — substitution of parties to a contract.

O

Officers — servants of the corporation.

Operating Agreement — contract between members of a limited liability company regarding the business's operation.

Organizational meeting — first meeting of the corporation.

Organizer — promoter of a corporation.

Ostensible authority — apparent authority.

Outstanding shares — shares held by members of the public.

P

Paid-in surplus — amount above par paid for stock with a par value.

Par — amount below which the directors may not sell a share of stock.

Parent corporation — corporation that owns a controlling block of stock of another corporation.

Partially disclosed principal — agency relationship is disclosed, but not the identity of the principal.

Participation rights — preference giving the shareholder the right to receive both a preferred and a common stock dividend.

Partnership rights or interests — rights to manage, to assets, and to income, profits, and losses.

Payables — name given to all liability accounts.

Piercing the corporate veil — legal doctrine permitting the court to attach the personal assets of a shareholder to satisfy corporate obligations.

Power coupled with an interest — supported by legal consideration.

Preemptive rights — the right of a shareholder to purchase newly issued shares of his or her class of stock in the same proportion as his or her current ownership before outsiders may purchase the shares.

Preferred stock — share with rights different from common stock.

Preincorporation share subscription — offer to purchase shares of a corporation yet to be formed.

Premium — paying more than the face value for a debt security to reduce the actual rate of return.

Principal — the person from whom the agent's authority derives; or trust property.

Principal-agent relationship — relationship in which one person has the ability to enter into contracts on another's behalf.

Private placement — arranging for the sale of a security to a small group of investors.

Professional corporation — corporation formed to provide professional services.

Professional limited liability company (PLLC) — a limited liability company for professionals.

Promissee — person to whom a contract promise is owed.

Promissory note — short-term loan.

Promoter — organizer of a corporation.

Proxy — authorization by a shareholder to have someone else vote the shares.

Proxy contest — two or more persons seeking a shareholder's proxy.

Proxy solicitation — request to a shareholder to give his or her proxy to the person making the request.

Public offering — sale of securities to the general public.

Q

Quasi-preemptive rights — preemptive rights granted by court action; no longer available in New York.

Quo warranto — action by Attorney General to revoke a corporate charter.

Quorum — minimum number necessary to have a valid meeting.

R

Real Estate Investment Trust (REIT) — tax provision for real estate trust.

Record date — day on which the shareholders who are permitted to assert specific rights are identified.

Redemption rights — the right to compel the corporation to repurchase shares of stock.

Registered limited liability partnership (RLLP) — a limited liability company for partnerships.

Registration Statement — document required to be filed with the SEC.

Regular meetings — corporate meetings required by statute.

Remainderman — person in whom legal and equitable titles merge.

Renunciation — agent's act to terminate agency.

Residual owners — common stock owners.

Resolution — document indicating Board of Directors action.

Respondeat superior — tort doctrine holding a master liable for his or her servant's torts.

Restated certificate of incorporation — superceding document that incorporates a certificate of incorporation and all of its amendments.

Retained earnings — profit or loss resulting from the operation of a business.

Revised Uniform Limited Partnership Act (RULPA) — current New York limited partnership law.

Revocation — principal's act to terminate agency.

Risk free interest rate — interest rate paid by government backed securities.

S

Schedule C — the form used by sole proprietorships to report income.

Scrip — document representing a fraction of a share of stock.

Section 1244 stock — tax election for qualifying small businesses.

Securities Act of 1933 — federal securities law.

Securities and Exchange Commission (SEC) — government agency regulating securities.

Security — proprietory interest in a business.

Senior securities — bonds and preferred stock.

Service mark — government grant of exclusive use of a name designating a service.

Sham corporation — corporate format used to attempt to shield the owner's personal liability.

Share — stock.

Shareholder — owner of a corporation represented by owning a share of stock.

Shareholder derivative suits — lawsuits brought by a shareholder for injury to the corporation.

Shareholder pooling agreement — contract among shareholders to vote their shares as a block.

Shareholder restrictive agreement — agreement limiting the ability of a shareholder to alienate his or her shares.

Share of stock — document evidencing ownership of a corporation.

Share subscription — offer by potential investor to purchase shares of stock.

Short-form merger — merger resulting when one corporation owns 90 percent of the voting stock of another corporation.

Short-term capital gain or loss — amount realized from the sale of a capital asset held for no more than six months.

Sinking fund — account maintained as security for bondholders.

Sole proprietorship — person who owns and operates a business on his or her own.

Solicitation — formal request, or any part of a continuing plan leading the way to a formal request, for a proxy.

Special agent — agent for a particular act or transaction.

Special meetings — corporate meetings called for a particular purpose.

Staggered Board of Directors — Board of Directors whose members are elected at different intervals.

Stated capital — account representing the consideration the corporation has received for the sale of its shares.

Statute of Frauds — law requiring certain contracts to be in writing to be enforceable.

Stockholder — another term for "shareholder."

Structural change — any transaction affecting a corporation's certificate of incorporation.

Subchapter S corporation — tax election for qualifying small businesses.

Subsidiary corporation — corporation controlled by another corporation.

Surplus — excess.

Survivor corporation — corporation that continues in existence after a merger.

T _____

Target corporation — corporation taken over in a merger.

Tax Identification Number — issued by the IRS for income tax purposes.

Tenancy in common — form of multiple ownership of property with divisible portions.

Tenancy in partnership — title for partnership property.

Tenant in common — title holder to a tenancy in common.

Trademark — government grant of exclusive use of a name designating a good.

Treasury shares — outstanding shares reacquired by the corporation and maintained on its books with no dividend or voting rights.

True value test — test used to determine the adequacy of the consideration the directors accepted for shares of closely held corporations with no quantifiable assets.

Trust — fiduciary relationship.

Trustee — person who holds legal title to a trust.

U _____

Ultra vires — beyond the scope.

Underwriter — the process of arranging the sale of securities to the public.

Undisclosed principal — third person believes agent is acting on his or her own behalf.

Uniform Limited Partnership Act (ULPA) — former New York limited partnership law.

Uniform Partnership Act (UPA) — statute governing general partnerships.

Unrestricted, unreserved earned surplus — source of funds for a corporate dividend.

V _____

Variance — permitted divergence from zoning regulations.

Vicarious liability — one person being held legally responsible for another's actions.

Voluntary dissolution — corporate termination brought about by the wishes of the owners.

Voting trust — trust created for not more than ten years in which the trustee has the authority to vote the shares and the beneficiaries receive the dividends.

W _____

Warrants — long-term options to purchase shares of stock at a stated price.

Watered stock — stock sold for consideration not even nominally equivalent to its par value.

Workers compensation — state statute granting relief from fellow servant exception.

Workers Compensation Board — government ageny that administers workers compensation.

Z _____

Zero coupon bond — bonds that make no periodic distribution of interest.

Zoning — government regulation of land use.

Zoning board — government agency administering zoning laws.

Index

Corpus, 75
Cottrell v. Albany Card and Paper Manufacturing Company, 169
Coupon bond, 133
Crane Co. v. Anaconda Company, In the Matter of, 90
Creator, 75
Cross Properties, Inc. v. Brook Realty Co., Inc., 202

DBA form, 27
Debenture, 132
Debt security, 131, 132
    maturity date of, 132
Debt-equity ratio, 131
Deering Milliken, Inc. v. Clark Estates, Inc., 167
Depreciate, 176
Depreciation, accelerated, 176
Diamond v. Oreamuno, 152
Discount, 133
Dissolution of corporation, 210
    articles of, 226
    certificate of, 211
        form for, 219
    involuntary, 211
    voluntary, 210
Distribution(s), 165–178
Dividend(s), 165–178
    cumulative rights in, 140
    noncumulative rights in, 140
    taxation of, 175
    types of, 171
Doing Business As form, 27

Earnings, retained, 166
Equitable title, 75
Equity, 166
Equity security, 131, 136
Equity-debt ratio, 131
Erie County Sav. Bank v. Grove, 10
Estate planning, in sole proprietorship, 27
Exchange(s), 203
Executive committee, 89

Fellow servant exception, 3
Frankowski v. Palermo, 119
Fraud(s)
    absence of, test for, 144

statute of, 40
Freeze out, 162
Friedman v. Beway Realty Corp., 204
Frolic of his own, 3
Funding, difficulty of, in sole proprietorship, 27

Gallagher v. Lambert, 183
Garzo v. Maid of the Mist Steamboat Company, 122
General partnership(s), 39–65
    benefits of, 47
    creation of, 40
    detriments of, 47
    income of, 43
    losses of, 43
    management of, 42
    operation of, 44
    profits of, 43
    termination of, 46
Gitlitz v. Commissioner of Internal Revenue, 96
Gonzalez v. Chalpin, 48
Gross loss, 166
Gross profit, 166
Gurney's Inn Corp. Liquidating Trust, In re, 76

Haenel v. Epstein, 120
Heffernan v. Marine Midland Bank, N.A., 17
Hiring, negligent, in master-servant relationship, 4
Holder of record, 92

Income statement, of business, 166
Incorporation
    certificate of, 84, 111
        amendment to, 197
            certificate of, 198
            form for, 126
        restated certificate of, 198
Incorporator, 118
Insider trading, 151
Interest rate, 132
    risk free, 132

Joint and several liabilit(ies), 44
Joint liabilit(ies), 44
Joint stock company, 71
Joint tenancy, 42
    four unities of, 42